Sin and Grace

Henry Danhof

Herman Hoeksema

originally published in Dutch
under the title *Van Zonde en Genade*

Translated by Cornelius Hanko · *Edited by* Herman Hanko

Reformed Free Publishing Association
Grandville, Michigan

This translation is of *Van Zonde en Genade* (Concerning Sin and Grace), a
hardcover book written in Dutch and published [in 1923] by H. [Henry]
Danhof and H. [Herman] Hoeksema with no mention of publication date
or publishing company name. The printer was the Dalm Printing Co.,
Kalamazoo, Michigan.

Reformed Free Publishing Association
4949 Ivanrest Ave SW
Grandville MI 49418-9709 USA
Phone: 616-224-1518
Fax: 616-224-1517
Website: www.rfpa.org
E-mail: mail@rfpa.org

ISBN 0-916206-73-4
LCCN 2003093351

For unto you it is given in the behalf of Christ,
not only to believe on him,
but also to suffer for his sake.

Philippians 1:29

Contents

❦

Editor's Introduction

❦

Van Zonde en Genade (Concerning Sin and Grace), the book from which *Sin and Grace* was translated, has long been out of print. As the number of people able to read Dutch steadily declined after the publication of *Van Zonde en Genade* in 1923, there seemed to be no market for a reprint, even as important as the book is for an understanding of the origin and doctrinal position of the Protestant Reformed Churches in America.

It must have been about ten to fifteen years ago that my father, Rev. Cornelius Hanko, long retired from the active ministry, was looking for something to do that would be of benefit to the churches. He asked me what I thought about a project he had in mind: the translation into English of Henry Danhof and Herman Hoeksema's *Van Zonde en Genade*. Because he was fluent in Dutch and because he needed work to keep him occupied, I readily agreed that the book should be translated. I was a bit skeptical whether he was able to do it, though. He was, after all, in his eighties, very nearly blind, and weary with the burdens of many years in the ministry. But if it could be done, it would be well worth it.

I got out his copy of *Van Dale's Woordenboek*, the authoritative dictionary of the Dutch language; set up a word processor; installed a program that would enlarge the text on the screen of his monitor; and encouraged him to do what he could.

It was not long after this, a couple of years at most, that a typed manuscript was handed to me. It was relatively large, numbering nearly 300 pages. Although I had originally read the book in the Dutch, I read it once again in my father's translation. It impressed me even more than it had when I first had read it. It was difficult to know what to do with the manuscript, but I thought it important enough to prepare a few sections of it for publication in the *Protestant Reformed Theological Journal*.[1] These articles were read by a couple of men who were on the Book and Publication Committee of the Board of the Reformed Free Publishing Association (RFPA). The articles were apparently sufficient to whet their appetites, and they asked if they could read the whole translation. I was hesitant to give them the manuscript, because it had parts missing; it had serious mistakes due to misreading by a man with such failing eyesight, and the translation was a very literal translation of literary Dutch, which would make it difficult for today's readers to comprehend.

Nevertheless, the RFPA men saw the value of the manuscript and insisted that it had to be published. Their arguments were convincing and unanswerable. They appealed to the fact that it was part of the Protestant Reformed heritage and that new generations would have to read it if they were to understand the issues which led to the formation of the Protestant Reformed Churches.

≪∞≫

It is significant that the book was written in 1923, one year before the Synod of the Christian Reformed Church (CRC), meeting in Kalamazoo, Michigan, adopted the "three points of common grace." Both Revs. Danhof and Hoeksema were ministers in good standing in the CRC at that time. Rev. Danhof was pastor of First CRC of Kalamazoo, and Rev. Hoeksema was pastor of Eastern Avenue CRC, Grand Rapids, Michigan.

A year prior to the adoption of the three points, the common grace controversy had even then been raging in the church. *Van*

---

1. Herman Hanko, "Concerning Sin and Grace," *Protestant Reformed Theological Journal*, 31, no. 2 (April 1998): 24–42.

Zonde en Genade was written within the context of that controversy. Its two authors had both grown up in the Netherlands, immigrated to the United States, and studied for the ministry here. Much of the church business of that day was still being carried on in the Dutch language. In fact, the official Acts of Synod of the CRC were never completely published in English until 1930.[2]

The fact that common grace should be a bone of contention in the CRC is due to the history of the doctrine. To understand this history, we must go back a century before the book was written.

The roots of the controversy lay in the history of Reformed churches in the Netherlands. From the time of the Reformation of the sixteenth century, the Reformed Church in the Netherlands, *Nederduitsch Hervormde Kerk* (NHK) was a "state church." A state church is a denomination in which the government exercises a great deal of control. The NHK was the only church officially approved by the government. The state subsidized the church to a considerable extent: it supported the entire educational system; it helped with the payment of ministerial salaries and the care of the poor; and it supported retired ministers who were no longer able to work in the churches. In that church, a minister could not take a call without the permission of the state, and all ecclesiastical assemblies, including diaconates, did their work with state representatives frequently present.

An important element of the concept of a state church was that all the citizens of the Netherlands were technically members of it and were baptized by the church, married in the church, and buried under church supervision in church cemeteries. The local parish was responsible for the spiritual welfare of every citizen within its borders. Such a church is known as a national church.

The NHK, however, had become apostate. The apostasy had set in early—as early as the last part of the seventeenth century.

---

2. The Calvin Archives at Calvin College, Grand Rapids, Michigan, has English translations of all the Acts prior to 1930.

It continued and became worse until the true people of God were unable to worship God anymore in their local churches. Worldliness had destroyed piety, and false doctrine had ruined the preaching.

In 1834 God brought reformation to the church in the Netherlands. Under the leadership of Hendrik De Cock and a few other ministers, a new denomination was formed, faithful to the truths of God's sovereign grace as taught in Scripture and outlined in the Reformed confessions. Although this new denomination went under different names during its early history, it was generally known as *De Afscheiding* (The Separation or The Secession).

This reformation attracted mainly the lower class of people, the ordinary day laborers, the poor and uneducated, yet people who were pious and godly and were starving for the pure preaching of the Word. The movement soon faced many troubles, among them disagreement over the question of common grace. The common grace to which some in the Secession churches held included two elements: a general attitude of favor which God has towards all men, and a general well-meant gospel offer in which God expresses His desire to save all who hear the gospel. There were some among the leaders of the Secession who held to this doctrine, although Hendrik De Cock, the first minister to leave the state church, did not.

When the members of the churches of the Secession of 1834 immigrated to the United States, those committed to common grace brought their views with them. They were the immigrants who, settling in what was later to become Holland, Michigan, became the founders of the CRC. Their version of common grace was soon taught within the CRC.

I say "version," because another version of common grace soon began to be taught. It was introduced in the church by Dr. Abraham Kuyper (1837–1920). After his conversion from modernism, Kuyper also led a reformatory movement in the NHK. This was in 1886. This is the Kuyper of *Dat De Genade Particulier Is* (That Grace Is Particular), the book in which he vigorously and cogently defended the doctrine that God's grace is sovereign and for the elect alone.[3]

That Kuyper should turn his attention to common grace is understandable only in terms of the religious situation which prevailed in the Netherlands. It was common belief in the glory days of the Netherlands that the Dutch were a chosen people of God to whom had been given great favors and blessings. Accompanying these special favors of God was the calling of this small republic on the shores of the North Sea to be the source and fountain of a worldwide Reformed influence, flowing into all nations and causing the Reformed faith to be universally adopted.

This vision, shared by Kuyper, was the explanation, at least in part, of several aspects of his life. It explains why he resigned his position as minister to organize a political party, to run for the Second House in Parliament, and to aspire later to the office of prime minister. It also explains why Kuyper was originally not in favor of the union between the churches of the Secession of 1834 and the churches which followed his leadership out of the apostate state church. He was especially critical of the Secession churches because they had repudiated all official relationships with the state, had established congregations and a denomination free from state control and support, and had insisted on a free church rather than a national church.

Kuyper thought that separating from the NHK was a serious mistake on the part of the Secession churches. His churches, he believed, should never do this. In the church of Amsterdam, of which Kuyper was a pastor until he resigned, the entire citizenry of Amsterdam was on the membership rolls, even many years after Kuyper's reformatory movement. He called his movement the *Doleantie* (aggrieved ones), because he expressed by that term his conviction that he and those who followed him were

---

3. The English translation, by Marvin Kamps, is titled *Particular Grace: A Defense of God's Sovereignty in Salvation* (Grandville, Mich.: Reformed Free Publishing Association, 2001).

still members of the state church but were "grieved" by its apostasy. There was no official decision by them to secede from the state church, as had been made by De Cock and his consistory. But the later union in 1892 of the *Doleantie* churches with most of the *Afscheiding* churches cancelled Kuyper's claim by effectually separating the *Doleantie* from the NHK.

It is at this point that Kuyper's common grace became important. Kuyper had to have some explanation for the fact that within the NHK were countless unbelievers who, as citizens of the Netherlands, were and remained members. He had to have some explanation for the idea that all the members of the NHK could work together to establish the Netherlands as a land where the Reformed faith influenced and determined the character of every institution of society and its culture so that the country could exert its influence throughout the world. Kuyper found this in his doctrine of common grace.

Several things must be noted concerning this Kuyperian common grace. In the first place, it differed from the common grace as held by some in the Secession churches. The defenders of common grace in that tradition held to a general attitude of God's favor towards all men, manifested especially in the well-meant gospel offer. This is the common grace set down as dogma in the "first point" of common grace as adopted by the CRC Synod of Kalamazoo in 1924.

Kuyper's common grace had to do with culture. Kuyper made especially five points in his development of common grace. The first was that his new doctrine had to be distinguished from the common grace teaching found in the Secession churches, a common grace with which he did not agree. To emphasize the difference, Kuyper even used a different term: *gemeene gratie* instead of *algemeene genade* (The two terms cannot be distinguished in any English translation; and, ironically, in his definitive work on common grace, *De Gemeene Gratie,* he often used the two terms interchangeably).

Second, Kuyper's doctrine taught that if common grace had not intervened after the fall of Adam, man would have become a beast or a devil, and this world would have become a wasteland. The result would have been that the development of culture would have been impossible. Common grace, given to man after the fall, was found especially in the bestowal of the Holy Spirit, who restrained sin and produced good works in the wicked, but all without saving them.

Third, Kuyper taught that because of common grace, the cultural mandate not only remained in force, but was capable of being carried out in society by a cooperative effort on the part of believers and unbelievers. The result was that two streams could be found in history: the stream of common grace and the development of the cultural mandate, and the stream of special grace and the salvation of the church. Kuyper insisted that the former was as important, if not more important, than the latter. Indeed, so crucial to Kuyper was the stream of history characterized by the workings of God's common grace that the fruits of that culture would be preserved in the New Jerusalem!

This view formed the theological basis for the cooperation of all citizens in the Netherlands, backed up by a government which gave official sanction to the Reformed churches. It would enable all to labor together to make the Netherlands the fountain of Reformed culture, which would send forth a mighty stream flowing into all lands.

Fourth, Kuyper himself recognized the fact that his doctrine of common grace was a novelty and an innovation. He found hints in other Reformed writers going back to Calvin, but he insisted that he was really the author of this doctrine (as indeed he was), and that it now remained for the church to develop his thought further. This claim was completely contrary to the assertion of the Synod of the CRC in 1924, which virtually adopted Kuyper's common grace in the second and third points of its decision, but which added that these doctrines had been held by "Reformed authors of the most flourishing period of Reformed theology." Kuyper would have disagreed.

Finally, when the Dutch who had followed Kuyper's reformatory movement came to this country, they brought Kuyper's views along and attempted to implement his vision in North America. They pleaded for involvement in all aspects of American society so that they might influence society's institutions and cause the Reformed faith so to dominate that all of American life would be permeated by its principles.

❧

The two different camps, each with its own version of common grace, found a home in the CRC. Because the followers of Kuyper were among the more educated people in the Netherlands, they soon occupied positions of leadership in the denomination in America and became influential at Calvin College, Grand Rapids, Michigan. But the differences between the immigrants from the Secession churches and those of the Kuyperian churches were sharp and deep. The two groups not only did not get along in the Netherlands (even though both bodies merged in 1892), but they did not get along within the CRC either. The antagonism was so strong that many feared a church split.

I recall that in my own years at Calvin, one professor especially, strongly Kuyperian in his outlook, spent more time talking about these days of struggle and controversy than he did about the material in the course he was supposed to be teaching. He extolled the virtues of Dutch culture, insisted that this culture was Reformed, and pleaded with his class to do in America what the Dutch had done in the Netherlands. He spoke of the ferocity of the struggle and reflected in his own critical comments the bitterness in his own soul toward the people from the tradition of the Secession churches. In *Sin and Grace* many references are indirectly made to these things I have described. It is difficult for the modern reader who is quite unaware of these things to understand many of the allusions of the authors. It is hoped that this brief historical resume will be of assistance.

If I may make a parenthetical remark at this point, it is of interest to observe that this division within the CRC had important repercussions for subsequent history. From the perspective of the CRC and the believers in common grace, the divisions were healed and the unity of the denomination preserved by the adoption of the three points of 1924. The first point, as I mentioned, was the common grace of the Secession churches; the second and third points were purely Kuyperian. The breach was healed by adopting one decision which approved both kinds of common grace.

From the viewpoint of the origin of the Protestant Reformed Churches, the division between the two groups was healed by a *repudiation* of common grace. Over against common grace, Rev. Herman Hoeksema taught that God's grace is always saving, always sovereign, and always particular. Throughout the history of the Reformed churches in the Netherlands, there were those in the churches of the Secession and among the followers of Kuyper who never held to any kind of common grace, insisting instead on the truths of sovereign and particular grace. These Hoeksema brought together from both traditions by repudiating Kuyper's dangerous innovation and by emphasizing what the church of Christ had emphasized throughout its history.

༒

A second important event, this time in the CRC itself, forms part of the historical background of *Sin and Grace*. This was the Janssen controversy.[4]

---

4. For a detailed description of the Janssen controversy, see Herman Hanko, "A Study of the Relation between the Views of Prof. R. Janssen and Common Grace," 1988 Master of Theology Thesis for Calvin Theological Seminary, reproduced as a syllabus for seminarians at the Theological School of the Protestant Reformed Churches, Grandville, Michigan. See also Herman Hanko, *For Thy Truth's Sake: A Doctrinal History of the Protestant Reformed Churches* (Grandville, Mich.: Reformed Free Publishing Association, 2000), 38–42, 128, 129, 145, 159, 168; and footnote 9 on 104.

Dr. Ralph Janssen was professor of Old Testament at Calvin Theological Seminary. In his instruction he introduced higher critical methods of Old Testament exegesis. A few examples will suffice. He held that on the basis of the scientific principle of the conservation of matter and energy—that is, that the amount of matter and energy in the creation is constant—the water which came from the rock in Kadesh was always present in the rock. The miracle did not consist in water created by God to provide for Israel's thirst. The miracle consisted in Moses hitting the rock in just the right place where the rock was thin. The water gushed out from a rock broken by Moses' blow. The stories of Samson, Janssen said, were myths invented to illustrate spiritual truths. Just as the Greeks had their heroes and invented mythical stories about them, so did Israel. The monotheism in which Israel was instructed by Moses was actually learned from surrounding nomadic tribes. Moses, convinced of the truth of this view, conveyed it to Israel.

Now, the important point is that Janssen justified his views on the basis of Kuyperian common grace. He insisted that scientific discovery, elemental religion among heathen, and a knowledge of God as the only God could come from unbelievers because of the operations of the Holy Spirit working a common grace in the unregenerate. Janssen insisted he was simply applying the doctrine of common grace to biblical studies.

At the 1922 Synod of the CRC in Orange City, Iowa, the views of Janssen were condemned, and Janssen was relieved of his position in the seminary. This was done on the basis of a thorough examination of Janssen's teachings by an official committee in which Revs. Danhof and Hoeksema played a leading role.

The interesting part of this committee's work and subsequent synodical decisions was that the issue of common grace was never addressed. The reason for this is undoubtedly due to the fact that there was disagreement among the committee members and the delegates to synod on the question of common grace, while the condemnation of Janssen's higher critical views was more widely approved.

Nevertheless, many supporters of Dr. Janssen remained in the church. These supporters, in every case strong proponents of Kuyperian common grace, were infuriated at Janssen's condemnation. In their anger they resolved that the opponents of common grace in general, and Danhof and Hoeksema in particular, would have to follow Janssen out of the church. Common grace was the issue which would serve as an effective tool to remove them.

∾

Van Zonde in Genade was written in 1923. No agreement or consensus had been reached on the question of common grace within the church. Many did not even know what the issues were; many were confused about the common grace which was a part of the tradition of the Secession of 1834, and the common grace of Kuyper. Others, firmly and unwaveringly committed to the truths of sovereign and particular grace, wanted no part of common grace in any form.

The efforts to secure the condemnation of Danhof and Hoeksema relied on Kuyperian common grace. Even though the common grace of the tradition of the Secession churches was widely held in the CRC, Danhof and Hoeksema's book deals only with Kuyperian common grace. This must not be construed as an indication of their approval of a general attitude of favor towards all men expressed particularly in a well-meant gospel offer. Their disagreement with that view was also well known, but Kuyperian common grace was the issue which had to be addressed.

Kuyperian common grace was at the top of the church's agenda because of the recent Janssen case in which the implications of cultural common grace had introduced higher criticism into the seminary. Hoeksema had written a series of articles in *The Banner*, the weekly of the CRC, in which Kuyper's views had come under sharp criticism.

But it was also Kuyperian common grace that became the means by which Hoeksema's opponents attacked him. Rev. Jan

Karel Van Baalen had opened the controversy soon after the condemnation of Janssen with a book in which he charged those who denied common grace with Anabaptism, or world-flight. Van Baalen's book, written in Dutch, had the title *De Loochening der Gemeene Gratie: Gereformeerd of Doopersch?* (The Denial of Common Grace: Reformed or Anabaptistic?). Danhof and Hoeksema answered the charge of Anabaptism with a booklet entitled "Niet Doopersch maar Gereformeerd" (Not Anabaptistic, but Reformed).

Prior to the writing of *Van Zonde en Genade*, the authors seemed to think that the error of common grace could be stopped, and that the flood of worldliness in the church could be reversed. They took comfort in the condemnation of Dr. Janssen, who had appealed to common grace in support of his higher critical views. They based their optimism on the fact that Kuyper's views of common grace were so obviously contrary to Scripture and the confessions, and that the charge of Anabaptism was so obviously ridiculous, that a book laying out the biblical teachings on this subject would convince almost everyone. And so *Van Zonde en Genade* was written and contained an extensive refutation of Kuyper's views. The judgment of the authors was, however, naive; history proved them wrong. Kuyper prevailed.

⤞⥈⤝

While other volumes can be found with extensive quotes from Kuyper's untranslated work on common grace, *Van Zonde en Genade* contains the largest number of quotations from the three-volume work which Kuyper wrote in defense of his views. Thus, *Sin and Grace* has historical value. Anyone who wishes to know what Kuyper actually taught on the subject of common grace can find it in copious quotations in this book.

In close connection with the description that *Sin and Grace* provides of Kuyper's views, the book also contains the most extensive analysis of the errors in Kuyper's common grace doctrine that is to be found in English.

The authors of *Van Zonde en Genade* go to great lengths to show that Kuyper's views were not only innovative and new to Reformed theology, but that in fact they were contrary to the historic Reformed position as outlined in the Reformed confessions. Danhof and Hoeksema also show beyond doubt that Kuyperian common grace is, above all, contrary to Scripture. They do this by pointing out how few are the texts to which Kuyper appealed in support of his doctrine and by offering the correct exegesis of the few texts to which he did refer. There is much historical material in the book. There is also important exegetical material.

In proving the fact that the Reformed churches since the time of the sixteenth century Reformation held firmly to sovereign and particular grace, the authors give a ringing endorsement of the Secession of 1834. This is heart-warming, because even in Reformed circles the Secession is openly criticized. This endorsement is found, to cite but one example, in a reference Danhof and Hoeksema make to the Secession:

> We learned to marvel at and regard Mother Church highly for her repeated effort to guard the principle of election by grace, regardless of disapproval, mockery, and scorn.
>
> At the roots of their spiritual life, the churches of the Secession, in our estimation, were thoroughly sound although they were limited in gifts, manpower, and means. They walked in the footsteps of Augustine, the Reformers, and the fathers of Dordt, according to the demands of their time, revering the gospel in the midst of a crooked and perverse generation.

The authors refer to two characteristics in this endorsement. They refer to the strong emphasis on sovereign and particular grace found among most of the leaders of the Secession. They also refer to the fact that the Secession shook free from a state church and established within the Netherlands a free church, that is, free from government control. By this latter characteristic, the fathers of the Secession rooted the antithesis in sovereign election and reprobation—the decree of God which in its execution cut through the citizenry of the Netherlands itself and was such a high wall of separation that cooperation between the wicked and the righteous in that country was impossible. Kuyper broke down that wall and paved the way for all the Dutch people to cooperate. The important truth of the antithesis comes through loudly and clearly in the witness of the Secession group.

Sin and Grace points out that in Kuyper's early days, the doctrine of sovereign and particular grace was preserved, as powerfully set down in his *Dat De Genade Particulier Is*. In fact, Kuyper's position on particular grace was originally the foundation for the establishment of the Free University of Amsterdam.

It is interesting that already in a book published in 1923, Revs. Danhof and Hoeksema prophesied that if Kuyperian common grace became the teaching of the church, worldliness would be the result. "[Common grace] brings the church and the world into mutual fellowship," they said. And the authors claim that this is, in fact, the intended purpose of common grace, as penned by Kuyper himself:

> The very purpose of common grace is to maintain the relation between God's people and the world. It directs itself toward the life of that world. It upholds the glory of God's work of creation in that world. And it cooperates with particular grace to make possible the penetration of the Kingdom into that world.

Perhaps the most interesting aspect of *Van Zonde en Genade* (and for Protestant Reformed readers, the most important) is the clear statement of the authors' positive view of God's purpose in creation and history. Although the book was written by men who never gave separation from the CRC a thought, the fundamentals of Herman Hoeksema's theology are all to be found in the third chapter, in which the positive truth of particular grace is developed. All that the Protestant Reformed Churches have confessed in the years of their existence, all that these churches have maintained as a distinct and separate denomination, are found in seminal form here. If anyone wishes to know what is distinctively Protestant Reformed, this book is must reading. It is impossible to set down in a few brief paragraphs what that important chapter contains. Nevertheless, the heart and soul of the positive teachings of Herman Hoeksema are all there.

The authors proceed from the viewpoint that Scripture teaches that God's purpose from the very outset of creation was the glory of His own name through the work of His Son, our Lord Jesus Christ. They point out that all history, including the fall of our first parents, is subordinate to that one purpose. The glory of God through Christ is realized through the salvation of a church chosen from all eternity out of free grace, redeemed through the blood of the cross, rescued from this present evil world by irresistible grace merited on the cross and sovereignly given, and called to live in the world a life of the antithesis by *spiritual* separation from the wicked world. This antithesis is a separation expressed in a witness to the cause of God's truth as revealed in sacred Scripture. To accomplish this, God makes His people His own covenant people, whom He forms through the Mediator of the covenant, whom He takes into His own covenant fellowship, and whom He calls to walk as His covenant people.

This truth is the explanation of history—not a realization of the original cultural mandate through a common grace operating in the world, but the final redemption of the whole creation through the work of Christ in the salvation of the elect by sovereign and particular grace. This world-and-life-view is thoroughly biblical; reaches back into eternity; spans the centuries, giving meaning to all that happens; and carries us into the final perfection of heaven itself where all shall be to God's glory forever. This view puts steel in the spines of those who suffer persecution for the cause of God, gives courage to those who seek to live an antithetical life, and demolishes every charge of Anabaptism.

In this connection a word must be said about the repeated reference of the authors to God's *organic* dealings with the human race, with the church, and with the creation as a whole. In a rather lengthy chapter, in which the two authors spell out "Our Viewpoint," they develop their idea of this subject. It is not an exaggeration to say that this *organic* idea forms the soul of all Hoeksema's theology, even in his development of the doctrine of the covenant of grace. When put together with Hoeksema's strong emphasis on sovereign and particular grace, one has the kernel of all Protestant Reformed theology as developed in later years. I dare say that Protestant Reformed theology cannot be understood apart from this organic conception, already taught and partially developed in 1923 by Danhof and Hoeksema.

⌒∞⌒

There are many places in which the authors add spice to the book by answering specific criticisms of their views.

Hoeksema's denial of common grace was well known in the churches, and even before the book was written, his views attracted criticism. Two such critics are answered in this book. The first critic wrote in *De Wachter*, the Dutch denominational weekly paper. The writer, Rev. Henry Wierenga, criticized Hoeksema's denial of common grace by attempting to show that Hoeksema was holding a position contrary to the fathers at Dordt. In support of this contention, Wierenga quoted from various foreign delegates who had submitted their opinions to the synod. These opinions were supposed to prove that the fathers of Dordt believed that God's common grace gave all men the light of nature by which they were able to do good in the sight of God.

The trouble was that Wierenga quoted delegates from the province of Bremen in Germany, who were sympathetic to the Arminians and who did all they could to support the Arminian position. It was a position rejected by the synod itself.

The second critic was Dr. Valentine Hepp from the Netherlands. A minister of the CRC had written Dr. Hepp (who held the chair of theology in the Free University) asking his advice on how to deal with a minister in the CRC, Hoeksema by name, who denied common grace.[5]

Hepp's suggestion, which he printed in *De Reformatie*, was that the writer of the letter deal patiently with Hoeksema, because apparently Hoeksema had no knowledge of the Reformed faith as developed in the Netherlands over the centuries. Hoeksema was himself relatively young and did not know very much yet, but given time, he would mature, learn more about these things, and modify his views.

As Hoeksema recounts this, one can sense how he restrained himself and said only that Dr. Hepp would have to excuse them if they said that this brought a smile to their faces.

There are times when the book is eloquent in its defense of sovereign and particular grace; there are times when the book is intensely moving. Consider this paragraph:

> It must not surprise us at all that throughout the ages it is precisely the doctrine of grace that has been contradicted. If we have learned from experience to taste that eternal election is meant for us, that we are God's children, and that God wills to be our Friend; if we have learned that the bonds of God's covenantal mercy have drawn us out of the estrangement and the bondage of sin and out of all the power of the enemy—then we have discovered indeed that the mystery of election is great. Then the humbled heart praises God's mercies, and the mouth rejoices: "I am once again the possession of the Lord." Then the Pelagian in us dies, and we, as far as we are concerned, desire to be saved only by grace. Then we understand men like David, Paul, Augustine, Luther, Ursinus, the Reformers in general, and the true martyrs. Then the doctrine of grace is indispensable for us, but also gloriously pleasant.

∽∾

Because Kuyper repudiated the unbiblical view of common grace, he wanted a term to distinguish his view from the tradi-

---

5. The query sent to Dr. Hepp was almost certainly sent by Rev. Jan Karel Van Baalen.

tional view. Kuyper wanted to emphasize that common grace was more a restraint of sin in the hearts of men which enabled them to do good in the sight of God. So, rather than call his common grace by the more traditional name, *algemeene genade*, to avoid confusion he chose the term *gemeene gratie*, even though that term also means "common grace."[6]

I have chosen to retain the English term *common grace* in the translation of this book for two reasons. The first one is that although Kuyper meant something different from the traditional view of common grace, his view was nevertheless a view of the grace of God that made God's grace common and general rather than sovereign and particular. In that respect it was essentially no different from the traditional view in its deepest meaning. That this is true is evident from the fact that the Synod of the CRC in 1924 adopted both the traditional view of *algemeene genade* and Kuyper's *gemeene gratie* in one decision on common grace without any effort to distinguish between the two.

The second reason is that Kuyper himself, in his work *De Gemeene Gratie*, sometimes uses *genade* rather than *gratie* and does so for no apparent reason. It seems as if he himself thought in terms of *genade*, even though he was writing about *gratie*. On occasion I have indicated in a footnote the fact that the word *genade* is used; it seemed to be another reason why the term common grace could be a proper translation in spite of Kuyper's own distinction.

In the days in which Kuyper's work was written and when Danhof and Hoeksema penned this book, the Dutch literary style was extremely cumbersome. It involved long paragraphs, often covering several pages, long sentences within the paragraphs, and complicated sentence structure. We have simplified this literary style to a considerable extent. We have broken lengthy paragraphs into

---

6. The Dutch words *genade* and *gratie* both mean "grace." For a more detailed description of the difference between the two terms, see Herman Hoeksema and Herman Hanko, *Ready to Give an Answer: A Catechism of Reformed Distinctives* (Grand Rapids, Mich.: Reformed Free Publishing Association, 1977), 51–62.

shorter ones and lengthy and complicated sentences into several simpler sentences.

All references to other books put into the body of the text by the authors, I have moved to footnotes to help maintain the flow of the thought. I have also included in the footnotes some biographical and historical information which the authors assumed the readers of their time knew, but which may be names and allusions unknown today. Bracketed information in the text represents additional information or explanation by the editor for the benefit of today's reader, and occasionally an aside by the authors within a quotation. For some of the longest chapters, subheads have been added, whereas the original had none.

I have tried to make the translation as accurate as possible and have attempted to maintain the style of the authors, but I have, admittedly, not always been successful. In the interests of making the book as understandable as possible to the modern reader, I have sometimes had to make compromises. I do not apologize for this. It is more important that many read and understand this important book than that the exact rendition of the original Dutch be retained.

The book as originally written had only scant bibliographical references, and sometimes none at all. I have tried to track down the incomplete references but have not always been able to find them. Further, the quotations are from books in the Dutch language, and it is impossible to tell what editions were used by the authors. Where I have given bibliographic information, it is from editions available to me.

The persevering reader will be amply rewarded. To those who love the Protestant Reformed heritage, reading this book will provide a deeper understanding of the truth confessed by the Protestant Reformed Churches and a deeper appreciation of the great gift God gave in preparing men to lead the denomination in the rich paths of that truth.

I am appreciative of the RFPA, which has not only agreed to publish *Sin and Grace*, but has also enthusiastically urged me to prepare it for publication. May God, by means of this book, be pleased to give to those who love Protestant Reformed truth a greater appreciation for its heritage, and may He give others who read it a sense of the importance of the biblical truth that God's grace is always particular, always sovereign, and always for the glory of His own great name.

HERMAN HANKO
Professor Emeritus
Protestant Reformed Seminary

Preface to *Van Zonde en Genade*

⚜

As we promised, we now present in the following pages our view of the free grace of God. We include a criticism of the position that was taken especially by Dr. A. Kuyper on so-called common grace, and which many brethren promoted as one of the foundations of a sound Reformed life-view.

Many have eagerly anticipated the publication of this book. Some of our opponents who disagree with us on the subject of common grace have even begun to show signs of impatience, and some of the bread-eating prophets among them assured our people that we would never publish the book we promised. They forgot how much work we have—more than enough to keep us busy without occupying ourselves in writing books. In the meantime, however, we carried on with our work of writing and can now offer something to our people.

This is not the last that we intend to write on this subject, for it is too broad, too extensive, and too important for that. In the future we hope now and then to offer more on the subject of the free grace of our God.

Since our last booklet was published, there has been little development in the doctrine of common grace.[1] There are still those

---

1. The booklet, in reply to a work by Jan Karel Van Baalen, is Danhof and Hoeksema's "Niet Doopersch maar Gereformeerd" (Not Anabaptistic, but Reformed). It was published in Grand Rapids, Mich., with no year of publication given, but presumed to be 1923, the same year that they published *Van Zonde en Genade*.

who consider it their duty to follow the course laid down by Dr. A. Kuyper, especially in his book *De Gemeene Gratie*. These even emphatically insist that Kuyper's view is fundamentally Reformed. They lay more and more emphasis on the importance, all-inclusiveness, and all-controlling significance of common grace. Living in the delusion that common grace is not only an all-controlling life-view, but also a fundamentally Reformed view, they put forth their best efforts to introduce it more fully into our churches.[2]

Thus it follows naturally that these common grace zealots opposed us more strongly than anyone else—just because we set ourselves firmly against this position of Dr. A. Kuyper. However, our opponents could not even be content with that. Perhaps they might have been able to put up with those who think that they can take a sort of neutral position on this issue, who are not fanatical about the theory of common grace, and who even often warn against misusing or exaggerating the doctrine. Yet such men as Van Baalen,[3] J. Groen,[4] Van Andel,[5] Kuizenga,[6] and others would never be satisfied with that moderate position; eventually, they would also oppose those who try to remain somewhat neutral.

Nevertheless, it is in the nature of the case that these defenders of common grace especially want to render harmless the strongest opponents of common grace. We do not blame them for

2. The reference is, of course, to the Christian Reformed Church (CRC), in which Revs. Danhof and Hoeksema were ministers.

3. Van Baalen (1890–1968) was minister of the CRC in Munster, Indiana, beginning in 1920. He was a strong supporter of Janssen and a prolific defender of Kuyperian common grace. He had studied at the theological school in Kampen, the Netherlands, from 1909–1914 and at Princeton Theological Seminary from 1914–1916.

4. Johannes Groen had been minister at Eastern Avenue CRC, Grand Rapids, Michigan, prior to Hoeksema's coming to that congregation as pastor.

5. Henry J. Van Andel was professor of the Holland language and literature at Calvin College and a strong Janssen supporter.

6. I have been unable to identify Kuizenga.

that. What we think less honorable is the fact that they do not hesitate to speak of "erring brethren," and they continue to do so, even before they have tried to understand the issue. They should not think it ill of us that we have an entirely different view of the issue involved. We are not the ones who depart from Scripture and the confessions; rather, it is Dr. Kuyper who has gone in an unreformed direction in his *De Gemeene Gratie*. We consider it our calling to point the attention of our churches to the error of his view in order that we may be kept from further departure.

The history of the controversy is as follows.

Apart from an expression or an accusation here and there in the former *Christian Journal* and in *Religion and Culture*,[7] the first attempt to defend the theory of common grace and to expose us as false teachers was made by Dr. R. Janssen after he was attacked for his unscriptural instruction in our theological school. Yet he never offered more than a few vague and general charges. He never attacked us on the basis of principle. He simply assumed that the teaching of Kuyper on common grace was obviously Reformed, and so he never attempted to prove the doctrine using Scripture and the confessions. Partly for this reason, and partly because of the practical objection that Dr. Janssen at one time wanted to charge far too many men before an ecclesiastical tribunal (It would hardly do to depose almost all of our ministers!),[8] the professor's word did not make much of an impression on our people.

In the meantime, there were those on Janssen's side who fearlessly raised the banner of common grace as if it were the real mark of a Calvinistic confession. Nor did they hesitate, without proof, to brand as "erring brethren" those who fought against this view. This sounded brotherly but was, in fact, far from it.

---

7. *Christian Journal* and *Religion and Culture* were two magazines published in the USA at the time of the common grace controversy. Both defended the views of Dr. Abraham Kuyper.

8. The reference is to Janssen's charge that most of the ministers in the CRC did not hold to Kuyperian common grace.

They themselves recognized the difficulty that confronted them. It was, after all, not such an easy task to show that the doctrine of common grace was really one of the pillars of our Reformed life-view. For, as strange as that may seem, our confessions actually do not say a word about this doctrine. In fact, they even directly oppose every effort to make this doctrine an integral part of our Reformed structure.

In any case, they might have had the idea that those who denied the theory of common grace were walking in an improper direction, but they faced an enormous difficulty when they confronted the task of producing the evidence. That was not easy. They might have thought that we were showing some symptoms of suffering from Anabaptistic fanaticism, but to come to a sound and correct diagnosis of our ailment was a less simple task. It is not surprising, therefore, that the bold attempt of the brother from Munster (not in Westphalia, but in Indiana)[9] who attempted to expose our error was greeted with open arms. What a hearty reception his book received, especially when compared with the formal, somewhat chilly "pleased to meet you" with which our reply was greeted in the public press! Everything seemed to be perfectly clear. The problem was solved. With great relief they shouted, "Eureka!" And so nothing seemed left for us to do but to make our choice between repenting of our error or leaving the church.

But this also ended in a disappointment. The brethren who were attacked had before long prepared a booklet in which the brother from Munster was answered. Although there were no favorable reviews written, except by the faithful and alert editor of *De Hollandsche Amerikaan* [The Holland American], in an unbe-

---

9. A Munster in the province of Westphalia in Germany was taken over by Anabaptist radicals during the Reformation, but Munster is also the name of the city in Indiana where Rev. Van Baalen was minister of a CRC church. He is the "brother" who attacked the authors with his *De Loochening der Gemeene Gratie: Gereformeerd of Doopersch?* (The Denial of Common Grace: Reformed or Anabaptistic?) (Grand Rapids, Mich.: Eerdmans-Sevensma Co., 1922).

lievably short time the booklet was sold out, and a second edition had to be prepared. As we were assured by more than one party, the first glow of light that had risen in Munster was now dimmed, if not completely swallowed up in darkness. Indeed, nothing more was heard from Munster. And the pamphlet that Rev. Van Baalen promised to write if we did not repent, also remained unwritten. The brother thought it wiser not to risk a hasty venture out on slippery ice, but thought it best to wait until his skates were sharpened.

However, this did not end the conflict as far as the brethren on the other side were concerned. Oh no! They still continued to speak of "erring brethren," even though they must have realized that they had no basis for such talk. A few even had the boldness to call us by that name publicly at an ecclesiastical gathering. They even called for help from the theologians of the Netherlands. Although some of our opponents had said at times that we here in America should develop our own type of Calvinism, and that Amsterdam[10] could not think for us, they now asked the Dutch to supply reinforcements from the capital city of the Netherlands and to take up the battle against us. But in general it may safely be said that they have had no success. No one risked entering into a discussion of the basic principles—not even Dr. Hepp.[11]

We, the writers of this book, stand completely on the opposite side, but we do not want this to be misunderstood. Some have written to us with the good intention of showing us that we were opposing a *wrong application* of common grace. Others also felt that the debate was a matter of words, but this is not so. We are deeply convinced that Dr. Kuyper led us in a fundamentally wrong di-

---

10. The reference is to the Free University of Amsterdam, founded by Dr. Kuyper.

11. Dr. Valentine Hepp was a noted theologian in the Netherlands and a professor at the Free University of Amsterdam. He is one of the two ministers to whom the authors reply in their chapter 4.

rection when he wrote his *De Gemeene Gratie*. The great leader of
the Netherlands has written much with which we heartily agree.
When we read his *Dat De Genade Particulier Is*, we are generally of
the same mind. But in his *De Gemeene Gratie* he departs from the
Reformed confessions on the subject of the grace of our God.

Nor do we hesitate to add that he has also departed from the
historical line of Reformed thinking. Some make the distinction
between being confessionally and being historically Reformed.
They claim that even though we have not departed from confessional Reformed doctrine, we nevertheless have broken with the
historically Reformed line. That, too, we deny, unless they understand by *historically Reformed* something which is not even a half
century old. It is none other than Dr. Kuyper who departed from
the historical line of Reformed theology, a line to which he himself adhered even as late as 1879. This also we will try to show in
detail in this book.

Brethren, we are not motivated by the desire to vilify. That has
been done. No one has attacked the faith more vilely than Eisen
from Holland, Michigan, whose piece appeared in *De Wachter*.[12]
We are only sorry that the writer has never had the moral courage
to make confession in the same periodical.

No, we do sincerely love peace, but it is our deep conviction
and love for our Christian Reformed Zion that spurs us on to fight
to the finish. We write because we feel it our calling to warn our
people of the bitter fruit that must come from maintaining this
doctrine. Do we not see before our very eyes how an alliance with
the world is being justified by this doctrine? Are these defenders
of common grace not telling you that the men of the world enjoy
the fruit of common grace in the world's art, in the world's science,
in the world's pleasure and relaxation? Is it not true that by this

---

12. *De Wachter* (The Watchman) was the official Dutch weekly paper of the
CRC from 1868–1985. As first founded, it reflected the views of the Secession.
Eisen, meaning "demand" in Dutch, was an assumed name used by a *De Wachter*
writer.

doctrine a sphere is created in which light and darkness, church and world, go hand in hand, living out of one and the same principle, the sin-restraining grace-principle? Did not Dr. Janssen himself attempt to show us how his modernist view of Scripture can be supported on the broad basis of common grace? Dr. Janssen was not entirely wrong. If it is true that the light that is in natural man is no darkness, but is truly light, there can be no objection to allowing Scriptural revelation to arise out of that natural light. Then the line fades between sin and grace, nature and miracle, reason and revelation. And then there can be no principal objection to the demand that we put ourselves in the same position as the natural man, the position of natural light, to view and to judge Scripture from that position.[13] We do not intend, therefore, to quit halfway in the struggle that began with the Janssen case, but we believe that we must carry on the battle to the end.

It is because we hold these convictions that we have withdrawn from further cooperation with *The Witness*. After we fought together with them against the instruction of Dr. Janssen, our ways parted. The brethren from *The Witness* still hold to common grace.[14] They not only speak of it, but they defend that viewpoint. It is true that they oppose much that comes from the hands of

13. These are references to Dr. Janssen's views that the religion of the Israelites was gained in part from the heathen because they, too, possessed, by natural light, elements of the truth. Dr. Janssen also attempted to explain the miracles in a natural and scientific way. He claimed that common grace enabled the ungodly to develop truth in science which the Bible could not contradict. And Dr. Janssen took an empirical approach to Scripture in keeping with the scientific method. In doing this he denied that Scripture is the object of faith.

14. Herman Hoeksema was a writer for *The Witness* with many of the same men with whom he cooperated in securing Dr. Janssen's expulsion from the seminary. But the issue of common grace, though it was Janssen's theological basis for his critical views of Scripture, was not so much as mentioned in the committee report and the decisions of synod. The reason was, undoubtedly, as Hoeksema states here, that there was already then disagreement on the question of common grace.

the common grace fanatics. They also opposed the instruction of Dr. Janssen. Yet they try to follow Kuyper's common grace. This seems to us to be impossible, and it will prove to be of no help to us in the end. We would once more end up where we do not want to be. Since there was no room in *The Witness* for the development of our sentiments, we have simply withdrawn to continue the struggle alone to get at the deepest principles of the Janssen matter.

We do not deceive ourselves into thinking that the task we have in mind is an easy one. We understand very well that to oppose men like Dr. A. Kuyper and Dr. H. Bavinck,[15] if only because of the impression their names make, seems an almost impossible task. But this does not relieve us of our duty, our serious calling before God and our churches. We are serious concerning this matter. The truth of God, the emphasis of the time-tried confessions that grace is particular and never common, spurs us on to the battle. Although the task of pointing out the right path in a clear and orderly fashion may seem almost impossible when great men have led the church in the wrong direction, yet faith is the substance of things hoped for and the evidence of things not seen. Our trust is upon and our prayer is to the Lord our God. May He crown our weak efforts with His indispensable blessing in order that our people may remain faithful to the God of the covenant and may continue to reveal themselves as the party of the living God in an evil world!

THE WRITERS

---

15. Dr. Herman Bavinck was a contemporary of Dr. Kuyper. He was one of the great theologians of the Netherlands and a professor with Kuyper at the Free University.

1

A Historical Review

❦

What prompted us to take our present stand against a certain doctrine of grace?

Was it world-flight? Was it perhaps a reaction against a craving for the world—a well-intended Anabaptistic avoidance of the world?

No, not that!

Listen!

A small church of the Secessionists at Ulrum, province of Groningen, the Netherlands, recently had to be replaced by a much larger building. According to the papers in Holland, the entrance to the small church bore an inscription on a stone on its left side that read, "Man Nothing." Engraved in granite on its right side were the words "Christ All in All."

That entrance was too narrow for many people.

Dutchmen with a broader outlook and wider inclinations chose the state church.[1]

Only the "common folk," who were *scarcely* saved, and entered

---

1. The state church in the Netherlands was the Nederduitsch Hervormde Kerk (NHK). In effect, it was an established church, that is, sanctioned and supported by the government. For additional information, see also footnotes 8 and 48 in this chapter. See also text about the state church in the Editor's Introduction.

the church *through many different forms of persecution*, sang the following:

> This is Thy temple-gate, O Lord,
> The just shall enter there;
> My Saviour, I will give Thee thanks,
> O Thou that hearest prayer.[2]

We had our sojourn among them.

However, the inscription on the wall of the small church was not to our liking either, at first. It sounded so humiliating: *Man Nothing!* And that second part, *Christ All in All*, completely excluded man's own righteousness. Certainly we readily confessed intellectually that salvation is of the Lord and that our salvation is entirely by grace, but the full spiritual light of that truth did not immediately penetrate our hearts. Only very gradually did we learn to agree with the watchword of the reformers:

> God's Spirit, working in my heart,
> Exposed to me my sin;
> God's law demanded holiness,
> But I was vile within.
> I should be clothed with righteousness;
> Instead, foul rags were all my dress.
>
> This truth profound He taught to me:
> That of myself there's naught.
> Christ's righteousness supplanted mine;
> He Satan's downfall brought.
> Now death and grave are beaten down,
> And I receive the victor's crown.[3]

---

2. No. 318, second stanza, a versification of Psalm 118 in *The Psalter: with Doctrinal Standards, Liturgy, Church Order, and Added Chorale Section*, Revised ed., PRC (Grand Rapids, Mich.: William B. Eerdmans Publishing Company, 1998), 276.

3. The English versification was made by Thelma Westra of Jenison, Michigan, at the request of the translator. The Dutch source is not known.

Then we also understood the inscription at the entrance of the small church. It was directed against the Pelagian in every one of us. It was the spiritual hallmark of the Secession. The truth that it is not of him that willeth, nor of him that runneth, but of God that showeth mercy was, as with Augustine and Luther, learned by experience and sharply impressed on the consciousness of our fathers. "God's eternal good pleasure"[4]—God's election by grace—was the heart of their confession, and all the issues of our life were from that heart.

That gave us reason to understand and love our Mother Church. Her constant watchfulness at the narrow gate, in spite of all the accusations that she was narrow-minded and Anabaptistic, only served as proof to us that she was spiritually healthy in the deepest principle of her life. The accusation was made that she was seriously sick. Such an accusation must be rejected as without any basis insofar as it referred to the spiritual principle out of which the church of the Secession lived.

However, the Secession understood far better than our forefathers the spiritual character of the life-roots of the church. This deeper understanding was the reason why the church of the Secession could break away from the idea of a people's church, or a national church, and take up the battle against all sorts of half-hearted religion and new inroads of the error of Pelagianism and Arminianism. This understanding enabled these churches to rise up in defense of the principle of election by grace.

When the state church sacrificed its honor to the principles of the revolution,[5] (as formerly Judah did, who married a daughter of a strange god and thus desecrated the Lord's holiness), the church of the Secession indignantly separated from the state church and,

---

4. *Om eeuwig welbehagen* is a very common Dutch expression, which literally means "because of eternal good pleasure."

5. The reference is to the revolution in church government that took place during the time of Napoleon's rule. For background on this, see D. H. Kromminga, *The Christian Reformed Tradition from the Reformation till the Present* (Grand Rapids, Mich.: Wm. B. Eerdmans Publishing Company, 1943), 72ff.

following their own life-principle, returned in 1834[6] to a doctrine and life ruled by the principle of election by grace. That is their honor. The Secession of 1834 was not an excursion down some byway, but a protest against departure in doctrine and walk, discipline and worship, and a return to the Reformed confessions and Church Order, as well as to the principles of the Reformation.

Apostasy in the State Church

In the previous period of unbelief and revolution, all certainties had been cast to the wind, but the truths of the sovereignty of God and His free election of grace were especially attacked. Even after the defeat of Napoleon and the return of the House of Orange,[7] the people still continued to drink from the cup of the pig's swill of the revolution. It is true that they avoided the worst extremes of the French Revolution, but they maintained its principles. Without completely denying the supernatural, every sharp distinction was erased. On the basis of mere human brotherhood, they sought fellowship with all the citizens of the land.[8] Among the more religiously inclined, a vague Christianity was maintained which was said to be more important than all the differences in the faith. All sorts of spiritual and unspiritual elements were brought together under one roof. Even the Remonstrants[9] requested union with the Reformed. Christian disci-

---

6. 1834 is the date of the Secession, which took place under the leadership of Rev. Hendrik De Cock, Albertus Christiaan Van Raalte, and others.

7. The House of Orange was the ruling monarchy in the Netherlands from the time of William of Orange ("the Silent"), who delivered the Netherlands from Spanish rule in the seventeenth century.

8. A state church, by virtue of the fact that it is established by the government, is one that is the only official, legal church of the country. As the one approved and legally established denomination, it is responsible for the moral and spiritual welfare of the entire citizenry. It is as if all the citizens are, to some degree, under the supervision of the church.

9. "Remonstrants" is another name for the Arminians in the Netherlands

pline grew lax, spiritual life was reprehensible, and rationalistic errors forced their way into the church. Van der Palm[10] praised the
changes as beneficial; J. H. Regenbogen[11] unashamedly taught his
rationalistic interpretation of the miracles, of sin, of repentance, and
so forth; and W. Hoving and P. W. Brouwer[12] could attack the doctrines of Holy Scripture, the Trinity, and the divinity of Christ without meeting much opposition. The Reformed doctrines of 1618–
1619 were despised. Some of the common people, especially of
Gelderland, still maintained the confession of the fathers, but the
majority of the leaders were bitterly opposed to it. Thus, finally, the
church permitted the government to replace the Church Order of
Dordt [Dordrecht] with a new set of regulations.

Over against this apostasy, the men of the Reveil[13] never did
return to the actual historical position of the Reformers. The cause
of their failure was not that their labors were largely limited to the
aristocratic and higher circles. Nor did they fail, as is sometimes
said, because the Reveil was not "a native plant." After all, the
Reformation of the sixteenth century did not have its origin historically in the Netherlands either. The failure was not, as the
proverb has it, that "the soil of the fatherland does not bear spiritual flowers." The reason for the failure of the Reveil to bring reformation was that this spiritual awakening did not have its roots
in the historically Reformed confessions, but rested on a founda-

---

who were condemned by the Synod of Dordt. This term comes from a document
they drew up called the Remonstrance, which Arminius' followers wrote in 1610
in the city of Gouda.

10. Johannes Henricus Van der Palm (1763–1840) was professor at the theological school at Leiden University in the Netherlands.

11. J. H. (Johan Hendrik) Regenbogen (1769–1814) was a professor at the
theological school in Franeker, the Netherlands.

12. I have been unable to identify Hoving and Brouwer, but it is clear from
the context that they, too, were modernistic professors in the state universities
in the Netherlands.

13. The Reveil was a reformatory movement in the Netherlands that never
separated from the apostate state church. It had its origin in Switzerland and
spread through Europe.

tion of a vague, general Christianity. There were men of faith
trained in the school of Bilderdijk[14] who, through the preaching
of the riches of the grace of God in Christ, fought untiringly and
heroically against the spirit of the age, but that did not make them
Reformed. Their ideal was not the Reformed church in the flourishing period of the Reformation; rather, in their heart, they
wanted a return to the church in the age of the apostles. In doing
this they were being unhistorical.[15]

The men of the Reveil, especially Groen,[16] were even less sympathetic to some of the Reformed doctrines established at Dordt
in 1618–1619, as, for example, the doctrine of predestination,
even though this doctrine is the heart of the confession. Thus, the
movement of the Reveil did not satisfy the orthodox people, who
were deeply interested in the doctrines and mysteries of the true
faith. The way to the heart of these reviled common folk was
through Dordt, and the Secession could not come until these pious folk[17] had led their leaders back along that time-tried path.

The Reformation of the *Afscheiding*

This became especially evident in the history of Rev. De Cock.
When he came to Ulrum in 1829, he was ignorant of the heart of
the faith in more ways than one. He was not well acquainted with

---

14. Willem Bilderdijk (1756–1831), a lawyer and leading figure in the
Reveil, founded a private theological school at Leiden.

15. The authors refer to movements that speak, sometimes rather piously, of
returning to the simplicity and innocence of the apostolic church. In doing this,
they deny two millennia of the work of the Holy Spirit of Christ, who leads the
church into all truth.

16. Guillaume Groen Van Prinsterer was a leading figure in the Reveil. Later,
with Dr. Abraham Kuyper, he formed the Anti-revolutionary Party.

17. Dr. Kuyper called the common folk in the church the "kleine luyden,"
which is an affectionate term for the people who, though mostly uneducated,
were the true spiritual remnant in the Netherlands and exhibited great piety. The
term literally means "small folk."

the content of the Canons of Dordt. But soon after he came, through his contact with some of the common members of his congregation, he began to do his own thinking. By studying Calvin's *Institutes* and the writings of van Zuylen of Nijveldt,[18] De Cock was won over to the old truth. From that point on, he zealously proclaimed the basic doctrines of the Reformed faith.

In order to overcome the ignorance of the Reformed truth among the people, De Cock wrote "The Conclusions of the National Synod of Dordt" and "A Compendium of Christian Religion." He also took up his pen to defend the true Reformed doctrine and to protect the sincere Reformed people against "two wolves"[19] who had attacked the sheepfold of Christ. At the same time he did battle with Professor Hofstede De Groot of Groningen, who declared in 1816 that the binding power of the confessions had been abandoned, and who felt free to attack the fundamental truths of Reformed doctrine. And De Cock finally, seeing for himself the close relationship between doctrine and walk, turned to the people of the Netherlands, urging them with warnings and admonitions to return to the faith of their fathers. He considered that to be their only salvation. Alas, it was an uneven struggle of one against many. Difficulties with the officials of the state church arose. De Cock was suspended, fined, thrown into prison, reviled, and deposed from office—all because in his ministry he attacked false teachers and fought for sound doctrine.

Due to these things, De Cock could also correctly write in the "Act of Secession"[20] that, in harmony with the office of all

---

18. Cornelis Baron van Zuylen of Nijveldt was the man who is sometimes called "the chain" that joined the Reveil to the Secession.

19. "Two wolves," meaning false teachers, comes from the title of a work by Hendrik De Cock: "Defense of the True Reformed Doctrine and of the True Reformed Believers, Attacked and Exposed by Two So-called Reformed Teachers; or The Sheepfold of Christ Attacked by Two Wolves and Defended by H. De Cock, Reformed Teacher at Ulrum."

20. The Act of Secession (*Acta van Afscheiding*) was the document drawn up and signed by Rev. De Cock, his elders, and deacons that made official their with-

believers (Article 28 of the Confession of Faith), he and his followers had separated themselves from those who were not of the
church and would no longer have fellowship with the state
church[21] until that church returned to the true service of the Lord.

In the same Act of Secession, they also expressed that they were
willing to have fellowship with those of the state church who were
truly Reformed, and that in every respect they wanted to maintain
God's holy Word, the time-tested Forms of Unity,[22] and all doctrine
that is based upon God's Word. Thus, the Secession was a means to
the establishment of a true Reformed church. It did not merely break
with the Synodical Association that had been decreed by King
William I, and with the related synodical administration, but it also
broke with the idea of a national or state church, and it returned to
the original principle of the Reformation: election by grace. The spiritual nature of the deepest life-principle of the church requires this.

The Basic Unity of the *Afscheiding*

The work of such men as H. P. Scholte, A. Brummelkamp, G. T.
Gezelle-Meerberg, S. Van Velzen, A. C. Van Raalte, and other leaders of the Secessionists was along similar lines. There was some difference in the views of these men in minor details, in their personal
gifts, manner of conversion, local circumstances, and the ways in
which events developed. One was more opposed to the false teach-

---

drawal from the state church. To see an English translation of the full text, consult Herman Hanko, *For Thy Truth's Sake: A Doctrinal History of the Protestant
Reformed Churches* (Grandville, Mich.: Reformed Free Publishing Association,
2000), 420–422.

21. By *Hervormde Kerk* (Reformed Church), the authors refer to the state
church.

22. The "Three Forms of Unity" are the creedal basis of the Reformed
churches: the Heidelberg Catechism (1563), the (Belgic) Confession of Faith
(1562), and the Canons of Dordrecht (Dordt)(1619). All of them are reproduced
in the liturgical section of *The Psalter*.

ings of the state church; another was more opposed to the wrong government of the church. One preached the fundamental truths of the Scriptures "in a rigidly Reformed way"; another called the people of the Netherlands to sorrow and repentance and to return to the God of the covenant and to the faith of their fathers. Some appealed to the synod to maintain the confessions, demanding that these, and these only, be made binding, as in the past, in order to force the anti-Reformed preachers to return to the Reformed doctrine. Others, also because of pressure from the congregations, allowed hymns to be sung or simply refused to submit to the ecclesiastical regulations. But no matter how much difference there was among them, they were all agreed that the state church could not meet the standard of Article 29 of the Confession of Faith, and that the salvation of the sinner is only by the free grace of God. The Secession, therefore, was not merely a return to the Church Order of Dordt, but above all, it was a return to the spiritual principle of election by grace as it had been defined by the Canons of Dordt.

This is evident from a sermon of De Cock on Ephesians 2:8–10, preached five days after the signing of the Act of Secession. But it is evident, too, from the slander of his enemies. In De Cock's sermon, among other things, he said this:

> Those good works, beloved, the Lord has prepared in advance for you to walk in them, and thereby you will know your calling—not by the works that the Pharisees do to be seen and praised of men, for they are mere glittering sins; but works which proceed from faith and the work of God's Spirit, and which the Lord Jesus has described (Matthew 5:3–10)—not as they were presented from this pulpit last Sunday, mutilated and corrupted in the Remonstrant manner by Rev. Smith.

In the following poem[23] De Cock was mockingly presented as a faithful defender of the Synod of Dordt:

---

23. The poem is quoted by J.C. Rullmann in *Een Nagel in de Heilige Plaats: de Reformatie der Kerk in de XIXᵉ Eeuw* (A Nail in the Holy Place: The Reformation of the Church in the 19th Century) (Amsterdam: W. Kirchner, 1912), 105.

Is Christ's sheepfold being attacked by two wolves?
Are the poor sheep the victims of claw and teeth?
Are there no faithful shepherds upon the walls of Zion
So that the small flock is being overpowered?
One man watches and fights with the shield of the Synod of Dordt.
Thus the pair of wolves are defeated by him!
He is the most faithful messenger of Bogerman
And an untiring defender of the doctrine of Gomarus.
He holds the balance of the number that perishes.
Those he damns irrevocably in misery.
He has the measuring rod of the number of the elect.
He knows the language of both; their lot is known to him...
Where may that twinkling star spread its light,
Through which the light of Gansvoort and Hugo De Groot is
    eclipsed,
Through which the light of Van der Palm and Borger must
    fade,
With whom no Bible interpreter of our time can compare?
That glorious light arose in Ulrum's congregation!
There the doctrine of Dordt was again newly planted.[24]

The other leaders of the Secession were spoken of in similar terms. Even though most of them were well-trained and educated men, and some even had a classical training, their detractors still generally referred to them as Bilderdijkians, Da Costians,[25] stuffed

---

24. The poem is a sarcastic picture of De Cock as one who thinks he has saved the church and has done a greater work than outstanding men in Dutch history. Identification of persons mentioned in the poem follows. Johannes Bogerman was the president of the Synod of Dordt (1618–1619). Franciscus Gomarus was the chief defender of the supralapsarian position at the synod. Gansvoort lived prior to the Reformation, but was an influential Dutch theologian who sought reform within the Roman Catholic Church. Hugo De Groot, a government official who lived at the time of the Arminian controversy, was a humanist with much political influence who defended Remonstrant theology. Van der Palm, as we have noted before, was a theological professor at Leiden University. Borger (1784–1820) was also a professor at Leiden.

25. Isaak Da Costa (1798–1860) was a Dutch poet and part of the Reveil.

shirts, precisionists, the pious, the backward, the orthodox, and the Dordtians. All of this, in our judgment, is convincing proof that the Secession was indeed a return to the doctrine of free grace, the actual principle of the Reformation, the real life-source of the church, the confession of the fathers of Dordt.

But the Secession did not settle the matter. Two hundred years separated the Secession from the Synod of Dordt. During that time there had been many changes. Political circumstances especially differed in the nineteenth century from those of the seventeenth. One must reckon with those changes in judging the Secession of 1834. Such changes had already begun during the period 1618–1795 when the Reformed churches dominated the life of the Netherlands. At that time already, there was a gradually growing laxity in maintaining true doctrine, although in the period of revolution that followed, the decay and deformation of the church advanced much more rapidly through the influence of revolutionary principles. The "Remonstrance," which had been driven out of the front door of the church by the decisions of the Synod of Dordt, forced its way in again through the back door in alliance with unbelieving science. This Remonstrance was influenced by the state, and it bent an ear to so-called autonomous science, which rejected God and His Word. Thus, before the fathers of the Secession could return to the historical line of the Reformed confessions, they had to reorient themselves. They had to enable the renewed Reformed churches to take their places, from a practical point of view, in the life of the nineteenth century.

This was far from easy. Quite suddenly churches were united which were actually quite different. Sharp differences separated the north, the south, and the central Netherlands. There was a difference between Frisians and Saxons, Celts and Franks, along with other external influences that brought unrest and strife in the churches. Labadistic[26] and Puritan influences were still active.

---

26. Labadism had developed from the teachings of Jean de Labadie, a teacher of mysticism, who led many away from the faith.

Scholte and De Cock differed from each other on their views of the church. The new Church Order of 1837 brought further confusion and separation. Scholte's request for recognition by the government and for the legal incorporation of his congregation at Utrecht created more division. For various reasons, some—both leaders and members—even refused to remain in the same denomination with the Secessionists.

Nor did those fully agree who remained together as a denomination. The differences between the "North" and the "South," between the "precisionists" and the "broad-minded," were not limited merely to formal and church-political matters, nor to the name and the historical continuity of the Secessionists.[27] There was also a marked difference in regard to various doctrinal truths, such as the covenant, election and reprobation, Christ's satisfaction for the elect *only*, a twofold calling, the impotence of the will of man, the offer of grace and salvation, the demand of faith, and the like. Similar questions, which are still current among us, date all the way back to the first days of the Secession, or even earlier. They certainly did not begin in our day. In their implications, however, all these differences bring us to the very heart of the matter: the principle of election by grace. But the men of the Secession did not settle these differences by their own synodical decisions. They obviously felt that all these differences had been sufficiently covered by the Canons of Dordt.

It must be granted that the Secessionists were limited in manpower and means, but they were not narrow-minded. Their aim was to continue on the path laid out by the fathers of Dordt. To

---

27. In the early years of the Secession, its churches debated at length the question of whether they should insist that they were the true continuation of the state church. They wanted to insist that they were, and that they had a right to the name. It was this very insistence of theirs, however, that was a reason for their being persecuted. When they finally agreed to abandon their claim, they were also given freedom by the state to worship according to the dictates of conscience. Abraham Kuyper was later critical of the Secessionists for repudiating their claim to be the lawful continuation of the state church.

depart in the direction of Munster[28] was out of the question. Nor was mere faithfulness to the past sufficient for them. They dared to adjust their practice to the demands of their time so that they had room to develop. And whatever principles they let slip through thoughtlessness in some unguarded moment, they recovered and held firmly to them.[29] With an eye for reality, but contending for the faith once delivered to the saints, they attempted above all else to preserve the old ways. Yet they were determined to shine as the light of the world in the midst of a crooked and perverse generation, maintaining the Word of life.

The same can be said of the immigrants. The leaders of the colonists, the pioneers and founders of the Christian Reformed Church in North America, were aware of their times and understood their calling. Imagine: the "naive" Van Raalte intended to establish a colony in the highlands of Java "in order to be busy there in mission work, and with a whole colony of men, women, and children to work there like a Williams among the inhabitants of the South Seas, and to establish that as a center for the spread of the gospel."[30]

Scholte's objection to colonizing South Africa was that they "would likely find among the churches there an attachment to the adopted Forms, but not so likely a living faith."

The "Constitution of the Zeeland Society for Moving to the United States" spoke of the debt the Netherlands owed to God, of oppressive ecclesiastical ties and persecution for the faith, and of not being in a position "to have their children instructed ac-

---

28. The "Munster" here refers to the town in Germany that radical Anabaptists captured in 1535–1536. Hence, to depart in the direction of Munster means to become Anabaptistic.

29. The reference is probably to the fact that a synod of the Secession churches, at the prompting of Rev. H. P. Scholte, abandoned the Church Order of Dordt, but in a few years they saw their error and adopted it once again.

30. The reference of this quotation is not given in the original text. It is evident from the context that the authors were proving that the Secessionists were zealous and neither ignorant nor incapable.

cording to their religious conviction."[31] All the immigrants acknowledged God's Word to be the rule and standard for their lives. They regulated their fellowship in the new world in harmony with that rule. It is true that the settlement in Pella under Scholte departed somewhat in the direction of Chiliasm and Darbyism,[32] and the colony in western Michigan initially manifested a kind of national religion as in the Netherlands, more or less patterned after the settlements of the Boers in South Africa, or after Israel in the dispersion. The consistories exercised influence over every aspect of life; the office bearers supervised almost everything. The aristocrat was too prominent in Van Raalte. However, in spite of these peculiarities, all due to the unique circumstances of the settlers, they were faithful to their beginning. And after they were formally organized in April 1848, they lived in harmony with the confessions and the Church Order of the Reformed churches. Even before they joined the Reformed Church in America, it could be reported of them that "They organized themselves into a Reformed Dutch Church with the usual standards of doctrine and church polity." And later, when many discovered that in the Reformed Church in America, the doctrine and church polity were not in every respect according to the decisions of Dordt, they returned in 1857 to the position they had forsaken in 1849, in order that they might keep fellowship with the churches of the Secession in the Netherlands, freely and independently according to the demands of life in this good land, but in the tradition of the fathers of Dordt.

They were not Anabaptistic, but Reformed.

The agreement for union in 1892 between the Secession churches and the churches that followed A. Kuyper was no differ-

---

31. No further details were supplied by the authors on the source of this quotation.

32. Chiliasm and Darbyism are forms of premillennialism and dispensationalism.

ent.[33] The points debated before the union did not deal with the actual basis for union. And so important was all of this that the two church groups joined their efforts to manifest themselves as *Reformed* churches. Only the question of training for the ministry created a problem, and that only for a while. Even then, though, the two groups maintained their own emphasis in their separate theological schools.[34] As far as theological instruction was concerned, the different emphases did not touch the heart of the truth: the principle of grace.

The same is true of the intra-confessional differences, concerning which the Synod of Utrecht formulated certain conclusions, which were also adopted by our Christian Reformed Churches in 1908.[35] As Reformed churches we walk in the way of Dordt.

A Brief Survey of the History of the Doctrine of Particular Grace

And so, we now face the question, What did the men of Dordt actually confess?

The answer to that question is that our fathers of Dordt took a positive position in the struggle over the question of the freedom of the sinner's will over against the absolute predestination of God. The principle issue was the relation between man's deeds and divine providence. The question was how the freedom of hu-

33. The reference is to the union in the Netherlands between the churches of the Secession and the churches that came out of the state church under the leadership of Dr. Kuyper. These two denominations merged in 1892 to form the Reformed Church in the Netherlands (*Gereformeerde Kerk in Nederland*).

34. The churches of the Secession had their seminary in Kampen, while Kuyper's churches had their seminary in Amsterdam.

35. These were adopted in the Netherlands in 1905 and became known as *De Conclusies van Utrecht* (The Conclusions of Utrecht). A translation of this document in English is given in Hanko, *For Thy Truth's Sake*, 427–431.

man acts and man's consequent accountability before God could be harmonized with God's absolute determination of all things. Dordt did not, in fact, adopt the "higher opinions" of the supra-lapsarians, who started from God's purpose in the fall, but they assumed the position of the infralapsarians. They answered the question of the relationship between the activity of fallen man and God's works, especially in connection with the restoration of the sinner.

To understand this properly we must go back to Augustine.

In the development of dogma, the question of the grace of God was first considered at the beginning of the fifth century. The church in the first four centuries assumed that in the conversion of the sinner, a certain cooperation took place between the work of grace and the human will, although no account was given of how this cooperation worked. But especially after Tertullian[36] there were differences between the East and the West over this question. In general, although there was still much hesitation and uncertainty, the universal sinfulness of mankind, its connection to the sin of Adam, and the unconditional necessity of divine grace in Christ unto salvation were acknowledged by all the ministers of the church.

But the influence of the British monk Pelagius brought a major change. Pelagius taught that the sinfulness of mankind is not caused by Adam's sin, and that even without the cooperation of the grace of God, by his own moral ability and by persistent strug-gle, man is able to raise himself to holiness and sinlessness.

In those days, Aurelius Augustine (A.D. 354–430), bishop of Hippo in Africa, in the struggle with Pelagianism, maintained, over against the doctrine of the free will of man, the truth that the counsel of God is determinative for all things. This preeminent church father taught that the entire human race sinned in Adam, "for he was the entire humanity." He did not regard the relation-

---

36. Tertullian was a church father of the third century who did much to lead the Western church into a biblical understanding of the doctrine of the Trinity.

ship between Adam and all humanity as a mere covenant fellowship, as was later true of many, but he taught that it was also an organic relationship: the entire human race was present in its first
father and shared with Adam in his guilt and depravity. All human individuals together form one organic whole.

> By procreation—not by imitation, as Pelagius had taught—Adam's
> nature, as it was after the fall, with its sin and guilt, dead and worthy
> of damnation, but also saveable, was passed on to his descendants.
> Divine grace, which is the only possible power that can deliver and
> save a person, joins itself to the remnants of the divine image that
> reveal a need of and susceptibility for salvation. Grace is therefore
> absolutely necessary; it is the beginning, the middle, and the end of
> the Christian life. It becomes man's portion, not because he believes,
> but in order that he may believe, for faith is also the work of God's
> grace. [Thus also] free will is restored, and manifests itself in a holy
> life in love.[37]

From this view of God's grace, [says Orr],

> Augustine was brought by the force of logic to the doctrine of an ab-
> solute predestination. Experience taught him that not all mankind
> attains conversion and salvation. Since a person can add absolutely
> nothing to his conversion, the basis for this difference must not be
> sought in him, but only in the eternal, sovereignly free decree of God,
> according to which He has determined, for the glory of His grace, to
> save some out of the entire human race, which has completely fallen
> into condemnation, and to leave others for the glory of His punish-
> ing justice in their deserved condemnation. The reason for this elec-
> tion rests only in the wise and hidden good pleasure of the divine will,

---

37. Augustine quoted in James Orr, *The Progress of Dogma: being the Elliot Lec-
tures Delivered at the Western Theological Seminary, Allegheny, Penna., U.S.A.,
1897* (Grand Rapids, Mich.: Wm. B. Eerdmans Publishing Co., 1952), 148.
I have been unable to locate the Dutch source of this quotation from Augustine
as it stands in the text. For Orr's full discussion, see 146–160.

leaving out of consideration faith, which, after all, is also a gift of God.[38]

The result of this struggle [between Augustine and Pelagius] was that pure Pelagianism was condemned at the Synod of Carthage in 412, again in 418, and also at the ecumenical Council at Ephesus in 431, but no positive decisions were made. The East insisted on cooperation between the grace of God and the free will of man in the conversion of the sinner. In the West, in Gaul (now France), the Pelagian struggle revived with the so-called Semi-Pelagianism of Cassianus, abbot of Massilia, and his followers. These Semi-Pelagians recognized "a causal relationship between the common sinfulness of men and the first sin of Adam, but nevertheless taught that the divine image was merely weakened, and especially that free will was not entirely extinguished, but rather weakened, and to such a degree that without divine aid the sinner could not attain to salvation and develop it."[39]

After a long, drawn-out struggle, a weakened Augustianism triumphed at the Synod of Orange in 529. This synod tried to avoid the severity of the doctrine of predestination by seeking the basis for reprobation not in the will of God, but in the rebellion of mankind.

For a short time the struggle concerning Augustine's doctrine of absolute predestination was revived in the eighth century by Gotteschalk and the defenders of his views, but the struggle ended without any definite conclusion.[40] A biblical doctrine of predestination was never ecclesiastically established.

At the time of the Reformation of the sixteenth century, particularly Luther and Calvin appealed to the statements of Augustine. The experiences of Luther's life, along with his study of the

---

38. Ibid., 152, 153.
39. Ibid., 160, 161.
40. Gotteschalk (806–868) died a martyr for his commitment to the truth of sovereign and double predestination.

epistles of Paul and the writings of Augustine, caused him to understand that the individual is by nature not free, and therefore is incapable of that which is good. Man is brought to salvation only by the free grace of God in Christ without any cooperation on his part. This acknowledgment, as in the case of Augustine, brought him in the beginning of the Reformation to confess the doctrine of predestination. Luther maintained this conviction especially over against Erasmus, who took the position of the Semi-Pelagians on the question of the freedom of the human will.[41] Calvin went even further than Augustine in his conclusions concerning the doctrine of predestination. But in Melanchthon, Luther's friend, we find a revival of Semi-Pelagianism as described above, namely, that there is a certain cooperation between the free choice of the individual and the grace of God in the conversion of the sinner. According to Melanchthon, the remnant of free will in the sinner consists in his ability to grasp the proffered grace by his own impulse, although that deed has no inherent merit.

The Formula of Concord (1577) brought an end to the struggle that broke out over the same question in Lutheran countries. It expressed agreement, over against Melanchthon, with those who wanted no cooperation between the grace of God and the will of the individual in the conversion of the sinner. It rejected most emphatically any and all cooperation in the work of conversion. But it did not adopt the logical consequence of this position, namely, the doctrine of predestination: that God ordains some unto salvation and the others unto damnation. For, according to the Formula, while an individual does not have an ability in himself to cooperate in acquiring grace, he does possess the ability to oppose and refuse it. Therefore, the Formula tried to maintain that: (1) God wills that all mankind shall be saved; (2) salvation is, in the absolute sense of the word, by God's grace; and (3) con-

---

41. Desiderius Erasmus, the prince of the humanists, split with Luther over the question of the freedom of the will. Luther's book *The Bondage of the Will* was an answer to Erasmus' defense of the freedom of the will.

demnation is the fruit of man's own guilt. It follows, then, that *particular* grace—as taught by Augustine, Calvin and the Reformed, and Luther—was actually abandoned. Predestination had as its object the salvation of people, but the fact that specific persons go lost can only be ascribed to bare divine foreknowledge.

Such a view could not possibly be the end of the matter. How is it possible that a sinner, who in no way is able to cooperate with the grace of God in his conversion, can still resist God in His desire to save all men? That is an inconsistency. The logical conclusion of this position, based on improper exegesis, is that God's work of grace, or at least His desire that all mankind be saved, is dependent upon the choice of the sinner. But then God must certainly also be dependent upon the will of the elect in saving them unto eternal life. Election and reprobation cannot be separated. We are confronted with a dilemma here, and we must make our choice. Does God elect and reprobate according to His own divine freedom, or does He elect and reprobate depending on the creature? The Reformed reached the first conclusion; the Arminians adopted the latter.

Earlier, at the very beginning of the Reformation, the Reformed had enthusiastically embraced the doctrine of God's free grace, and later established, in the Confession of Faith and the Catechism, the doctrine of God's predestination as absolutely independent of the sinful creature. Such a delight in God's saving grace also governed the Reformation in the Netherlands. Living out of the principle of free grace, the whole of the national life of the people, as well as of those in civil authority, professed this Reformed confession and used it for a high and holy purpose. Convinced of its truth, they took up the battle against Spain and Rome. The need to rebel arose out of the desire to be obedient to Zion's King. During that heroic period, the people of the Netherlands lived entirely out of the principle of saving grace, which, as far as the intent of Reformed people was concerned, was the principle of God's absolutely sovereign good pleasure.

The Synod of Dordrecht

In 1618–1619 our fathers gave an account of that doctrine of grace with deeper understanding. Reviewing the Confession and the Catechism, they confessed, in the light of the Scriptures, that God, absolutely independent of man, has chosen *a certain number of individuals out of the entire human race* unto eternal life. He did not do this in an individualistic and particularistic sense. That view would have flagrantly contradicted their entire view of life. Rather, they confessed that God has known His own from all eternity and has not made their salvation dependent upon anything in themselves, as the Arminians erroneously taught. The Reformed doctrine of the election of definite individuals does not exclude the idea that the elect are organically related to each other and to the entire creation of God, but definite election must be understood over against the Arminian idea of an election on the basis of foreseen faith and an objective, universal reconciliation.

The occasion for this confession was the revival of Pelagianism in the doctrines of Arminianism. Pelagius acquired a new generation of sons in the Remonstrants. That did not happen accidentally. There were in the Reformed Church in the Netherlands those who had never been entirely cleansed from the Romish leaven of Semi-Pelagianism. The doctrine of the *free will* of man was revived through their influence. Men like Anastasius, Duifhuis, Coolhaas, Herberts, Sybrandi,[42] and others, who came over to the Reformation with a Romish mentality, did not unconditionally assent to "God's reckoning of Christ's reconciliation according to pure and free grace."[43] They became the forerunners of the Arminians.

Moreover, the revival of the doctrine of free will was also indirectly related to a newly revived Arianism in the teaching of

---

42. These men were pre-Dordt defenders of views later taught by the Remonstrants.

43. Source of quotation is not known.

Socinianism.[44] To some extent it even arose out of the so-called
Renaissance, or rebirth—that revival of the study and adoption of
the teachings and life of the ancient Romans and Greeks. It was
mere humanism and was defended by such men as Erasmus and
Coornhert.[45] Because these movements are more distantly related, we can ignore them for the present. At Dordt the fathers
were more directly confronted with the question of the *character*
and the *extent* of God's grace, and that in connection with human
responsibility. Is God's grace *particular*; or is it *general*, that is, universal? That was the question.

The Remonstrants not only made *going lost*, but also *being saved*
dependent upon the sinner. They did continue to speak of predestination and election unto salvation, but according to them, this
divine election was on the basis of a foreseen faith. They taught that
faith may not be considered a gift of God's electing grace, but must
be regarded, at least in principle, as a contribution of the sinner
himself. Thus, God does elect and save but is dependent upon the
objects of His love. More particularly, God's action is dependent
upon His *foreknowledge* of the actions of mankind. Consequently,
an individual by nature cannot be incapable of any good and inclined to all evil. If his foreseen actions can serve as a basis for eternal election unto salvation, then they must be good in the sight of
God. So, too, God is able to condemn a person only on the basis of
His foreseen wrong deeds. According to such a presentation, God's
eternal election unto salvation takes place on the basis of foreseen
faith, and only the deliberate rejection of the gospel of Christ makes
the individual worthy of condemnation. By teaching that doctrine,
the Arminians also ended with the doctrine of Pelagius and a free
will that enables the sinner to merit with God.

---

44. Arianism, an ancient third and fourth century heresy condemned by
the Nicene Creed, denied the divinity of the Lord Jesus. Socinianism was a
rationalistic denial of the doctrine of the Trinity.

45. Dirk Coornheert (1522–1590) was a Dutchman who, like Erasmus, defended the freedom of the will and denied sovereign predestination.

However, this was never openly admitted by the Arminians. Rather, they pretended, as others did before them, that they merely wanted to avoid the harshness of some views of predestination, particularly of predetermination unto condemnation. First of all, therefore, they directed their attack against the so-called harsh statements of the supralapsarians, such as Luther, Zwingli, Calvin, Beza, Zanchius, Piscator, Perkins, Ursinus, Trigland, Gomarus, and others. The Arminians claimed that the teaching of these men came down to this: according to His eternal intent, God willed sin. This, they said, relieved the individual of his responsibility and made God the author of sin. However, it soon became evident that they also objected to the more infralapsarian presentation of God's eternal good pleasure as found in the Confession of Faith and in the Heidelberg Catechism. They were obviously opposed to the Reformed doctrine of predestination itself. First of all, they wanted to see the hard statements of the supralapsarians condemned; having done that, they also wanted the confessions to be subjected to revision. They then insisted on a completely free discussion of the mutual differences, preferably in a conference at which the decisions would be binding upon no one. The discussion, they insisted, should be only on the basis of the Word of God, which virtually implied a temporary suspension of the doctrine held by the Reformed churches. They also wanted the discussion to be held on the basis of God's general revelation in creation, such as the light and the right of nature, the remnants of the image of God in man, the use of the law, and the external preaching of the gospel.

All this was obviously with the intent, as far as they were concerned, of opposing the doctrine of the predetermination of God unto damnation. That is also why they would not hear of presenting their objections to certain points of Reformed doctrine in an ecclesiastical manner.

However, the delegates to the National Synod at Dordt were of a different mind. They certainly also wanted a discussion of the differences that had arisen among them, and they wanted this discussion to be held according to the Holy Scriptures. But they

wanted the differences treated by the lawful synod of the Reformed
churches and decided as *doctrinal differences,* so that the decisions
would be binding upon all. Also, the Reformed wanted them treated
without temporarily setting aside the existing confessions. The followers of Arminius, who were summoned to appear before the synod,
would not consent to such a treatment of the difficulties that had
arisen in the churches, because according to their assertion the synod
consisted mainly of the opposition and consequently could not sit as
judge in this case, which case was also synod's own. On the basis of
that objection, the grounds for which, according to the Arminians,
are found in nature itself, they refused to submit their views and convictions to the investigation and judgment of the synod.

Because of this refusal, the Synod of Dordt "briefly and faith-
fully" sought out the sentiments of the Remonstrants from their
writings. It then became evident to the synod that all the differences concerning God's predetermination in relation to human
responsibility invariably arose out of differing views over the freedom of the human will. They also learned that the Remonstrants,
in their view of sinful mankind, did not follow the teaching of Augustine, Paul, and Holy Scripture, but rather that of Pelagius and
the philosophy of the world. Therefore, the synod was able to condemn the opinions of the Remonstrants as tainted with the error
of Pelagius and as being contrary to the Word of God. It did this
in spite of the fact that the majority were infralapsarians and representatives of moderate Reformed theology, that some of the foreign delegates stood closer to Arminius than to Gomarus, and that
the representatives of the civil government worked hard for peace
and unity because of the precarious situation in the Republic of
the Netherlands and the consequent threat to Protestantism.[46]

We can do no less. Our conviction may be stronger than that

---

46. The reference is to the fact that although hostilities had ceased for the
most part, the nation was still technically at war with Spain, and the threat of
new hostilities was very real. Peace did not come officially until the Peace of
Westphalia in 1648.

expressed by Dordt, for the "high view" of the supralapsarians was not condemned, even though Gomarus, a supralapsarian, was only tolerated. But no one may believe less. Anyone who wants to lay claim to the name *Reformed* must condemn Arminianism, and with respect to God's predestination, must accept the Canons of Dordt as orthodox. In the Canons is found not the maximum, but the minimum of the Reformed doctrine of predestination.

In the Canons of Dordt the Reformed fathers chose a position over against the following Remonstrant opinions:

1. God's election and reprobation depend upon the foreseen faith or unbelief of men.
2. Christ died, according to God's intention, for all mankind.
3. The individual obeys the calling of the gospel and perseveres by his own free choice.
4. God's grace is resistible.
5. One can always lose the grace of God and therefore can never be certain of his salvation.

In brief, it comes down to this: God actually never elects or reprobates anyone, but has only provided a possible general atonement in Christ. God allows this to be proclaimed through the gospel, and thereupon He waits to see whether anyone is willing by his own free choice to accept in faith these glad tidings of salvation and thus to appropriate to himself the salvation in Christ. The lifeline that is cast out to the person through the preaching of the Word, if it is to save him, must be grasped by his own strength, and he must persevere in clinging to it to the very end. His ability to do all this lies in what is retained by the sinner after the fall. Thus, the doctrine of God's free grace is made dependent upon the individual's free will. Salvation depends upon the whim of the sinner, and therefore on less than a cobweb.

Over against this God-humiliating and man-exalting teaching of the Remonstrants, the Canons of Dordt declare as sound doctrine that:

1. The cause of the unchangeable and irrevocable decree of God's eternal predestination rests in His good pleasure. It applies to all mankind in their fallen state. It includes the two elements of eternal election and eternal reprobation, and it applies to the purpose as well as to the means of salvation.

2. The necessity of Christ's death follows from God's justice. The power and the sufficiency of Christ's death is determined by the excellence of the person of the Son of God. The gospel must be preached and presented without distinction, along with the command of repentance and faith. But God owes no one the gift of faith; and according to the divine decree, the quickening and the saving power of Christ's death extends only to the elect of all nations. This decree of God will certainly be realized.

Therefore, the synod rejected as error

> the teaching of those who use the difference between meriting and appropriating, to the end that they may instill into the minds of the imprudent and inexperienced this teaching, that God, as far as He is concerned, has been minded of applying to all equally the benefits gained by the death of Christ; but that, while some obtain the pardon of sin and eternal life and others do not, this difference depends on their own free will, which joins itself to the grace that is offered without exception, and that it is not dependent on the special gift of mercy, which powerfully works in them, that they rather than others should appropriate unto themselves this grace. For these, while they feign that they present this distinction in a sound sense, seek to instill into the people the destructive poison of the Pelagian errors [Canons II, Rej. of Errors 6].

The preaching of the gospel without distinction, and with the demand for faith and conversion, may not be regarded as the same as a general offer of grace and salvation, which a person by nature would be able to accept of his own free will.

3. Man has brought upon himself by his sin a darkness of his understanding, a hardness of his heart, and an impurity of his inclinations. All men have become slaves of sin, not by imitation,

but by the transmission of their depraved nature, and they neither can, nor do they, will to return to God. The light of nature cannot lead the individual to the saving knowledge of God. He cannot even properly use that light in natural and civil matters, but in various ways he completely pollutes it and suppresses it in unrighteousness. And because he does this, every excuse is taken from him before God. Even the law cannot save him.

But that which natural light and the law cannot do, God accomplishes by His Spirit and Word. Conversion is wrought in the elect by God, who penetrates into the deepest recesses of the individual by the powerful operation of His regenerating Spirit. However, this irresistible work of the Spirit of Grace at the same time arouses the individual to faith and repentance in such a manner that he also becomes active. Nevertheless, faith remains a gift of God, both as to the will to believe and the actual believing. But the using of this gift of faith by the individual is in harmony with his nature. The sinner does not cease to be a human being. Therefore, this work of God includes the use of means, so that the Word, the sacraments, and Christian discipline must be maintained.

4. By these means God causes His saints to persevere in faith even to the end. It is possible that sometimes, if one has angered God by his sins, he may for a while lose the awareness of God's grace, but God never completely deprives him of it. He does not allow His people to fall from His grace. This preservation follows from God's mercy, which is always new for them, so that through faith and the testimony of the Spirit they can actually be certain of their salvation.

The "Five Articles against the Remonstrants" reject as error these Arminian teachings:

1. That God decreed to save only those who would believe and persevere in that faith, in this way establishing the conditions for salvation; that election is made dependent upon each individual's use of the light of nature; and that God did not determine to pass anyone by.

2. That God ordained His Son as an expiatory sacrifice with-

out any definite decree to save certain individuals; that Christ merited from the Father only the right to establish a new covenant with mankind, with conditions, the realization of which would depend upon the free will of the individual; and that God was willing to give the benefits of Christ's death to all, so that now participation depends upon the will of the individual.

3. That original guilt is not sufficient unto condemnation; that as a result of the fall human nature is not corrupted, and the unregenerate is not completely dead in sin; that mankind can by nature make use of natural light in such a way that thereby he can attain to saving grace; that faith is not a gift of God, but an act of the individual; that grace unto regeneration is resistible; and that grace and free will cooperate, the will of the individual being most prominent in that activity.

4. That the perseverance of the believer is not the fruit of election, nor is it a gift of God merited by the death of Christ, but depends on the free will of the individual; that the true believers can fall away from grace and be guilty of a sin unto death, so that the elect can have no certainty of their salvation without a special revelation; and that the difference between temporal faith and saving faith is merely a matter of duration.

It is repeatedly pointed out in these rejections that the opinions of the Remonstrants are like the doctrines of Pelagius, as, for example, in the fourth rejection under the First Head of Doctrine, in the third and sixth rejection under the Second Head, and in the second rejection under the Fifth Head.

Thus, according to Reformed orthodox doctrine, it is established that:

1. God, absolutely independently from the creature, before the foundation of the world, out of sovereignly free good pleasure, has chosen a certain number of individuals out of the fallen human race unto salvation, has reprobated the others, and has determined all the means and purposes to accomplish these goals.

2. The sinner does not have a free will to choose that which is good. Even in natural and civil affairs he does not know how to use the light of nature properly, but pollutes it and suppresses it in unrighteousness. Because of these things, he is deprived before God of every excuse.

3. The sinner has not ceased to be a man. Sin has polluted and corrupted his nature and his way of life but has not touched his essence. The possibility of the application and use of the means lies in the fact that the sinner is still human. It does not lie in a remnant of original righteousness, which man lost completely. The work of God's Spirit in man is always in harmony with his character as image bearer.

That is the way the greatest Reformed synod established the confession of the truth that is according to godliness. Purely Augustinian and completely anti-Pelagian, the great synod confessed, according to Scripture, that God's counsel shall stand, and He shall do all His good pleasure. Since that time, complete agreement has reigned in the Reformed churches on the confession of election as such, although not as to its object and character. The dogma of election is the *cor ecclesiae*, the heart of the church. We live and work out of that principle of free grace.

This glorious principle should govern our whole life, for as G. Wisse Jr. correctly remarks,

> When thought out, the doctrine of predestination is in the broadest and deepest sense of the word an essential element of the Christian faith, a component of a theistic world view. Faith in God the Father is inseparably connected to faith in God's providence. It is the lofty idea that nothing happens by chance, but in prosperity and adversity, in joy and in sorrow, throughout the history of the nations, and in the sprouting of a blade of grass from the earth, in things large and small, we see nothing but the carrying out of God's eternal determinations. Nothing comes into existence or exists purely by itself.
>
> He who adopts the most accurate, and, according to the proper standard, the most consistent idea of predestination comes the closest

> to the essence of Christendom. Calvinism has maintained this truth
> with the most consistency.
>
> While every other branch of Christendom has more or less reck-
> oned with predestination, and adopted this idea for world history in
> its entirety and for life in this dispensation, Calvinism has drawn the
> line all the way and applied it also to the eternal state of mankind.[47]

Wisse is correct. Yet the fathers of Dordt did not draw out this
doctrine of God's eternal providence and predestination with
complete consistency, nor did they apply it to every sphere of life.
Their narrow conception of predestination, which they virtually
limited to the final destiny of each man, does not do justice to the
organic relationship of all things. They thought too much of the
person as an individual independent of the rest of the creation.
This gave the doctrine of predestination a much too individualistic and particularistic color. They virtually overlooked the fact
that the predetermination of God must be considered as directed
toward the final purpose of all things in their relation to each other
and not merely toward the determined end of His spiritual-ethical creatures. As a result, the organic character of the doctrine of
divine predestination was forced into the background. Eventually
this would have detrimental consequences for practical living.
Doctrine and life cannot be separated.

But life also precedes doctrine. This was the case with our fathers. Although theoretically they did not place the organic character of God's eternal election on the foreground, they did demand
a full-orbed life of devotion to the service of God. The fathers did
not derive this demand from the organic character of a life lived
out of the principle of election by grace. Rather, they insisted that
their life of devotion must be maintained in order to honor God's
name, as Scripture requires. Living out of the principle of their
personal election unto salvation, they tried to make even those

---

47. G. [Gerard] Wisse Jr., *Het Pessimisme* (Pessimism) (Kampen: J. H. Bos,
1907), 103, 104.

things which do not arise directly from the root of regeneration serviceable to the cause of the Son of God. That could be done only by connecting in a mechanical way the principle of the new life out of personal election unto salvation, with the glory of God as the final purpose of the full life of the whole creation. They actually proceeded from two principles, namely, personal election unto salvation, and the election of the people of the Netherlands to serve the cause of God's kingdom of grace. That faith in a national election served as a link to join the principle of the life of regeneration, which has its origin in personal election to salvation, to the glorifying of God as the goal of the life of the creature.[48]

Undoubtedly that was not done deliberately. In Article 12 of the Confession of Faith, the reasoning quite clearly follows the organic idea, but they seem to have proceeded from that rationalistic viewpoint for practical purposes.

Our fathers, with childlike naiveté and the clarity of faith and conviction, rejoiced in God's full, free, and glorious grace that made it possible for them to endure captivity and the suffering of death; and that rejoicing prepared them for a life of thankful devotion. However:

> The certainty of their personal election stood in close connection with the faith that the Netherlands, as another Israel, was chosen of God

---

48. To understand this paragraph, one must once again remember the situation in a country where one church is the established state church. The authors are saying that because of the established church idea prevalent in the Netherlands, the people of God could not live in society and in creation from the one principle of their election by grace. In other words, they could not live an organic life in which all life proceeded from one principle. The view of an "established church" presupposed that some lived out of the principle of the election by grace, while others, the rest of the nation, technically members of the established church, lived out of the election of the people of the Netherlands as a special people. The relation between these two people was mechanical in that it was only a general relationship in which all things served the glory of God.

to be the light-bearer of the purest and richest revelation, and to pro-claim before the whole world who God is and how God wills to be served. Thus, the nation was destined eventually to conquer the world to give mankind the freedom to serve God in every sphere of life according to His ordinances. The sincere and God-fearing element among the people of the Netherlands, a country that gave leadership to national life, felt themselves chosen for that holy task. Those who devoted their strength and life to that holy cause of God considered themselves to be fellow participants and heirs with that people.[49]

Naturally this was not a position and goal in keeping with the purely spiritual character of the New Testament, and for that rea-son it would necessarily end in confusion and disappointment, and even be detrimental to the people of God. The people of the Netherlands, as a nation, were not chosen for such a purpose, were not even chosen unto salvation, and therefore could not fight that spiritual battle.

Even though almost all the Reformers and the Reformed peo-ple of the Netherlands shared in such a view, this did not change the matter. It remains a fact that the Reformed element in the sev-enteenth century firmly believed that the people of the Nether-lands, in the national sense, were the spiritual people of God. They concluded, therefore, that they were especially fit to serve the cause of the Son of God.

The people of the Netherlands did not recognize that they, too, by nature, since Adam's fall, belonged to the fallen human race. They failed, therefore, to live out of the antithetical principles of sin and grace according to God's eternal decree of election and reprobation (the two parts of divine predestination). And so they did not conform their lives to the doctrines demanded by the Canons of Dordt. Rather, they tried to make the national life of the Dutch people flourish out of the personal electing grace of God

---

49. Lutzen H. Wagenaar, *Van Strijd en Overwinning* (Concerning Strife and Victory) (Utrecht: G. J. A. Ruys, 1909), 11.

in Christ. To do this, they leaned heavily on the strong arm of the magistrate, which "had to be a maidservant of God."[50] That magistrate was, by the Union of Utrecht, supposed to be committed to the Reformed religion.[51]

This view of the church and its relation with the magistrate is the reason why Prince Maurice convened the great synod of the Reformed churches at Dordrecht to settle the disputes with the Remonstrants. And when the decisions were made, he took a strong stand against the Arminians, who refused to submit themselves to them. Out of a similar erroneous position, almost all the foreign delegates at the synod considered the struggle of the Reformed people against the Remonstrants as a matter involving the government of the Netherlands republic. They not only granted to the civil government a certain right to deal with the spiritual matters of the Reformed churches, but thought that the Netherlands' government should promote the cause of the truth of the saving grace of God. This is convincingly shown by the way in which the foreign delegates concluded their judgment and advice to the synod. The conclusion of the judgment given by the delegates of the orthodox churches of Nassau and Wetteraw is one example of this general view. It reads as follows:

> Thus the God of peace and unity finish mightily that good work He has graciously begun by the esteemed States General Lords of the United Netherlands, and graciously accept the offering of praise that we daily offer upon the altar of our hearts.
> Only God's grace has eternally elected definite persons.
> Only God's grace has given definite persons to Christ.
> Only God's grace gives to definite persons the gift of faith.
> Only God's grace preserves definite persons.
> Only God's grace gives all things to us!
> Only God's grace directs all our affairs.

---

50. Source of quotation is unknown.

51. The Union of Utrecht (1579) was the agreement between the northern provinces of the Netherlands to form a republic.

> Let God's grace alone lead you, O Netherlands, along with the ex-
> cellent upon the earth, and crown your land with unchanging peace![52]

In this declaration the one saving grace of God is said to be that
out of which the nation of the Netherlands, including the magistrate, must live and work. According to that view, the life of
regeneration could never develop in a proper antithetical relationship over against the life that proceeds from the principle of
sin, as the New Testament and this present earthly dispensation
demand. The purely spiritual character of the life of grace faded
too far into the background.

That had to have dire consequences. Indeed, everything that is
not wrought by and according to the Spirit of Christ has no real
value for the cause of the Lord. The restraints of magistrates and
the natural bonds in which we live in the world do not advance
the kingdom of God. The life of regeneration cannot develop in
fellowship with the life of sin, but is directly opposed to it.

Post-Dordt Developments

That is also the lesson from the history of the Reformed
churches in the Netherlands after the Synod of Dordt. In spite of
all the synodical decisions, a large part of the population of the
Netherlands, even as in the past, continued to live an indifferent,
carefree, ungodly life. The favorable attitude of the authorities toward the Reformed churches changed as early as the time of Prince
Frederick Henry (1584–1647). The spiritual power of the Reformed people over the rest of the people of the Netherlands,
which before and during the Eighty Years War (1568–1648) gave
leadership to national life, dwindled according to the measure in
which the spiritual life of many declined and the breach between

---

52. *Acta of Handelingen der Nationale Synode* (Acts of the National Synod)
[original published in 's Gravenhage, 1620] (Leiden: D. Donner, [1887]), 571.

confession and life grew. By the end of the eighteenth century, this spiritual power of the Reformed people over the rest of the people of the Netherlands had virtually disappeared. Remonstrantism, supported by the state's involvement in the training of ministers of the Word, forced itself into the churches along with the worldly philosophy of Descartes and others. From these influences errors developed that led to the open rejection of God and His Word and brought the people of the Netherlands under the influence of the spirit of the world. Where once Reformed theology reigned, the scepter of autonomous science now held sway. The reformation of Dordt failed, and the failure must be ascribed in part to the wrong application of the principle of the doctrine of election by grace.

Having learned a lesson from this, the Reformed people of the nineteenth century tried to apply the idea of eternal predestination to their life more accurately. To do this they followed two paths. The churches of the Secession of 1834 felt compelled to break away from the state church to create a new church organization and to return both to the confession of the orthodox doctrine and to the Church Order of 1618–1619. Yet they did this without including in their position the older idea, so closely related to the concept of a state church, of the divine election of the Dutch people, which we described above. They were therefore committed to a life based on the principle of election by grace. Critics were of the opinion that this was virtual abandonment of the historical position and that a full human life could not develop out of that idea. Our judgment is that the Secessionists did take a proper position but were very narrow in their practical application of the principle of grace. They did not completely escape Puritan influence and the Old Testament way of thinking, nor did they lay sufficient emphasis on the organic character of eternal predestination.

A. Kuyper and the Free University

Another Reformed group in the state church wanted to continue more in the historic line. They strove for church reform within the state church. They wished to expel the idea of a people's church from the inheritance of the congregation of God's people, so that the original church of the fathers might once again be a mother to the Reformed folk and might restore to the Reformed churches their lost influence in the national life of the Netherlands.[53] The final fruit of the first attempt was the *Doleantie* and the union that followed between the *Doleantie* and the Secession churches.[54] The church of the fatherland (the state church) for awhile paid no attention. Many in the state church were not capable of discerning the sound of pure doctrine to the point where it would become necessary to withdraw from the church. Unlike the *doleantie* of the seventeenth century at the time of the Contra-Remonstrants,[55] which, in fact, was supported by the steel sword of Prince Maurice, this *Doleantie* was a failure, even though it was carried out as a historical imitation of the former *doleantie*.[56] One likely reason for the failure was the change in the political situation.

Even before the *Doleantie* of 1886, in order to preserve Christianity in the Netherlands, particularly in the sphere of higher

---

53. It is not entirely clear what is meant by this. It seems as if the authors mean to say that Kuyper, though disagreeing with the concept of a state church, nevertheless wanted a Reformed Church that would be influential throughout the Netherlands.

54. The reference here is to the churches of the Secession of 1834.

55. Prior to Dordt, when many churches had Arminian ministers, the faithful in these congregations were forced to worship separately from the congregation. They were said to be people of the *doleantie;* that is, they were, just as in the time of Kuyper, "aggrieved" by the sad condition in the church. These people were called Contra-Remonstrants because they were opposed to the Remonstrants (Arminians).

56. The term here, as well as in the *Doleantie* of 1886 led by Kuyper, refers to the grievances of those who were dissatisfied with the condition of the church. The authors speak of Kuyper's movement as a failure, not from the viewpoint of reformation in the apostate state church, but from the viewpoint of Kuyper's desire to establish the Reformed church as one influential in the state.

education, an effort had been made to establish a university on Reformed principles. They [its organizers] specifically did not want a state university, which likely would serve the interest of whatever party had control of the state. Nor would a school that would offer supplementary education satisfy them. No, the school to be established had to be Reformed.

> Over against an institution that had become the instrument of a spirit that was at enmity with Christ, they wanted to create another institution that would be an instrument for serving Christ in this life. "The foolishness of the cross" (that sharp expression of the apostle) had to follow from the pulpit to the classroom. And how could anyone allow the foolishness of the cross to be married to "wisdom of the world"?

That was what Kuyper said.

> ... And, in order that no one should mistake the significance of what he said, in the interests of honesty, he wrote his articles on particular grace.[57]

(We will return to these articles later.) Kuyper became the man of the antithesis, especially over against the irenic Beets.[58]

Kuyper had his early training in Leiden, the stronghold of liberalism in the Netherlands. However, when he came to Beesd,[59] well aware of God's unfathomable guidance in his own personal life, and having come into contact with orthodox individuals who surpassed him in knowledge of the Scriptures and set before him a well-organized world-view, he not only admitted that in Leiden the university had presented to him a caricature of the orthodox confession, but he

---

57. W. F. A. Winckel, *Leven en Arbeid van Dr. A. Kuyper* (The Life and Labors of Dr. A. Kuyper) (Kampen: J. H. Kok, 1904), 80, 81. In these two excerpts, Winckel comments on Dr. Kuyper's founding of the Free University.

58. Beets was a theologian and author in the Netherlands.

59. Beesd was the village in the Netherlands where Kuyper had his first charge as a pastor.

also said without hesitation that the spiritual life of the members of his congregation was out of the free grace of God. In principle he had by this admission returned to the doctrine of the fathers of Dordt, even as De Cock before him. For a time the so-called ethical tendency still appealed to him,[60] likely through the influence exerted upon him during his stay in Utrecht. This became evident from his work *De Menschwording Gods Het Levensbeginsel Der Kerk* (God Assuming Humanity: The Life Principle of the Church). But soon after this, voices from the hoary past reached his ear, voices that forced him to express himself in more Reformed terms. In such circumstances one would think that under the leadership of Kuyper, those who organized a school on a Reformed basis would present a strong front against the unbelief and the half-faith of science by proceeding from the organic-antithetical relation and development of the whole creation. In that way, in connection with but correcting the work of the past, they might once more restore the Reformed people of the Netherlands to a position of influence in the life and development of the nation, as had the fathers of the seventeenth century.

Originally the organizers of the Free University seemed to have had nothing else in mind. In connection with the organization of the school, they often spoke of "Reformed principles" in distinction from the Reformed confessions because they did not want a church school, and they felt the need of a foundation that was broad enough for the entire structure of a Christian and a Reformed science. Yet they also seemed to have given not a single thought to anything essentially different, at least in principle, from the Forms of Unity.

In any case, we on our part have always taken for granted that Reformed principles, as the foundation for the structure of a Reformed science, are essentially rooted in the Reformed confessions and in the Holy Scripture upon which the confessions are based. It might happen that while building the superstructure of the tem-

---

60. The *ethical* school of thought in the Netherlands emphasized Christianity as only a moral religion.

ple of science, there would arise a growing need for a "broadening out" of the confessions; yet, as far as we can see, there would be no need for any essential change. The foundation of gracious election would remain fundamentally the same. All Christian action would continue to develop out of the work of regeneration. God's grace would distinguish us from the world. And through the means of the school, we, as Reformed believers, would be far better able to defend the cause of the Son of God in the midst of a crooked and perverse generation. Through such a school, so we thought, the various rules regulating other related institutions and societies in the church and society would make certain that these organizations and institutions were based on Holy Scripture as the Word of God, and upon the Three Forms of Unity.

We saw this worked out in detail in the Constitution of the Free University at Amsterdam. Article 2 of the statutes of the Society for Higher Education on a Reformed Basis reads:

> The Society insists that all the instruction given in its schools must be based completely and exclusively on Reformed principles; and likewise, for instruction in Dogmatics, it recognizes the Three Forms of Unity as they were adopted for the Netherlands Reformed Churches in the year 1619 by the National Synod of Dordt, ascribing the same authority to them as the aforementioned Synod ascribed to the confessions of the Reformed churches, a fact evident from the proceedings and acts of the Synod.

In 1899 at Middelburg, Professor Rutgers gave a defense and explanation of this article that dealt with the certainty of the Reformed character of instruction at the university. We give the statement of Rutgers as it appeared in Rullmann's book:

> If we take a close look at the article, we see that it states, first of all, that all the instruction at the Free University is bound completely and fully to Holy Scripture; and this is done in such a way that no one can escape that connection. For, had the article said merely that the instruction is bound to Holy Scripture, no one would have been sure of

the Reformed character of the school. But the article speaks of Christian principles in general and of the Forms of Unity in particular. Every question in regard to Scripture is answered there, and everyone knows what is required of him. The article declares that Holy Scripture governs all the instruction in the Free University. There is no authority equal to Scripture, no matter what writing it is. But it is also established how Scripture must be regarded. Even the manner in which the authority of Scripture must be maintained is included.

But this article also informs us that no one may mine from the Bible and draw out of it for science what is not there. The article speaks of "Reformed principles." A Reformed person acknowledges that there is also a guidance of the Holy Spirit in the churches who, especially over against the various errors that arise, teaches us to understand ever more clearly the Word of Scripture so that our life becomes richer and fuller. He also leads the thoughts of mankind, at least of the believers, more and more into that which God Himself has revealed of His thoughts. And so as time goes on, a certain systematic confession arises; and in harmony with it arises a world-and-life-view historically called "Reformed." Thus, Article 2 expresses what this Reformed position is and insists that it must remain the character of the Free University.

In the third place, Article 2 also states that these Reformed principles, as far as Dogmatics is concerned, are developed in the Three Forms of Unity. This is expressed in the little word "likewise." Moreover, the article also states that the Forms of Unity do not stand on the same level with Holy Scripture. Yet they apply as long as they are not lawfully revised by the Reformed churches to conform more completely with the Holy Scriptures. Further, such authority should be ascribed to them as the Synod of Dordt itself gave to these Forms in 1619.

Even the non-theological sciences are bound to those Forms, insofar as the Forms deal with these sciences. This also is included in the little word "likewise," which tells us that these confessions contain "Reformed principles" to which, according to the beginning of the article, all instruction is bound. Besides, it is stated here that there are other Reformed principles, which are related to the Forms but are not expressed in them. By these also, the Reformed character of the instruction can be maintained.

If one should say that these Reformed principles refer to and are defined only for the department of theology and not for the other de-
partments, this is entirely correct. Yet it may not be forgotten that the
development of other principles for the other branches of knowledge
has hardly begun, while in theology Reformed principles have long
been thought out.[61]

On page 206 Rutgers makes mention of the university as an institution that "studies the sciences on the basis of God's Word and
that must carry over the treasures of science inherited from the
fathers to the younger generation, and as much as possible add
to it."

These Reformed principles, as defined in the Article referred to
above, guarantee, according to Dr. Rutgers, the Reformed character of *all* the instruction of the Free University, and at the same
time also maintain a proper view of the authority of the Scriptures.
We can do no better than that. Regardless of the question whether
some criticism might not be offered concerning this circular reasoning, Rutgers' elucidation and defense of the basis for the Free
University is sufficient to serve our present purpose. The basis for
the free institution for higher education at Amsterdam is *faith*.
More specifically, it is the faith of all who are Reformed. It is positive, very definite, and thus very exclusive. The non-Reformed
cannot build on that foundation.

Our views on this matter were confirmed in an article written
by Professor Dr. Hepp in *De Reformatie* of March 9, 1923, entitled
"Samenwerking van Alle Gereformeerden" (Cooperation among
All Reformed People). We quote only in part:

> Concerning the teaching of science at our university I shall say but
> a few words.

---

61. J. C. Rullmann, *Dr. F. L. Rutgers: In Zijn Leven en Werken Geschetst*
(Dr. F. L. Rutgers: A Sketch of His Life and Works) (Rotterdam: Libertas Press,
1918), 207–209. The quotation from Rutgers in the edition available to us was
not found on pp. 207–209 as cited by the authors.

It was never intended that our university should be a church school.

For reasons we will not examine now, it was forced against its will into an ecclesiastical corner.

But it is in harmony with its character to make room for all who stand on the basis of the Reformed confessions.

If it were possible for it better to manifest this character in practice, it would also serve its purpose better.

If at least some Reformed groups could agree on this matter, Reformed science would, to our mind, be well served.

We could present a stronger front over against unbelieving and half-believing science.

Thus the Free University desires to teach Christians, indeed Reformed people, the sciences. To attain that goal, it seeks the cooperation of all who are Reformed. To our mind, it is for this that Dr. Bavinck struggled to unite the theological school and the department of theology. He wrote:

A small group of men working together in one spirit, even if they teach only a small part of the sciences, can have a great influence throughout the land. The Free University has already proved this. But the influence would be much stronger if the theological school and the theological faculty were joined, and if all those who confess the Reformed truth would unite in support of one school. Then a rich blessing would flow from the university to all our churches, to the whole land and our people, and to every sphere of life. Then the glorious spectacle of a foolish God who is wiser than men, and of a weak God who is stronger than men, could be displayed anew before the whole world. Indeed, in Christ, who is the Head of the church, are hidden all the treasures of wisdom and knowledge. In Him dwells all the fullness of the Godhead bodily.

The history and the blessing of the Secession of 1834 would then be perpetuated and continued. For the work of God in the Secession consisted in this: He used it as a means to preserve in these countries the pure confession of His Word and to protect it from being intermingled with all kinds of theories and proposals of man. The Secession served that purpose.

Through the Secession, the church of the Lord was once again purely manifested in our fatherland. It was the first to establish, though with its limited resources, a school for higher education on the basis of God's Word, which even to this present day has bought abundant blessing.[62]

Thus, there can be no doubt, according to Bavinck, that the Secession and the *Doleantie,* rooted in one and the same spiritual life, stand with their schools on the foundation of the Reformed confessions. They both offer instruction in the Reformed sciences distinct from the unbelieving and half-believing sciences.

To prove this we produce one more witness.

I now consider it my duty to make clear the position that the Free University takes in regard to the certainty of science ... The Free University attempts to raise the structure of science to a higher level upon a predetermined foundation. In that respect it is accused by many of *vitium originis* [an error of beginning][63] ... That is, one establishes in advance as truth what ought to be the result of one's scientific research. That, if true, is certainly not scientific, and whoever so acts forfeits the right to join in any discussion ... I doubt if they who accuse

---

62. Herman Bavinck, *Blijven of Heengaan* (Remaining or Going) (Kampen: Zalsman, 1902), 87. Bavinck is referring to the theological school in Kampen, where he formerly taught and where theology was considered "the queen of the sciences." The Free University of Amsterdam, to which Bavinck moved, made theology one of the sciences along with such others as jurisprudence, the natural sciences, etc. The difference involved a question of what was called "encyclopedia," or the division of various branches of learning and the relation of these branches to each other. It was a bitterly divisive question in the Netherlands and was even an issue that lay, in part at least, behind the Janssen controversy at Calvin Seminary in the early 1920s. See pp. 53–57 of Herman Hanko, "A Study of the Relation between the Views of Prof. R. Janssen and Common Grace." It is interesting to note that the Form for the Installation of Professors of Theology used in the Protestant Reformed Churches calls theology "the queen of the sciences."

63. *Vitium originis* is a Latin name for the logical error defined in the next sentence.

us of this actually know what our basis is or have themselves given an account of it. Are those Reformed *principles* (I emphasize the word) something arbitrary? Or are they the result of thousands of years of thought in the Christian world that lived by the Bible as the Word of God?

We believe that nature is the creation of God, and in the certainty of that faith we investigate nature in order constantly to learn to know it better and in greater depth. We believe that God directs the life and lot of the nations, and in the certainty of that faith we search out history. We believe that justice is from God, and in the certainty of that faith we have a standard for our research into that which is right... Naturally I do not expect that we will ever attain to a point where we will so clearly understand and define such concepts as "state" and "justice" that, by our clarity and reasoning, we will persuade others who do not have the same basis to admit that our definitions are correct. Especially in the sphere of science, there is the antithesis. Faith in God the Father, creator of heaven and earth, governs the whole of life, including science. It is useless to build alongside of it a positivistic science[64]... All the generations of mankind have labored on the structure of science. That which the previous generations have seen and thought is taken up in the science of our day, tested, purified, and improved... I grant this, but the contention that our time more than any other is the era of scientific knowledge is mere boasting, something unworthy of science. We stand on a higher level of the scaffolding that serves for the building of the structure, but we cannot lay another foundation. That foundation is given by God Himself in His work of creation and in the spirit of man, whom He created after His own image. When out of pride man exalted himself in the place of God, God relaid that foundation in His special revelation. He did so because He does not relinquish the work of His hands. In our day the great danger that threatens is that man puts himself in the place of God. He wants to lay his own foundation and construct science according to his specifications. It will become evident, however, that his

---

64. Positivism is a philosophy maintaining that all human knowledge is, and can be, based only on what we are able to perceive with our senses. Thus it rules out all knowledge of God and of His Word.

structure is built not upon a rock, not even upon sand, but upon an
enticing swamp, and it will disappear into the depths. Therefore, because this danger was foreseen, the Free University was built and is
founded upon the eternal principles of the Word of the Lord, principles that are recognized and confessed by faith, and that prove and will
prove, in spite of faults and errors that cleave to us in our labors, a genuine certainty in science.[65]

Science as taught in the Free University is, therefore, faith-
science—Reformed faith-science. That cannot be doubted. This
results in an antithesis between the science of faith and the unbelieving philosophy of the world. It is, as Bavinck correctly remarks, that

> Christians can have no other conviction than that truth in the do-
> main of science can be found only when one proceeds from the con-
> fession that Christ is the Way, the Truth and the Life, and that no one
> can come to the Father, the origin and purpose of all things, but
> through Him. This confession does not stand opposed to science, for
> creation and re-creation have the same origin; grace does not nullify
> nature, but delivers and restores it. Christ did not come to destroy the
> works of the Father, but to destroy only the works of the devil. The
> confession that Christ is therefore advantageous to science delivers it
> from the lie and directs it into the proper channel. To be truthful, the
> name "Christian science" is a redundant expression. Science as such,
> since it arises out of creation, is neither Christian nor unchristian. Sci-
> ence has its standard in the truth. That which is true is scientific, even
> though the whole world should claim the opposite. That which is not
> true is unscientific, even though everyone maintains the contrary. But
> because there is so much sham and imitation in science, just as there
> is in everything else, God has granted to us His revelation as a guide
> and director, which in the practice of science directs our footsteps and
> protects us from error. Thus, Christian science is a science that
> searches out all things in the light of revelation and therefore sees

65. Dr. J. Woltjer, *De Zekerheid der Wetenschap* (The Certainty of Science)
(Amsterdam: Wormser, 1891), 24, 25, 28, 35–38.

them as they are in their essence. In the eyes of the world, this may seem like foolishness, but the foolishness of God is wiser than men, and the weakness of God is stronger than men. We cannot oppose, but we can maintain, the truth.[66]

In the light of all this, we believe we can conclude that the organizers of the Free University consciously and deliberately based their school on "Reformed principles" over against the whole scientific world of unbelief and half-belief. It was their purpose to manifest, in every area of human activity, the enmity God put between the "wisdom of the world" and the "foolishness of the cross." First of all, they tried to show what had always lived in the heart of a Reformed man and what Groen always insisted on: that the Holy Scriptures, which alone are capable of restoring health to our lives, do not just contain a Word of God for the soul, but that they lay the foundation for all human life and for the holy ordinances that must govern the entire life of mankind in the church, the state, and the government.

[The organizers of the Free University] chose a historical-scientific basis because that left plenty of space for growth. Yet they saw that if men abandoned their own principles and acted apart from the principle of regeneration through the grace of God, they were virtually free to go in any direction. Anyone who had any feeling for the life of faith and the struggle of faith experienced by the fathers in the sixteenth and seventeenth centuries had to understand this intuitively. The position of the Free University is historical and scientific, governing the whole of life, yet at the same time—and this must not be lost from sight—it is exclusive exactly because it is Reformed. Non-Reformed persons cannot stand on that basis. And because there are other principles, particularly those of sin and unbelief, out of which many live and work, the position of the Free University is antithetical.

---

66. The quotation is taken from the end of Bavinck's *Christerlijke Wetenschap* (Christian Science) (Kampen: J. H. Kok, 1904), 121.

Therefore, twenty-five years after its establishment, Bavinck could quite justly make this remark:

> If the Free University, now entering the twenty-fifth year of its existence, has from the beginning placed itself on a Reformed basis; and if now, in harmony with that basis, it is willing to work for the development of science, then, in spite of a lack of appreciation for its work, it can comfort itself in the thought that it fills a dire need in our time. To the person who ignores the fashions of the day but does reckon with the history of the ages, cultivating science in a Christian and Reformed spirit and working towards the development of science in all the different relationships of life, it will prove to be nothing exceptional and, still less, anything spectacular. Such a spirit is and desires that which all Christians have always wanted, that which our fathers regarded as a matter of fact and perfectly natural for the schools of instruction and science. This ideal does not want the universal, undoubted Christian faith to become as sounding brass. What this Reformed school of higher learning intends to maintain is in essence no different from the time-tried confession that the fear of the Lord is not a hindrance but an advancement of science—that it is the beginning of wisdom.[67]

One could expect that the fruit would match the seed that was scattered. The result of this broader and more powerful idea of life and action on the basis of Reformed principles could not possibly be a united fatherland, even though many had apparently considered that as an ideal. The result had to be an internally divided and torn Netherlands, not only in religion but in every sphere of life. The result could only prove anew that Christ did not come to bring peace upon the earth, but the sword.

Indeed, before the establishment of the Free University, unity and peace had been sought in the state church by silencing the truth that the Holy Spirit had taught the church of Christ

---

67. Herman Bavinck, *Christelijke Wereldbeschouwing* (Christian World-view) (Kampen: J. H. Kok, 1929), 95.

throughout the ages. Would it now not necessarily follow that where the gospel of the kingdom once more had free course, conflict could be stirred up? Surely not all the citizens of the Netherlands were believers, still less, Reformed! Grace is not common. Therefore, the antithesis would become manifest. And that is exactly what happened. But alas, this inevitable spiritual and good fruit did not sufficiently satisfy many people.

The Introduction of Common Grace

People sought for something different. Alongside the antithesis in the spiritual realm, they felt the need for a synthesis in the realm of the natural. They wanted a common basis upon which all humanity would be able to unite and work together. Naturally the Reformed confessions could not serve that purpose, for every person is not Reformed. The same applies to a general Christian life-principle. Obviously there are many non-Christians. These unsatisfied people could not attain their end without changing our life-principle. Life was divided so that a part of the life of the Christian was joined with a part of the life of the non-Christian, and those two parts that were joined were neutralized; that is, they were not allowed to be lived out of the deepest principles of life. Certainly these people maintained, along with Dr. J. Woltjer, that:

> The contrast between Athens and Jerusalem, between Greek and Jew, does exist . . . But the question is, in what sense? . . . Are we interested in the true knowledge of God and His worship? in proper self-knowledge? in the salvation of our souls? Then we do not go to Athens, but to Jerusalem, for we hold to the word of the apostle: "What advantage hath the Jew? Much in every way: chiefly, because unto them were committed the oracles of God." But if you are interested in so-called natural gifts—the beauty of a language, the excellence of a style, knowledge or science in the realm of this earthly life—go to Athens . . . Yet, even so, these gifts are intended to serve Israel. Thus the wisdom of the heathen is employed to build the house

of the Lord. This beautiful example truly shows how the church must employ all the gifts that God has given her in the works of the heathen. For Christ has broken down the wall of separation between Athens and Jerusalem, between Jew and Gentile, and put to naught the enmity in order that from the two He should make unto Himself one new man, making peace, in order that the new temple should arise, founded on the foundation of the apostles and prophets, of which Jesus Christ is the chief cornerstone.[68]

That is what Woltjer had already written in 1891, thirty years before our Professor Van Andel expressed similar ideas. He contended:

> Calvinism is the need of the world!
> For our leaders this means that they should pay equal attention to the Jachin idea of the antithesis and to the Boaz idea of Common Grace. We all believe in the antithesis, and it is up to us to make plain to the children of the covenant that they should be spiritually different from the world. But do we all believe in general revelation and Common Grace? The Jachin pillar stands firm among us. The Boaz pillar is shaky. The present minimizing—if not worse—of general revelation and Common Grace, whether it be serious or initial, is a grave danger for our Reformed life and principles. The Jachin of the antithesis and the Boaz of Common Grace belong together. We need men who are willing to be *witnesses of these two precious truths*, for the greatest enemy outside of the walls may be worldy-mindedness, Arminianism, Humanism; but the greatest foe inside the gates is the minimizing of God's general revelation and Common Grace, and the upshot of this: Pietism and Anabaptism.[69]

Woltjer implies that the elect out of Jews and Gentiles who are made into a new man in Christ cease to be Jew or Gentile and are

---

68. J. Woltjer, *De Wetenschap van den Logos* (The Science of the Logos) (Amsterdam: Wormser, 1891), 46–48.

69. Henry J. Van Andel, "The Foe within the Gates," *Religion and Culture* 4 (July 1922): 23–27, with quotation from p. 27.

brought into a union existing only in his imagination, a union of Athens with its worldly wisdom, and Jerusalem, the Old Testament covenant people, both possessing the words of God. Van Andel maintains that the left pillar in the court of Solomon's temple, Boaz, refers to God's general revelation and common grace. We are convinced that such an exegesis of Ephesians 2:14–22 and 1 Kings 7:21 is not yet permitted on any of our pulpits, but the direction of such thoughts and intents is clear.

Except for the principles of sin and grace, the latter of which is not common to all mankind, there must be, so they think, still another life-principle out of which every individual lives and that can explain the comparative good in the unregenerate. Instead of two life-principles, sin and grace, they speak of three: sin, particular grace, and common grace or common favor. Particular grace is naturally the possession of only a few people, but the other two principles are the common possession of all mankind. And it is on the basis of this communal life-principle of common grace, so they assert, that every individual can be pleasing to God during this present earthly dispensation, in spite of sin and despite the particular grace of regeneration. Man can accomplish one work, which although it cannot very well be regarded as spiritually good, still bears fruit for eternity and is essential to God's kingdom of grace.

Therefore, according to this view, there is a life proceeding from the antithetical principle of sin and grace, but only in a limited sense. The regenerated can in principle live out of particular grace in the sphere of re-creation, whatever that may be. But in the broad terrain of natural life, which all mankind share together, they live out of the root of common grace, even though they still carry around with them the principles of sin and particular grace. We must even desire that. In the area of the spiritual we must live our soul-life out of the root of regeneration, but in the sphere of natural life we must live out of the root of common grace.

Such is our duty. We owe that to mankind and to science. General human knowledge is not rooted in sin, but is, according to

Kuyper, nothing more than "a discovery of and a learning to know the secret of the *means of common grace,* which God has appointed and intended for us."[70]

It is also asserted that "Dogmatics did not come into existence without the help of human sciences. It gradually entered the Christian church with the aid of the natural sciences, which were developed in Greece and in Rome through God's common grace, and even to this present time common grace forms the basis for our formal development and civilization." In that case, could not the "science of revelation" reimburse the "science of nature" for past services? The development of human life in general, which comes out of common grace, must therefore be promoted by our influence as far as possible in order that its fruit may serve for the advancement of the eternal kingdom of God's grace. The Free University, therefore, desires to *cooperate* in the development of general human knowledge on the basis of "Reformed principles." By neglecting that calling it would certainly make itself guilty of "Anabaptistic world-flight."[71]

These ideas have never been sufficiently investigated by Reformed leaders, according to Kuyper's introduction to his *De Gemeene Gratie.* Reformed principles suffered great loss because of the faulty development of the doctrine of common grace. After 1650 there was actually no dogmatic development at all. After that first flourishing period, not one man with original talent arose in the area of dogmatics. In a narrow-minded way theologians picked away at the polemics that had been recently carried on by the Arminians. They found themselves outside the spiritual activities of their time. They therefore had very little influence upon human life in general after that first flourishing period. However, a favorable change took place in the Netherlands toward the end

---

70. Abraham Kuyper, *De Gemeene Gratie* (Common Grace), (hereinafter referred to as *DGG*), 3 vols. (Amsterdam: Höveker & Wormser, 1902), vol. 2, 509.

71. Winckel, *Leven en Arbeid van Dr. A. Kuyper,* 300. The quotations are interspersed in this paragraph.

of the previous century. There was an awakening of historical research in the Reformed principle of life. Kuyper says:

> The question became urgent, what must be the relationship of the
> Christian life, as we know it, to the life of the world in all its expres-
> sions and variations? And how can we restore our influence upon life
> in general, which at one time was so extensive, and now is so sorely
> lacking?[72]

We are therefore not alone in our "Anabaptistic world-
flight."[73] Ever since 1650 the *Reformed element* has been narrow-
minded. But now they are going to try to restore their influence
upon human life in general, just as they formerly had done but
since 1650 had so sorely neglected to do.

How did they go about restoring their influence on human life?
Kuyper continues:

> It seemed that the Reformed people chose as their guideline the apos-
> tolic teaching that "all things are yours and ye are Christ's," and had
> deliberately thrown themselves, with unusual talent and with an all-
> conquering resilience, into the full life of humanity as it existed in the
> midst of the turmoil of the nations.[74]

We have already pointed out that a very wrong idea lay at the
basis of this mighty activity of the fathers. That wrong idea was
that the people of the Netherlands, like Israel of old, were God's
people, and, in close connection with this, that the steel sword of
the civil authorities must be put into the service of the spiritual
cause of the Son of God. But Kuyper's opinion was that the basis

---

72. Kuyper, *DGG*, vol. 1, second page of unnumbered "Voorwoord."

73. The authors are referring to the charge of Anabaptism that the proponents of common grace leveled against them. The authors' detractors surpassed
Kuyper in this respect, for Kuyper never made this charge.

74. Kuyper, *DGG*. The authors do not supply the volume or pages here or in
short quotations in several paragraphs that follow this.

for their view was also the doctrine of common grace, something that directly followed from the truth of the sovereignty of the Lord, "which is and remains the most fundamental idea of all Reformed thought."

It is difficult to understand how the doctrine of common grace can be deduced from the sovereignty of God. It is certainly not the question whether God is sovereign, but whether all humanity possesses grace out of which they can live and act. Most certainly, the sovereignty of God extends to all things. But it is exactly for that reason that the child of God who lives out of grace, in keeping with the character of this present dispensation, may not lay claim to all things with the sword of the magistrate.

But what difference does that make, as far as a common source of life is concerned, out of which all humanity should live together? It certainly makes no difference whatever! All humanity is not of Christ!

Kuyper actually has something entirely different in mind. That is evident from what he goes on to say. God is sovereign also in the unbaptized world, "and therefore Christ's church on earth may not, nor may the child of God, simply withdraw from this life." Since God works in this world, the child of God must also work in it, thereby glorifying the name of the Lord.

We answer, "Of course, Dr. Kuyper, the child of God must do that, and he also wants to do that!" That is also, as we showed earlier, what the Secessionists wanted. But God's child must defend God's cause with spiritual weapons in a world that is at enmity with God. And that can never be done with a grace that is common to all, but only by the grace of God in Christ Jesus. Only he who is of Christ's party can fight for God's cause. That is our position. Therefore, we do not agree, since it certainly does not follow, when Kuyper adds, "Therefore, it all depends upon a revival of the rich and basic thought embodied in the doctrine of common grace." We contend that the fathers did not hold to that kind of doctrine. On the contrary, they attempted, even though they did not succeed, to place the entire life of the people of the

Netherlands in the service of the cause of Christ. They never based their Christian action upon a grace that was common to all. One ought not twist a weighty matter such as this into its very opposite. That clashes with history. And Paul's words in 1 Corinthians 3:21–23 simply do not mean a grace exists that is common to all; rather, it means that those who are in Christ are heirs of all things, and therefore in principle possess all things and can use them in the Lord's service. It is not surprising, therefore, that Kuyper later admitted that he could not find in this text a clear definition of the so-called doctrine of common grace. He said that he carefully gathered "all the historical and doctrinal material related to this doctrine and organized it under this one principle," and that he has offered it to every Reformed church in every country. They will then be compelled to pass judgment upon it. But they will also be compelled to pass judgment on the purpose that Kuyper had in mind in his work, namely, the breaking down of all spiritual and ecclesiastical isolation, something which Kuyper himself declares to be anti-Reformed.

Further, it is impossible to speak of a Reformed dogma of common grace that is according to the confessions. The Reformed churches have never yet, when assembled as a synod, closely examined the different views of various individuals, clearly formulated a doctrine of common grace, and incorporated it into their official confessions. Nor have other churches done anything like this. Historically, there is actually no such thing as a doctrine of common grace. No one can even boast of a partially formulated Reformed tradition of the doctrine. The Remonstrants spoke of common grace. They meant by it the good gifts in nature, but they connected it with salvation. Their ideas, however, were condemned by the Synod of Dordt as reeking of the doctrine of Pelagius. That we certainly cannot use. Moreover, the same term is commonly used for various purposes, by à Brakel (among others), to refer to the general, non-saving works of the Holy Spirit.

But that has nothing to do with what is now offered us under the name of common grace. What is now offered would make it possible for all mankind to live a good communal life in the natural sphere. That is something new. Kuyper is correct when he himself remarks,

> The idea of the *gratia communis* [common grace] has up to the present been poorly and scantily treated in the Christian church. There is no writing that can be referred to from Roman Catholic, Lutheran, or Reformed theology that specifically or incidentally deals with this subject in a precise way. The Catholics do not deal with it; the Lutherans only touch upon it; the most information is found in Reformed theology. *Calvin, Zwingli, Voetius, and later writers fail to give their own, independent treatment of it.* The subject must be developed from the bottom up and set in its proper organic relationship to everything else. The various aspects touched by this subject must be properly systematized.[75]

Therefore, no one may simply brand those who do not teach common grace as unreformed or Anabaptistic. On the contrary, the views of anyone who does teach it must be tested in the light of Scripture and the Reformed confessions. The confessions, likely, will not be of much value in this research, for, as has been remarked in *The Christian Journal* of November 30, 1922, there is no reference to common grace in the confessions from which one could draw any definite conclusions, except for a few expressions, and those mostly from the mouths of, or in relation to, the Remonstrants.

However, as we see it, some definite conclusions can be drawn from the principles of the doctrine of predestination, which are clearly defined in the confessions and more extensively developed in the Canons of Dordt. So, too, the agreement and the relationship between that which is already established as being Reformed,

---

75. Abraham Kuyper, "Locus de Magistratu," *Dictaten Dogmatiek* (Dictated Dogmatics), second ed., 5 vols., vol. 5 (Grand Rapids: Sevensma, [no date]), 27, 28.

and that which is now presented to us as a new discovery, should be defined. But even apart from that, the current common grace question is an extra-confessional matter, especially in its present state of development. Thus, a judgment will have to be made mainly on the basis of the Scriptures.

It is therefore greatly to be deplored that some have regarded their own personal opinion as Reformed dogma and have dragged through the mud the names of those who hold a different view. Dogmas, according to Kuyper himself, are interpretations of God-given truth, and thus they are not human sophistry or working hypotheses.[76] The church must first discover the revealed truths from God's Word and more closely define them in articles of faith before we can accuse one another of being unreformed. We agree in this respect with the adage that the disciple far surpasses his master; but the master himself—Kuyper—is by no means without fault. In almost all of his later writings, he uses the expression "Reformed dogma" with respect to common grace. Occasionally he does admit that his research offers only a first attempt at an answer to the present question, and he says that he wants it to be regarded as such, but for the rest he proceeds from the assumption that the problem is solved and that ever since Calvin, one can speak, also in a historical sense, of a Reformed dogma of common grace.

Actually, Kuyper only wiped off the dust. To find a solution to the present struggle, and to pave the way for any future development, he says:

> It was necessary that a serious and accurate study once more be made of the ancient dogma of common grace, to dig it out of the dust of the ages and place it before us in a clear light. Anyone who locks himself up inside the circle of his own ecclesiastical institute [as if anyone ever consciously or willingly did that—the authors] is satisfied with a study of particular grace. But he who is called to take action in the scientific, civil, and pedagogical spheres [it clearly seems to be a question of

---

76. Kuyper, *DGG*, vol. 2, 25.

spheres—the authors] must have acquainted himself with the institutions that lie outside the institute of the church, and specifically that area that remains beyond the horizon of our faith. That, too, is covered by God's grace in Christ. Thus we take that marvelous doctrine of common grace seriously inasmuch as it clarifies for us God's control *outside* the life of the church.[77]

It is our conviction that the entire creation is God's and that the child of God in his fellowship with Christ receives anew all things from the hand of his Father. Therefore, he may not withdraw himself in his daily activities from any sphere whatever. But what connection does that have with the idea that through common grace, all mankind is able to live a good life before the face of God? That is exactly the question.

As to God's control over life *outside* the church, the fathers, according to Kuyper, had certainly maintained this. Yet, Kuyper insists, the believers of the nineteenth century knew very little about the fathers of the past (as if that has anything at all to do with the present question!). But, says Kuyper, from this ignorance

we can explain the fact that throughout this entire century, believers have attempted to set themselves dualistically over against the world and thus have developed spiritually in a one-sided way. No one gave a thought to reconquering the higher realms of science and of civil life, and of becoming involved in the life of the state. In their spiritual desperation, they did not dare to aim higher than the retrieval of true spirituality for their own life. Therefore, they locked themselves up in that sphere. They left whatever lay beyond to itself. They applied themselves especially to practical activities. No one had the slightest idea nor smallest conception of the calling of holy theology to give leadership in the realm of all scientific principles and for the entire life of the people.[78]

---

77. Kuyper, *DGG*, vol. 3, 7.
78. Ibid., vol. 3, 6.

We already pointed out the historical inaccuracy of this state-ment. The power and gifts of the faithful were undoubtedly limited. This was also true of the influence they had, especially because of the tremendous changes in the circumstances of their lives. Yet the Secessionists did not consciously and deliberately withdraw them-selves from life. They did not again assume the wrong and unspiri-tual position of the fathers of the seventeenth century. But suppose for the moment that what Kuyper says is true. What does that have to do with the idea that there is a grace that is common to all and out of which all mankind lives? The question is not whether a be-liever must live a full life, but whether everybody, as the result of a common grace, lives a life that is good in the sight of God.

As might be expected, Kuyper did not fully succeed in con-vincing all the brethren of the correctness of his view, as much as that was his desire. Some even raised the objection that "The Free University increasingly becomes a school of common grace, and saving grace is subordinated to it and thus weakened."[79] Kuyper answers this objection by saying that if this is their objection, there rests upon the brethren "the moral and very serious obliga-tion to point out a better way that is in keeping with their view-point. Then they must also offer the principles that establish rapport between life within and life outside the church institute. And they must do this in such a manner that it is evident their theory is deduced from Reformed principles and fits in with the whole of our Reformed confessions."[80]

That is still, then, the situation today. According to Kuyper, anyone who comes with a different proposal violates history, first of all, and is considered guilty of opposing Kuyper's own words.

Thus, the obligation will also rest upon us to point out a better way, for we share the objections of the brethren mentioned above. We, too, can see that the Free University is becoming increasingly a school of common grace, and that saving grace is being subjected

---

79. Kuyper reports this objection of some in Ibid., vol. 3, 1.
80. Ibid., vol. 3, 7.

to common grace and thus invalidated. This is proved by what we read in Kuyper's *Dictaten Dogmatiek*.

> All five faculties of learning have this in common: they are rooted in *gratia* [grace] and, moreover, in *gratia communis* [common grace], but in relation to the *gratia specialis* [particular grace], they differ completely.
> Thus, theology as a science is also rooted in the *gratia communis* insofar as it:
>
> 1. receives from *gratia communis* the means to investigate and to draw conclusions scientifically;
> 2. still finds in the sinner, through *gratia communis*, the *scintillae religionis* [remnants of religion] by which the sinner is able to benefit humanity;
> 3. finds its own absolute necessity, because it [as the *science* of theology] is not absolutely necessary for the salvation of the elect, for fighting the powers of destruction, and for challenging all humanity to reveal its full strength. Humanity must manifest completely its full development, which according to the counsel of God was given to man as a life task to the praise of His name. In this way it is exactly like the other faculties of learning.[81]

And then he adds:

> It is impossible to carry out any real action in the realm of religion and in theological research unless one has an insight into the natural condition of mankind. In nature itself there must be something that can serve as a basis; otherwise, nothing can be accomplished by *gratia specialis*. Some ministers do suggest that through regeneration the *semen religionis* [seed of religion] enters a person, but this denies God's Word and is empty chatter. It is therefore to the great credit of Calvin that he taught that the *semen religionis* is present in all sinners and is that to which the Word of God joins itself.[82]

---

81. Kuyper, "Locus de Magistratu," in *Dictaten Dogmatiek*, vol. 5, 98, 104. The authors sum up what Kuyper is saying on these two pages.

82. Ibid. The quotation was not found on page 23, as supplied by the authors, in the edition available to us.

Reading on, we find this:

> In contrast to *gratia specialis*, which is definitely directed toward the salvation of the elect, *gratia communis* must be understood as that gracious operation of God whereby after the fall in paradise, God has restrained the immediate and complete operation of the destructive power of sin, made possible a human society even in this sinful world, assured the fallen human race of steady development, and has thus created a sphere in which special grace could unfold. It thus guarantees a continuation of paradise in the *regnum gloriae* [kingdom of glory].
>
> This *gratia communis* works from paradise on, but received a definite form and an external sanction in the covenant with Noah. It is as the light of the sun that manifests itself in the midst of a gloomy creation and is therefore symbolized in the rainbow.
>
> It has five parts:
>
> 1. The restraint of Satan and the powers of destruction.
> 2. The tempering of the curse that is upon the creation because of sin.
> 3. The checking of sin in the individual.
> 4. The arrangement of different systems for families, nations, and governments, and the distribution of gifts for every aspect of human life.
> 5. The preparation for *regnum Christi* [kingdom of Christ] and the means whereby this preparation is made useful for the life of the church."[83]

Reading this kind of thinking, we understand the language of Rev. Van Baalen that appeared in his latest pamphlet on preaching. There must be some influence, he said, of common grace upon the sinner if one is able to preach the gospel to him. Such statements make our heads swim. We do not find a trace in Holy Scripture or in the Reformed confessions of the common grace which is first ascribed to science and is then applied to the sinner. In my judgment we have here the very thing that Kuyper himself wanted

83. Ibid., 23.

to avoid in the university: to permit the "foolishness of the cross" to be married again to the "wisdom of the world." The kind of language which Kuyper used to describe science may leave something to be desired, but it harmonizes very closely with what Scripture says of the Christ of God. According to the Word of God, the Father mandated the Son with the task of destroying all the work of the devil, accomplishing the salvation of man, and re-creating all things. See Ephesians 1:8–10, Colossians 1:15–20, Colossians 2:8–15, 1 Corinthians 15:24–28, and Hebrews 2:7–9.

Kuyper's description of common grace also strikes us as strange when we compare it with what he says elsewhere, especially in the fourth volume of his *Uit het Woord* concerning the "small sparks" and "remnants" in the sinner.[84] We will discuss this in more detail later, but we most emphatically refuse to be responsible for what he writes about common grace. Kuyper does not seem to reckon in the least with God's eternal purpose in regard to all created things, but he proceeds from the idea that the creation, in spite of sin, the curse, and death, will attain to its original purpose by means of science and common grace. We, on the contrary, see the actual plan of creation realized in the plan of redemption in and by Christ in spite of the wisdom of the world, which is made foolishness by God. Regarding the *semen religionis* [seed of religion], to which Calvin refers, and here included by Kuyper in the *scintillae religionis* [remnants of religion], one must be very careful that he does not re-introduce naked Pelagianism with its banners flying. On this point we gladly subscribe to what G. Wisse Jr. says:

A person originally has a heart that is created in such a way that it is directed towards God. It is indeed so completely inclined toward reli-

---

84. The authors refer to *Dat De Genade Particulier Is* (That Grace Is Particular), which was volume 4 in a series of books entitled *Uit het Woord* (Out of the Word) (Amsterdam: Höveker & Wormser, [no date given, but printing soon followed publication of the *De Heraut* articles that make up this book, and the last of these articles appeared June 13,1880]). The reference of the authors is probably to chapter 6 of that volume.

gion that when a man says that he has done away with the living God and then still experiences in his self-worship that he is not able to find life, he either sets himself against God or bows down in worship before that which is no God.[85]

Later we will show in more detail that Kuyper himself teaches that those whom God separates from His people fall upon their knees before idols as a result of the darkness that floods their souls. We will deal with this later because we are, in the nature of the case, compelled to consider extensively the theory of common grace itself.

For the present, we will only remark that Kuyper applies common grace in a mechanical way to the organic life of creation. He does not allow it to arise organically out of the principle of regeneration, but makes it a basis for regeneration—something psychologically impossible. In Kuyper's view, the life of creation goes on without a new root of life and independently of God's work of salvation. But the life rooted in the grace of Christ is in a particularistic and one-sided way applied exclusively to the spiritual aspect of a person and limited only to eternal salvation. The organic idea is lacking. Life is first divided into different spheres, which are then joined again in a mechanical way.

In that way not only does the organic relation of everything to every other creature become impossible, but the same can be said of the life of regeneration and the life of sin. Neither one nor the other can develop organically. To this must be added that evidently the development of creation does not actually arise organically out of any genuine life-principle. This would be possible only if man is not dead by nature, or if one brings a dead man back to life through common grace. Neither one is directly taught by Kuyper, although one or the other is absolutely necessary to maintain his theory.

In any case, it will have to be accepted that the unregenerated

---

85. Wisse, *Het Pessimisme*, 24.

sinner, if only through common grace, can will and can do that which is good in the sight of God in the realm of natural life. This must even be considered as a condition for the bestowal of saving grace upon the elect in Christ Jesus. Without common grace, as we saw above, nothing can be accomplished by *gratia specialis* [particular grace].

But do these men not realize that in this way they are doing what Rome does, and virtually what Luther did with baptism, and what the Remonstrants did by enabling the light of nature to make use of the law and the external preaching of the gospel? They once more enthrone the free will of man. Limit that, if you wish, to natural life. Is not all human activity and the entire direction of life turned about and corrupted by sin? If so, how can a man, without regeneration, still accomplish that which is good in the sight of God? It is certainly as plain as day that anyone who allows the sinner, apart from regeneration, to perform that which is good in the sight of God—wherever, whatever, and by whatever means—moves in the same direction as Pelagius, the humanists, and the Remonstrants, but not in the direction of Augustine, the Reformers, and the fathers of Dordt.

Further, by an unwarranted separation of the different spheres of life and an unnatural union of disparate spiritual elements, Kuyper runs the risk of a false dualism. He removes the offense of the cross in the broad area of so-called natural life—in the family, in society, in government, and in the realm of science and art. He makes it impossible, as far as he is concerned, for the wisdom of the world to be made foolishness by the preaching of the gospel.

We ourselves are fully convinced that this entire discovery of Kuyper is the fruit of a superficial and faulty conception of the mutual relationship and development of things. We believe that the doctrine now being promoted among us of a so-called common grace (the above summary forms the principal basis of this doctrine) is in flagrant conflict with the Scriptural doctrine of the election of grace, with the nature of a life out of sin, and with the idea of reprobation in history. Besides that, it is anti-confessional and contrary to history. Moreover, this doctrine, if it is not opposed, will weaken nearly all real Christian action and send a tidal wave of world-conformity through our churches. We fear that even the danger of Pelagianism is not completely excluded. "Already," says Rev. T. Bos in his discussion on common grace, "the real distinction between 'common' and 'general' grace is reasoned away by some, and common grace is exalted to a position where it becomes the basis and root of special grace, so that the development from the one to the other is considered possible."[86]

We refuse to be reckoned with those who think that they need only to warn against a one-sided emphasis on what is to them the good doctrine of common grace, though we do readily grant that wrong conclusions have been drawn from Kuyper's argument by people who always prefer to "walk along the edge." The prediction of Rev. Gispen has been fulfilled in these people: "They will discuss common grace so long that particular grace will be forgotten."

We also raise our protest against such misuse of Kuyper's work. But that is not our main objection. We object to Kuyper's presentation of common grace itself. And that objection is a matter of principle. We are not concerned with merely some points of minor significance, but with the very heart of the matter, the real question involved. We are not finding fault with names, terms, conclusions, or consequences. Between Kuyper and us there is a difference in principle.

We have repeatedly and publicly expressed this difference without any reservations. We have never hesitated wholeheartedly to admit this, even when others looked at us out of the corner of their eyes or tried to make capital out of it for their own departures from the truth. For some time our basic presentation of the organic relationship and development of things has remained unanswered.

But with the Janssen case, which aroused violent emotions, a change came. This did not happen immediately, but only when we

---

86. T. Bos, *De Dordtsche Leerregelen* (The Canons of Dordt) (Kampen: J. H. Kok, 1915), 144.

began to reveal our objections to the teachings of the professor and were placed on committees to deal with the case. Then it was soon being rumored that we ourselves were not sound in doctrine and thus would hardly be able to judge the scriptural and confessional purity of the instruction of another man. It was almost completely in that connection that the pending question of common grace began to be discussed in our circles. If both parties maintain their position on common grace and define their position clearly and accurately, then this weighty matter can be decided in the ordinary ecclesiastical manner. However, a great deal of preparatory work must still be done.

In the meantime, one thing must not be lost from sight. The Janssen case as such had no connection whatever with the present issue. We want our readers to understand what we mean. The instruction of Dr. Janssen was closely related to his view of common grace, which, as we see it, does not essentially differ from that of Dr. Kuyper. But in our criticism of his instruction, common grace was not considered, not by the various committees, nor by the curatorium,[87] nor by the synod. Common grace was left out of the discussion. There was no formal charge against Dr. Janssen's view of common grace, and Janssen's opponents and the synod did not want to allow their attention to be drawn away from the main issue, namely, Janssen's view of Scripture and Scripture's interpretation. Apart from anything that in any way was related to his view of common grace, the instruction of Dr. Janssen itself could not possibly be considered Reformed.

Therefore, once synod did condemn Janssen's instruction on what they deemed sufficient grounds, it must not be said that our view of grace is the cause for Janssen's condemnation. That is entirely wrong. One need but consult the official documents. Such a disposal of the case would not have been generally acceptable. What? Would the entire synod have changed the accepted views of common grace because of the opinion of two delegates who,

---

87. The "curatorium" was the theological school committee.

moreover, were already branded? No, indeed, we did not have such an influence upon the synod. We say this for the sake of the synod. The synod of our churches ought not be dragged through the mud in such a manner. It must be understood that criticizing us, or even condemning us, cannot lead to a restoration of Dr. Janssen. In other words, the Janssen case and the common grace issue are two separate matters.

But that does not change the fact that after all, there still is a very real connection between the instruction of Dr. Janssen and the accepted view of common grace. If there were a close connection between the instruction of Dr. Janssen and *his* view of common grace, that would not be so serious. In that case, one could simply say that he differed with Janssen's view. But as we see it, an almost inseparable connection exists between the instruction of Dr. Janssen, together with others in our circles, and the accepted view of common grace, in spite of all the differences of detail. We would almost dare to say that the two stand or fall together. They are related to each other as the root and the branches, as the foundation and the superstructure. There is no doubt about it, as we see it, that Dr. Janssen and his friends are of the same mind. Their plan for the future, which is not completely a secret to us, betrays this. But also their tactics, which are sufficiently evident to many, show us that they are rallying all their available forces toward that one goal.

Therefore, those who do not agree with that group but still want to defend the doctrine of common grace must prepare themselves. No one must imagine that this is merely a matter of saying that he is not in agreement with the particular teaching of this one or that one, and of merely being on guard against a one-sided overemphasis of this doctrine. In that case, one could quietly proceed on the assumption that this doctrine is clearly defined in the mind of the church. But that is by no means the case, and therefore that may not happen. If it does happen, one leaves the church in a very arbitrary position. A great deal could then be taught with an appeal to common grace, and the consequences could not be ignored. No, the issue must be thoroughly studied. A fundamental life-principle is involved here. And principles carry through with necessary consequences.

There is also the practical aspect. The practical application of an opinion very often results in it becoming an established doctrine. At this point, the development of the doctrine has only approached the stage of personal opinion, as we have seen above. A synodical decision on the subject is either far off or never will happen. But that does not prevent the development and application of it in daily practice. Experience has already taught us that. During the past twenty-five years the life of Reformed people has been steeped in the principle of common grace. Supporters even appeal to the Scriptures to prove the contention that God in Christ has made Jerusalem and Athens one. They contend that they have found reconciliation in the New Testament church between "the science of revelation" and "the science of nature." Christianity may in one sense form a contrast to heathendom, yet it is also the fulfillment of it. Actually, they say, the wisdom of the Greeks gave support already in the old dispensation, like the pillar Boaz in Solomon's temple. They cannot imagine maintaining a high school or a college except on the basis of common grace. It naturally follows that the elementary school, the family, society, and the state must also have common grace as their foundation, for not one of those arises out of the principle of regeneration. Thus, the sphere of particular grace shrinks to a very small size, while the area of common grace broadens out extensively.

As a matter of fact, if this presentation is correct, we actually live out of two principles: particular grace and common grace. Therefore, our activities in life must be divided into different areas or life-spheres in keeping with these different principles. Then those who oppose these views and want to live out of only one principle are very really "the foes within the gates." But that will have to be determined, for if the doctrine of common grace is erroneous, then it is our calling and duty to oppose it. Then the doctrine of common grace, as far as its significance for life is concerned, would become no more than a theory encouraging world-conformity.

It is our conviction that this latter happens to be true. Hence, we deliberately looked at matters from the viewpoint of so-called common grace. Having entered in through the narrow gate of the righteousness of God in Christ Jesus, we consider ourselves to be well aware of the craftiness of the human, sinful heart, and we would not dare to refrain from being spiritually watchful. We learned to marvel at and regard Mother Church highly for her repeated effort to guard the principle of election by grace, regardless of disapproval, mockery, and scorn.

At the roots of their spiritual life, the churches of the Secession, in our estimation, were thoroughly sound although they were limited in gifts, manpower, and means. They walked in the footsteps of Augustine, the Reformers, and the fathers of Dordt, according to the demands of their time, revering the gospel in the midst of a crooked and perverse generation.

The same can be said of the Reformed colonists who came to this country from the Netherlands, even though their very peculiar circumstances exposed certain weaknesses. The churches in the Netherlands that united in 1892 also stood on the basis of the Canons of Dordt. Along with the churches of the sixteenth and seventeenth centuries, these churches lived out of the principle of election by grace.

But they did take a different attitude toward the people of the Netherlands as such. They wanted to be the historical and confessional continuation of the Reformed church of the fathers, but they broke away from the idea of a national church and similar conceptions. This took place through the means of the great change of circumstances in the Netherlands,[88] but as we see it, it was also a matter of principle. In any case, they officially lived under no other rule than that of election by grace. However, that

---

88. The reference is to the change in the political situation in the Netherlands under Napoleon.

unity of life-principle was disrupted by the introduction of Kuyper's peculiar doctrine of common grace, not with regard to salvation, but in regard to life here on earth. This temporal life had to be lived out of two principles, particular grace and common grace. The supporters of common grace wanted to assure the Reformed people of a restoration of the lost influence which the fathers of the past exercised upon the society in the Netherlands.

However, this attempt to govern all spheres of life by the application of Reformed principles ended, in practice, in a dualistic kind of life among them. They began to speak of these things in connection with the establishing of the Free University. Under what they considered Reformed principles, they evidently also included, at least later, the doctrine of common grace, even though this was never officially stated. In practice this position ended in dualism, for they saw life as originating in two principles—of particular grace and common grace. Instead of governing the lives of others by a powerful life drawn from the principle of grace, they split their own life in two to fit the demands of different life-spheres, as they said.

In the confessional-historical sense this cannot be called Reformed. Yet this theory increasingly controls life in our circles. The result of it is world-conformity. The idea of being a stranger and pilgrim on the earth gives way to world-citizenship. They envision that by common grace, everyone can live a good life in this world before the face of God, and they say it is our obligation to raise that general human world-life as high as possible. In our opinion this view can only lead to the theory of world-conformity, which is already widely evident in our daily practice.

Especially for that reason we feel compelled to express our position, which is contrary to this view. Over against Kuyper's presentation of common grace, we present a plan for a life of mutual relationships which includes all mankind, but we desire to set the boundaries of the principle of election by grace as they frame our practical life in its broadest expression and in all its variations. Thus, we have in mind a plan for the life of God's people as representatives of the cause of the Lord in this world. We will, then, first give a brief sketch of the views of the defenders of the theory of common grace as it affects the relationships of life and human development, but we will do so with our criticism. After that, in a plea for the principle of election by grace, we offer for consideration our own positive view.

2

A Critical Investigation

❧

Introduction

We now are confronted with the question of how to understand the development of created things in their relationship to one another. We may not limit the question, for in a broader sense the point at issue is our relationship to the world. The relationship between all things is governed by the original and natural unity of all creatures and their present spiritual differences that result from the principles of sin and grace. It will be necessary, therefore, for us to look into the organic development of all created things in their natural unity and to look into the spiritual differences which divide all things.

Every attempt to deal with this problem runs the risk of getting lost in details, so that one cannot see the forest because of the trees. On the other hand, this broad perspective we take is in complete harmony with the practice of the Scriptures, which sees all things (always *all* things) in relation to both creation and re-creation, in their connection with each other, and in their connection with Christ and His kingdom. Christ is "the image of the invisible God, the firstborn of every creature: For by him were all things created, that are in heaven, and that are in earth, visible and invisible, whether they be thrones, or dominions, or principalities, or powers: all things were created by him, and for him: And he is before all things, and by him all things consist. And he

71

is the head of the body, the church: who is the beginning, the firstborn from the dead; that in all things he might have the preemi-
nence. For it pleased the Father that in him should all fulness
dwell; And, having made peace through the blood of his cross, by
him to reconcile all things unto himself; by him, I say, whether
they be things in earth, or things in heaven" (Col. 1:15–20).

The historical development of created things, in the mutual re-
lations of their natural unity, and in their spiritual estrangement
and differences, takes place completely according to the will and
counsel of God's providence in Christ Jesus. That counsel will
stand; God will do all His good pleasure. No one among us would
deny this at all. Nor will any of us deny that we are bound to the
Scriptures as the Word of God for the knowledge of this historical
realization of God's eternal purpose for His creation.

Agreement with A. Kuyper

Happily, there is even more agreement between Kuyper and us,
and we cheerfully acknowledge some of those points of agreement
which are directly related to the subject at hand.

First of all, let it be said that neither Kuyper nor we intend to
set up a system of philosophy and then use Holy Scripture for
proof. Nor do we intend to reason on the basis of a natural knowledge of God and then try to find proof that the revelation in God's
Word is in agreement with it. No, we intend to reason on the basis of the Scriptures; apart from them we know nothing with any
certainty. We agree with Kuyper when he says:

> Apart from Scripture, it becomes clearer every day that we know noth-
> ing about the living God with precision and accuracy. The heathen do
> "know His eternal power and Godhead"; even the strongest atheist
> must sense in life's moments of anxiety a shuddering of fear of the liv-
> ing God that grips his heart. That knowledge removes every pretense
> of excuse offered by the one who denies God. But knowledge, which

is conclusive, saving,[1] pure—though only natural knowledge—is not sufficient for the sinner. We therefore may pay no attention whatever to those who would devise a god apart from Scripture and according to their own imaginations. As conflicting as man's inclinations and intentions are, it is wrong to ascribe such human activities to a creature and then call that creature god. That is a mere guessing game, involving only assumption and imagination, without any basis for certainty... Indeed it is one or the other: either we have all revealed truth in the *Scripture*, or there is no revealed truth.[2]

Our wisdom is in the Word of God.

Moreover, Kuyper, and we with him, desire to take into consideration the guidance of the Holy Spirit in history. He says:

> Scripture always remains Scripture; that is, throughout the ages it remains the only fountain out of which our knowledge of God's purpose is drawn, and it is the only standard that may determine the accuracy of our insight into that truth. However, the enormous labor that the church of all ages devotes to digging up and sorting out the treasures of that Word does not allow for human arbitrariness, but depends upon the Holy Spirit. That is, under the guidance of that Holy Spirit, the church of Jesus Christ is constantly compelled to defend the truth over against wrong and false opinions. This means that all ideas, even those that have but little credence, must be subjected one by one and at appropriate times to the judgment of the Holy Spirit in the believing church. As a result, the church's knowledge of the truth steadily matures, becomes purer, clearer, and so the church of Christ in our own day is able to claim the treasure of the lessons taught her by history, and is thus able to walk in a clearer light than was ever formerly granted to the church. But then, it goes without saying, one must be

---

1. It is not clear what Kuyper means by the word "saving." The Dutch has *zaligmakend* and may mean only "able to make happy." The authors of the book would not have quoted Kuyper favorably if Kuyper meant to teach that *natural* knowledge is able to save. And, indeed, the remainder of the quote effectively shows that such was not Kuyper's position.

2. Kuyper, *Dat De Genade Particulier Is*, 53, 54.

willing to listen to that history, not, as so often happens, by completely
disregarding the history of the work of the Holy Spirit, nor by always
bringing up the same naive ideas which were exposed as untenable and
unscriptural centuries ago by theologians of the first rank.[3]

Kuyper wants the truth that grace is particular to be included
in the doctrine of the Christian church, and he wants it to be established, according to the Word of God, that not *all* men are
saved. In a time when the preaching of a *Christus pro omnibus*
[Christ for all], the doctrine that according to the will of God and
His own intention, Christ died for all mankind, head for head, soul
for soul—when such preaching was common, Kuyper maintained
over against this that the foundational doctrine of divine sifting,
by which the children of Adam are distinguished from each other,
did not need to be laid again. The Christian church has always
been right in confessing the doctrine of particular atonement on
the basis of God's Word.

Concerning the working out of this sifting, Kuyper goes on to
say in the same work:

> The work of reconstruction for which Jesus came to earth is reck-
> oned not from Abraham, but from Adam ... Christ is *sent into the world*
> to *uphold the world,* in order that He should *save the world.* However,
> He does not save all. No, He goes to war against "the Prince of the
> world." He will also soon judge the world, and the prince of this world
> is already judged. In the world Jesus makes a division between that
> which joins itself to the world and that which belongs to God out of
> the world.
>
> The world, insofar as it lives out of its own nature and follows its
> own impulses, does not share in Christ's love, but is under judgment.
> So emphatically is this true that the Savior excludes "the world" from
> His prayer: "I pray for them: *I pray not for the world,* but for them which
> thou hast given me out of the world"... A "conversion of the world"

3. Ibid., 123.

is impossible, for the Holy Spirit, through whom alone the world can come to conversion, is the One whom "the world cannot receive, for it does not see or hear him!"... Therefore, open enmity also reigns between Jesus and the world.

When Jesus dies in His blood on Golgotha, His own "shall weep and lament, but the world shall rejoice" with devilish enjoyment of another's misfortune. The world hates Jesus, and it will hate His disciples, because they are not of the world, but Christ has chosen them out of the world... From among the unholy of this world, Jesus separates a portion of mankind to become a higher organism. He grafts them into another root and causes them to live for a time in the world. But He preserves them, that the world may not again overcome them, and then at death He places them in a better world, with many mansions, full of glory!...

This sifting is not limited to any status, age, race, or origin, but regulates itself exclusively according to faith in the Son of God... One believes this only through regeneration, and only they who are given to the Son by the Father attain to regeneration.[4]

Here we have the doctrine of predestination as was confessed by those at Dordt, with its emphasis on particularism.

By *world* Kuyper understands the entirety of all created things, put together like a mechanism, a structure, or an organism. We listen, then, as he continues:

> God first *makes* this organism a *part* of all created things. Then it finds its higher expression in *the world of mankind,* as the noblest part of the entire work. Further, through sin the world changes into an instrument that is deliberately used *against* God. And finally, through Christ, it becomes both a false and a true organism, of which the first must be put down and the other must be placed over it...
>
> That is the reason why sometimes I find the world *in the service of God,* and at other times I hear it spoken of as an organically formed

---

4. Ibid., 117–120.

power that stands *opposed to God*...This is all in harmony with what Jesus and His apostles have in mind. The judgment of the curse rests upon that sham world that must be put down, but the entire world is upheld so that the nucleus of the organism of the world may be saved and glorified. Thus it appears, on the one hand, that Jesus is the Savior *of the world,* but on the other hand, that He says, "I pray not for the world"...At one time, "I am the light of the world," and on another occasion, "The world cannot see me." Or if you will, in one place, "The Lamb of God that bears the sin of the world," and in another place, "I have overcome the world!"...

When Scripture speaks of the large Christian organism, which we call the mystical body of Jesus, or the living church, as it still lives in this present world, then the church stands diametrically opposed to the world. Then the world hates her, and she must fight the world. She must be crucified to the world, and the world to the church. It is a life and death struggle, a struggle that must and will end with the world subdued by the church, condemned by it, and conquered through Jesus...

And, conversely, Scripture points out that in that church the nucleus of the world is saved. God's plan, which appeared to be defeated through sin, still continues and comes out right, and the organism of the world, though from a different point of view, still operates as God had intended...Then, obviously, we see the opposite: that the world is not judged, but is *saved;* not conquered, but *rescued;* not damned, but *reconciled.*[5]

Here we have Kuyper's organic-antithetical view of the history of the elect-reprobate world, according to God's eternal good pleasure.

Reformed language!

Kuyper refers us to God's decree as an explanation of this twofold eternal result of world events in history: "Therefore hath he mercy on whom he will have mercy, and whom he will he hardeneth" (Rom. 9:18).

---

5. Ibid., 230–232.

He also refers to the Canons of Dordt:

> For this was the sovereign counsel and most gracious will and purpose of God the Father, that the quickening and saving efficacy of the most precious death of His Son should extend to all the elect, for bestowing upon them alone the gift of justifying faith, thereby to bring them infallibly to salvation, that is, it was the will of God that Christ by the blood of the cross, whereby he confirmed the new covenant, should effectually redeem out of every people, tribe, nation, and language all those, and those only, who were from eternity chosen to salvation and given to Him by the Father [Canons, II, 8].

Therefore, the synod could truthfully add to this doctrine in the Rejection of Errors that the contenders for common grace, "while they feign that they present this distinction, in a sound sense, seek to instill into the people the destructive poison of the Pelagian errors" [Canons, II, Rej. of Errors 6]. And for this doctrine one finds, according to Kuyper, "a cloud of witnesses" in history, both before and after the illustrious Synod of 1618–1619.[6] He shows from examples in history[7] that this "cloud of witnesses" (Augustine, Calvin, and the Dordt synod—with the exception of Martinius[8] of Bremen) "does not know of a grace that is *not* particular . . . Departures from that doctrine came later, and came into the Reformed churches from the outside."[9] Thus Kuyper and we also agree that the saving grace of God, also in the objective sense, is not common, according to Scripture and the Reformed confessions.

Moreover, we want to show here that between Kuyper and us there is no essential difference over the idea and the historical revelation and operation of God's grace.

---

6. Ibid., 4, 5.

7. Ibid., 5.

8. Matthias Martinius, a delegate at Dordt from Bremen, openly sided with the Arminians.

9. Kuyper, *Dat De Genade Particulier Is*, 8.

Kuyper understands by the term "grace" *sovereign and particular favor*. Grace, he says, "almost always signifies in Scripture the *unrestrained* mercy of God."[10] Bavinck sums up all the covenant blessings under it: grace is that attribute

> whereby God, though as our Creator He owes us *nothing*, nevertheless presents us with all sorts of temporal and spiritual good. At the same time "grace" includes the idea that the *gracious character* of that grace becomes far more evident when it involves a damn-worthy sinner, but the reason is that in the sinner its *unrestrained* character becomes the more evident. As such, the term *grace* in the absolute sense does not imply that the recipient is a sinner.[11]

In this connection we briefly point out that there is no essential difference in the use of such words as grace, mercy, lovingkindness, pity, compassion, favor, love, goodness, and the like; neither Scripture, nor the confessions, nor the Forms, nor the Psalm versifications, nor any Reformed writers of importance, make a distinction.

Regarding the historical revelation and operation of God's grace, Kuyper writes:

> And thus we come to the third part of our apology for "particular grace," where we must show that *Scripture actually teaches particular grace*. To be able to know what is involved in this matter of grace, there is but one way open: *We must ask God Himself . . .*
>
> When we turn to holy Scripture, we do not find anywhere a chapter that treats the subject of grace directly, and which tells us concisely, completely, and in its logical relationship all the specifics concerning grace. God uses a different method in the Scriptures to instruct His people.

---

10. Abraham Kuyper, *E Voto Dordraceno: Toelichting op den Heidelbergschen Catechismus* (According to the Will of Dordt: Explanation of the Heidelberg Catechism), 4 vols. (Amsterdam: Höveker & Wormser, 1904), vol. 2, 327.

11. Herman Bavinck, *Gereformeerde Dogmatiek* (Reformed Dogmatics), second ed., 3 vols. (Amsterdam: Wormser, 1892), vol. 3, 660.

The Lord always walks the path of history; that is, He begins with *something*, and adds some *more*, and, after that, gives something *more explicit*, causing that something explicit to be followed by something still *clearer*, in order finally to place before the eye of the soul a clearer revelation of the truth at its very best and in all its *completeness*.

That revelation, enlightening and clarifying God's truth, is not given in such a way that over and over again formulas and definitions are handed to us. Such definitions are brief and rare. The main point is rather that the Merciful One, to show us what grace is all about, lets us *see* grace, very really *grants* and *demonstrates* it, in order that in the *operations* of that grace by which grace is experienced, and the manner in which it is increased, He enlightens us concerning its origin and nature...

We see that grace is shown in paradise, since God on his part addresses fallen man, seeks him, shakes him awake, and places him before his just and holy judgment.

It becomes evident from God's interference

that grace has already begun to work,...that favor and mercy are shown toward Adam by covering his shame, and by giving him another son for Abel. But obviously, this passage does not tell us whether this grace was intended for all Adam's descendants, or only for a portion of them...That only becomes evident when immediately after the fall the banner of the covenant of grace is displayed from afar to a sin-laden, utterly miserable humanity, and that, in fact, blessings are bestowed upon them out of this covenant.

Moreover, if we appeal to the history *immediately following* paradise, that is, to the immediate descendants of Adam, we are at once confronted with the horrible fact that Cain committed fratricide by killing Abel, hardened himself against all external admonition, gulped down the curse, and produced a generation that was *completely outside the dispensation of grace*...

There is most certainly nothing here in favor of common grace. Rather, from the beginning a *separation* takes place, which passes through the human race and divides it, so that the holy line of the work of grace is not drawn through the heart of *everyone*, nor does it reach the ear of *everyone*, but only reaches a *part* of those who are born of women, and thus shows a *particular* character.

There is a generation, *on the one hand*, in which the fear of the Lord dwells, and there is, *on the other hand*, a generation which seeks its strength in wickedness. Even in that *better* generation we discover little of a "common grace"; rather, evil increasingly overpowers the good, until at last the entire generation is cast out by the God of all grace . . .

But Noah found grace in the eyes of the Lord . . .

Here we actually are confronted with the fact that God the Lord, instead of advancing in every possible way the cause of the work of grace upon all mankind, that is, upon every soul among them, rather wipes from the face of the earth all existing humanity, confers grace only upon one family, and out of Noah, as the second progenitor, causes an entirely new generation of the children of men to arise.

Anyone who maintains the "paradise gospel," namely, anyone who believes and confesses that the covenant of grace was already established in paradise, is not confronted with strange reasoning, with doubtful expressions, nor with a biased presentation, but with an undeniable, definite *act of God* that shows irrefutably that in the main course of the history of God's accomplishments, the plan of His work of grace is *not* directed toward or intended for the salvation of every soul . . .

After the flood we do indeed read of the establishment of a covenant with Noah and the *whole* human race that came from the patriarch, and we readily grant that the covenant with Noah forms a link in the revelation-chain of the covenant of *grace*. But whoever would conclude from that, that the grace of God was destined and intended by God for *all mankind*, and that in the sense of "grace unto salvation," would be sadly mistaken . . .

On the contrary, even as before the flood, so after the flood the dispensation of grace was of a particular character. Indeed, of the three sons of Noah, the blessing did *not* come to Ham and his descendants, but only the *curse*. Of the two remaining sons, Shem very definitely becomes the bearer of the covenant promise, and Japheth has no prospect of salvation except through Shem. Thus, even as in Adam's time, there is a deep chasm running through our race by which mankind is torn apart, so the one part *is indeed* enriched with God's grace, but the other part is not.

The attempt at the building of the tower of Babel to frustrate this division and to keep the race together was nothing less than a deliberate assault of sinful rebellion and pride. Whenever mankind wants to remain one and work for a common cause, it is God who *scatters them*... The calling of and favor shown to Abraham even more strongly and emphatically contradicts the teaching that "Christ died for the sum total of all mankind." The great significance of God's work upon, in, and through this father of believers is, indeed, *the election of one, with the rejection of all the others, in order that only in later years God might cause salvation to come forth from that one to the descendants of the others*...

Through the separation of the "family of grace," those outside of that family who at that time were still living upon the earth were placed outside of the dispensation of grace. They were given over to the natural development of the evil within them, and in such a way that darkness was poured out upon the spirit of man, a darkness which blinded the heathen before the face of the living God and brought them on their knees before idols... Compare this to what we have written above... It must be granted that a Rebekah, a Leah, a Rachel, were brought out of Mesopotamia, to be granted a share in the blessing of Abraham. It may not be ignored that those who were born within the house of the patriarchs were lightened with the light of grace, and that Melchizedek experienced fellowship with God. But this does not change the main fact that grace concentrated entirely in Abraham's family circle, and that which was not related to or came in contact with it, steadily died out and became ripe for destruction.[12]

Thus Kuyper spoke *before* he wrote his *De Gemeene Gratie*. In connection with the Mosaic dispensation, we read:

The essence of the dispensation of grace in the Sinaitic form of the covenant of grace is *a confining of grace within the boundaries and limits of Israel's existence as a nation*, and, inseparably connected with that, a *withdrawing and withholding of that grace from all the nations on the face of the earth for centuries to come*.[13]

---

12. Kuyper, *Dat De Genade Particulier Is*, 93–100.
13. Ibid., 102.

Let us clearly understand this. We know very well that Kuyper is dealing here with saving grace, and not with so-called common grace; and we know that he is speaking against the universalists. But we are calling attention to Kuyper's presentation concerning the unity and development of all things. Plainly and clearly he presents here the organic-antithetical line. The covenant of grace is already presupposed in paradise. Saving grace, not common, comes to Adam and Eve from that covenant grace. And the covenant with Noah forms a link in the revelation-chain of the covenant of grace. The dispensation of grace after the flood shows the particular character of the covenant of grace just as consistently as before the flood. Blessing does not rest on Ham and his descendants, but the curse. Even as in the days of Adam, a deep chasm is made in our race by which mankind is divided. And by the separation of Abraham, all those who are placed outside of the dispensation of grace are now given over to the natural development of wickedness that is inherent in them. In this way, darkness, which blinded the nations before the face of the living God, was poured out upon the spirit of mankind, and it brought men upon their knees before idols; thus they are given over to dying away and becoming ripe for destruction.

This entire line of reasoning is in the organic-antithetical line.

The same applies to Kuyper's view of the character of sin. The sin of Adam in paradise is, according to Kuyper,

> in principle, *apostasy* and *rebellion* against the sovereignty of the Lord. But that is not all. When Adam fell and lifted up his hand against God, the Catechism says that his fall concerns *you*, for the man who fell was your *forefather*, and, in fact, your first forefather. When he fell, you also fell, for that first forefather had received of God a being, and in that being a *nature*. Now that being remained unchangeable; but that nature, which determined the character of his life, naturally and immediately underwent a change as soon as he forsook God and fell . . . Thus *man's* very *nature* was changed by this sinful act. It was turned around, and life that is in mankind began to operate in a different manner. Since that time, the change in the course of life within man becomes

a fading, a withering, and a dying existence. Our Catechism says that man's nature (not his being) became depraved.[14]

If you had, if I had, if all the descendants of Adam had, apart from him, been able to take anew out of God's hand a new human nature, then at the time of our birth, our nature would be pure again, and it would again depend upon us whether we would corrupt our nature . . . But this was *not* God's plan. His plan was that hope should arise not for an individual, but for a human *race;* that is, for all those who are from one blood, a humanity . . . This is why each individual after Adam did *not* receive his human nature directly from God, but from God *through* Adam. And since Adam no longer had a pure nature, neither he nor Eve could give a pure nature to the human race . . . Therefore, the same nature that was in Adam was passed along "to all his descendants."[15]

Because we were in Adam, we sinned when he sinned. His sin was our sin, and the guilt which he acquired by this original or root sin was our guilt . . . All sin after that is the continuation of that first sin . . . That is what is so appalling about Adam's sin: by it *he creates sin as something new.* He struck the first spark which set everything afire.[16]

But this is not the end of the matter, because an indescribably terrible result of sin is that *sin breeds sin.* Just as it is not in your power to set afire a single barrel of gunpowder in a storehouse without the first spark in the storehouse starting a fire which would cause everything to explode, so that everything was destroyed, so it is in your heart. Sin is like a fire, and no one has the consequences of sin in his own power. Sin once committed becomes a habit, lodges in the deepest inclinations of our being, puts something inscrutable in our nerves and in the cerebral membrane, and repeatedly arouses us, so that we walk in the flame and sparks that we ourselves have lit. This is horrible, but it is nevertheless a fact. The drunkard knows it, and the lustful person

---

14. Kuyper, *E Voto Dordraceno,* vol. 1, 47.
15. Ibid., vol. 1, 48, 49
16. Ibid., vol. 1, 61.

Sin and *Grace*

knows it; the liar knows it, the thief knows it, and the hothead knows it. A sin never remains isolated.[17]

In the meantime sin is not something unique in this or that person, but is something that is common to our race as a whole. A unique human sin does not exist. All sin proceeds from the original sin of Adam and is connected with the thread of life to that first sin, and continues to be fed by it. All sin is and forms an organic whole, and this organic whole is not in one person, but is, in fact, in the whole human race.[18]

Therefore, there is no such thing as an isolated, an independent, a swiftly passing transgression of Adam. It is a *basic* transgression, a *root* sin, a poisoning of himself in the deepest *principle* of his life. Adam could not commit a sin just once, and then continue his walk in holiness. But as soon as he committed a sin, even though it took a moment, his walk in holiness was immediately and permanently lost.[19]

Here Kuyper takes the organic point of view in regard to sin. Sin develops organically in our generations from the sinful life-principle out of which it began to live in and by Adam, and it reaches its completion in the sum total of the sinful deeds of all human individuals. It goes without saying that God's grace in Christ must harmonize with this organic character of sin.

But something very important is added. Sin is committed, according to Kuyper, by means of the creatures in the creation.

A sinner does not walk outside of the creation to commit sin in order to carry out his evil deed somewhere outside of God's creation and apart from the Lord. He cannot do that. It is true for all sinners that in Him they live and move and have their being. From moment to moment it is God who upholds them with His almighty hand, who continues to give them strength, who gives them the ability to think and

17. Ibid., vol. 1, 68.
18. Ibid., vol. 1, 94.
19. Ibid., vol. 1, 45.

to use their senses; and even in carrying out their evil, they are doing so with a power that belongs to God. All sin is committed before God's face, with the means that He gave—as it were in the very hand of God, by which He upholds all nature.[20]

In Kuyper's *Dictaten Dogmatiek* we hear similar language. There it is said that the unique character of sin is this:

1. When sin is allowed in Adam for a split second, it has the power to corrupt the entire person for all time.
2. This active *principium* [principle] also has the power to infect and corrupt the entire person.
3. It has the power to make each one who is born a bearer of that sinful human nature, a vehicle of that sin.
4. It has the power to affect completely each person, destroy whatever it can, and then corrupt the person in all his deeds and in his entire life.

Thus we are conceived and born in sin, because we stand guilty in Adam. But the sin itself also causes *reatis* [guilt]; and this aspect of the original guilt is given far too little attention. In regard to the original sin we do not have a *labes* [corruption] and a *culpa* [guilt], but a twofold *culpa,* a *culpa* which precedes the *labes* and which follows it.[21]

What Kuyper means is that Adam made himself guilty through sin; that this guilt is punished by God with death both in soul and body; but that through sin a permanent sinful disposition comes into existence, an evil habit, an inclination of the soul from which proceed the actual sins that again make us guilty before God in a fuller measure.

Also here Kuyper maintains the organic line.

---

20. Ibid., vol. 1, 395.

21. Kuyper, "Locus De Peccato" (Locus concerning Sin), in *Dictaten Dogmatiek,* vol. 3, 72.

It is self-evident that from this point of view there is no possibility of any positive, good development in the unregenerate. Concerning the unregenerate, Kuyper says:

> Now we face the question, What about the *rudera*, the remnants? Mankind is corrupt in all his ways, but retains "a few remains," as Article 14 of the Confession teaches. The Ethicals are, amazingly, in full agreement with that part of the Confession, but they forget what follows: "...for all the light which is in us is changed into darkness." Those remnants are measured out by the Ethicals, looked at through a magnifying glass, and finally become the entire person.
>
> On the contrary, the Confession teaches in regard to these *rudera* [remnants] that no good remained in the *nature* of the person, for as far as the nature is concerned, the person is completely sinful, so that his intellect and his will are not capable of performing anything that is good. These *rudera*, however, do have significance for man's being. Nature and being are thus to be distinguished. The nature is *id quod nascitur*, [that which brings forth] the activity. Being is that out of which the operation proceeds. That the will is corrupt does not mean, therefore, that the *voluntas* [will] becomes *nolunta* [incapable of willing], that is, that the person can no more will... Then the being would be injured. But the operation of the *voluntas* always functions negatively, is always wrong in the person...
>
> These *rudera* were formerly called *scintillae* [glimmerings] in the Confession, but in the translation, followed by the Synod of Dordt, the word is changed to *vestigia* [vestiges]. That clarifies the concept, something important to us. *Vestigum* means that once there was a person, but that person is now gone. Thus, if we say that a vestige of the righteousness of God can still be found in us, that does not mean that a particle of that righteousness remains in us, but exactly the opposite, that not one bit of it remains.
>
> The word *rudera* was not employed by the fathers to signify that one could still live in the remains of the ruins, but to state that the house itself has completely collapsed and only the ruins remain to give us some idea of the former beauty. The word *scintilla* does not mean that the fire can again flare up, but that there are only cinders of the *burned out* fire. Sparks remain, but they can do nothing but die out...

> The Synod of Dordt, 1618, says: "There remain, however, in man since the fall, the glimmerings of natural light, whereby he retains some knowledge of God, of natural things..." (Canons of Dordt III/IV, Art. 4). This seems to be in conflict with Article 14 of the Confession, but instead, the same figure is twice employed, but for different purposes. In the Confession, Article 14 speaks of the *lunem justitiae originalis* [the light of original righteousness]; while the Canons deal with the *lunem naturae* [the light of nature], that which is in man by nature, but apart from sin.[22]

Therefore, according to Kuyper, the idea of the "small sparks" comes down to this: our confessions teach that there remains in sinful mankind nothing of the original righteousness: not in his will, nor in his mind. In that regard, the light that is in him is darkness. The substance, as such, of his ability to know and to will is not corrupted, for sin left the human essence untouched, but the operation of these abilities is always negative and is wrong. It can still be seen that righteousness was there, but the righteousness itself is lacking. However, apart from sin, apart from the operation of the human nature, which is always wrong, there is still some natural light in the individual.

This should be compared with what we quoted before from Kuyper in regard to the *scintillae religionis* [glimmerings of religion] and the *semen religionis* [seed of religion], to which Calvin refers. We must, indeed, keep this in mind when later we consider the term *civil righteousness*, but we can already understand that it is impossible that anything done by a man as a citizen of a country, or done in civil matters, is righteous before God.

We consider these quotations sufficient for our present purpose. They could easily be multiplied from the various works of Kuyper and from others. With a few minor exceptions, we can readily agree with the basic view presented in these citations. But how anyone can fit a system of common grace into these views is a mys-

---

22. Ibid, 84, 86.

tery to us. We can neither see the necessity, the logic, nor the possibility. How can anyone in the position defined above possibly allow the sinner, in whom the light of original righteousness is turned into darkness, to do that which is good in the sight of God without the work of regeneration? An essentially positive and good development of human life in general, and of the creature in particular, is simply impossible without regeneration. This is true without even considering the negative development of the human race because of sin. The difficulties are found in the psychological[23] aspects of the matter. Therefore, we want to consider the main problems in the theory of common grace from the viewpoint of the sinner's existence and soul-life. But we will do this later.

We do not intend to enter into all sorts of details, which, for that matter, would be virtually impossible. Nor are we, by ignoring all the details, attempting to sidestep the difficulties. Rather, we are looking for them, because the problem we face deals precisely with the most fundamental principle of the spiritual-ethical development of the children of Adam's race in its natural unity and spiritual diversity.

Common Grace and the Fall

The question is, therefore, how do the proponents of so-called common grace conceive of the development of the sum total of all created things after the fall of mankind? And how do they view these things in connection with the working of God's regenerating and saving grace in Christ?

We will let Kuyper speak first. In his *Dictaten Dogmatiek,* he says:

---

23. By "psychological" the author does not refer to the present day meaning of that term, but rather to the biblical ideas of man's creation; that is, he was created with body and soul.

Taking as our hypothesis and foundation that the world is sustained and develops cosmically by common grace, the covenant of particular grace enters into the world, even as common grace, to maintain the honor of God over against Satan. But, in distinction from common grace, particular grace is essential and eternal...

God must first restrain sin; otherwise the covenant of grace is superfluous. If the covenant of grace saves sinners, then there must be such a common grace. Sinners enter the world from father and mother by birth. If no common grace had entered in, the fall would immediately have resulted in the death of Adam and Eve. The objects of the covenant of grace would not exist apart from the *gratia communis* [common grace]. There would be no elect... But it is not only necessary that those objects, those persons, exist; they must also be somewhere. They must be in this world. And if that is to be, this world must be habitable. The desert pictures to us what the whole world would be if the curse had been carried out. We can thank common grace that there is a world. However, in the world one still finds whole areas that are not habitable, as for example, at the north and south poles. But there are also habitable places. That is a condition for the covenant of grace...

Christ has also willed that His covenant of grace would be revealed in a church. And again that church cannot exist apart from common grace. Thus, in every respect common grace is indispensable for the covenant of grace.

Yet it may not be said that it is a *praerequisitum* [prerequisite] of the covenant of grace, that is, that it is present only for the church... It has a goal of its own, namely, that God, by the restraint of sin, and in spite of the opposition of the devil, causes His work of art to appear... But just because the covenant of grace presupposes *gratia communis* [common grace], there must be a binding cement between the two, a tendon that joins the two. This organic unity lies in the origin and the ultimate purpose of both. The origin of both lies in the Mediator of creation and of redemption. They are both out of Christ, but out of Christ who is first of all the eternal Word, and second, the incarnate Word. The purpose of both lies in the defense of the glory of God over against Satan. Indeed the purpose of *gratia communis* is to preserve the development of God's work over against Satan, and to preserve the development of the covenant of grace in order to destroy the works of Satan.[24]

Thus, Kuyper's presentation briefly comes down to this:

1. After the fall the world exists and continues its cosmic development through common grace.

2. Without this common grace, the fall would immediately have resulted in the death of Adam and Eve, and therefore the covenant of grace would have been impossible. Therefore, the immediate purpose of common grace lies in the covenant of grace.

3. However, the final purpose of common grace is the full manifestation of God's artistry in the creation.

4. The organic unity of common grace and particular grace lies in Christ, who is both creation-Mediator and redemption-Mediator.

With respect to the first point, it must be remarked, first of all, that Kuyper, strictly speaking, does not permit the creation after the fall to continue and develop through common grace. He distinguishes between creation, providence, and common grace. Creation, he says, is the *causing* of things *to come into existence;* providence is the *upholding* of those things. The development of things after the fall is not directly the fruit of common grace.[25]

> Rather the main point of the relationship between "common grace" and "providence" lies *in the process of gradual development*, which only by "common grace" can be used for the carrying out of God's providential plan. Without "common grace" there would be preservation and government, but no *divine rule* in providence. Ruling is really a directing toward a determined purpose and a realization of the means to attain that goal. It is to steer the ship and cause it to move forward, so

---

24. Kuyper, "Locus de Foedere" (Locus concerning the Covenant), in *Dictaten Dogmatiek*, vol. 3, 131–138.

25. In this sentence, the authors sum up what Kuyper wrote in *DGG*, vol. 2, 380.

that it advances, makes headway, and finally glides into the haven which is its destination.[26]

Looking at it this way, we must distinguish between two aspects of common grace, namely, between its constant operation and its progressive operation. By the first, God restrains "the destructive power *in nature,* in order that it does not at once destroy the world." At the same time, He arrests "the destructive power of sin *in the human heart* to make civil righteousness possible on earth among sinners and heathen."[27] That is its constant operation. But without anything more, there is no *divine government.* There is no management that directs things to a certain goal. The ship has no course to follow. There must be a certain process in our lives and in the life of the whole world. That process of the development of all things originates through the progressive operation of common grace. By it God brings human life to an ever richer and fuller development. And the individual man appears on the scene as *instrument and co-worker* of God. God works in and *through man.* And the result of it all is that the rule of man over the creation expands and becomes more established.

> Civilization, enlightenment, development, and advancement are not from the Evil One, but from God. From the Evil One comes only the wrong, immoral and wicked influences, against which we Christians must set ourselves with all our power. But the attainment of a greater rule over nature is a gracious gift of God, for which we must thank Him, and for which we, as children of God, must exert ourselves. At creation God Himself planted the rich seeds of majestic development in humanity, and it was the will of God from the beginning that these seeds should be fully developed by man's rule over nature. Satan wanted to restrain that development by sin. But then God intervened with His "common grace" in order to raise humanity to its high and

26. Ibid., vol. 2, 596.
27. Ibid., vol. 2, 600, 601.

> rich development, in spite of sin, even through a way of blood and tears.[28]

Thus, when he speaks of cosmic development, Kuyper actually means man's rule over God's creation.

Without entering into everything that is assumed in this position, we want now only to point out that, according to the reasoning of Dr. Kuyper, cosmic development would not have been possible if God had not interfered with his common grace, for then death would have been the immediate consequence of the fall of Adam and Eve. That is a constant refrain in Kuyper's argument. If that supposition falls away, then, as we see it, his entire mechanical plan for the dualistic development of the whole creation would fall with it. If man is dead in trespasses and sin, then without regenerating grace in Christ he cannot attain to a mastery of the world that is pleasing to God. Since his nature, according to Kuyper himself, always acts negatively and is perverse, he would turn this mastery of the world against his Creator. He would increase in unrighteousness. Kuyper's mechanical scheme for the development of things would, as we see it, certainly have to give way to our organic view if we should succeed in showing that the Word of God never makes mention of such an interference of God by means of a so-called common grace. Rather, it speaks emphatically of condemnation, curse, destruction, and enmity. But Scripture also speaks of the grace in Christ that immediately began to operate in paradise—something which Kuyper himself, as we showed above, wrote earlier and still believed at a later date.

There is an abundance of proof for the idea that mankind *did* die immediately after the fall.

> The LORD God commanded the man, saying, Of every tree of the garden thou mayest freely eat: but of the tree of the knowledge of good

---

28. Ibid., vol. 2, 603, 604.

and evil, thou shalt not eat of it: for in the day that thou eatest thereof thou shalt surely die (Gen. 2:16, 17).

And when the woman saw that the tree was good for food, and that it was pleasant to the eyes, and a tree to be desired to make one wise, she took of the fruit thereof, and did eat, and gave also unto her husband with her; and he did eat (Gen. 3:6).

Man died. Both Adam and Eve died. Here is our proof: The Lord God, who cannot lie, had said, "In the day that thou eatest thereof thou shalt surely die." Would He say that, and not do it? Would Kuyper want to maintain that?

But you want proof that man *is dead*. We will furnish it.

And you hath he quickened, who were *dead* in trespasses and sins; wherein in time past ye walked according to the course of this world, according to the prince of the power of the air, the spirit that now worketh in the children of disobedience: among whom also we all had our conversation in times past in the lusts of our flesh, fulfilling the desires of the flesh and of the mind; and were by nature the children of wrath, even as others. But God, who is rich in mercy, for his great love wherewith he loved us, even when we *were dead* in sins, hath quickened us together with Christ (by grace ye are saved) (Eph. 2:1–5).

And you, being dead in your sins and the uncircumcision of your flesh, hath he quickened together with him (Col. 2:13).

Verily, verily, I say unto you, He that heareth my word, and believeth on him that sent me, hath everlasting life, and shall not come into condemnation; but is passed from death unto life. Verily, verily, I say unto you, The hour is coming, and now is, when the dead shall hear the voice of the Son of God: and they that hear shall live" (John 5:24, 25).

And if Christ be in you, the body is dead because of sin; but the Spirit is life because of righteousness. But if the Spirit of him that raised up Jesus from the dead dwell in you, he that raised up Christ from the dead shall also quicken your mortal bodies by his Spirit that dwelleth in you (Rom. 8:10, 11).

> Jesus said unto her, I am the resurrection, and the life: he that be-
> lieveth in me, though he were dead, yet shall he live: and whosoever
> liveth and believeth in me shall never die. Believest thou this? (John
> 11:25, 26).

These are the facts that God's Word gives us. The very day that
Adam and Eve ate of the forbidden tree, they died, and in them
the entire generation of the children of men died. All mankind remains in death in time and in eternity, unless they are quickened
by God's Spirit in Christ, who is the resurrection and the life.
Those who are regenerated have in their spirit passed from death
into life and will never die, not even when they lay aside their
mortal body, which has not yet been quickened, in the hope of the
resurrection of the flesh in the day of Christ Jesus.

One certainly should not confuse dying with the separation of
soul and body. The separation of soul and body has no connection
whatever with the essence of death, since the accursed in hell will
have to bear the burden of the wrath of God against sin in both
soul and body, that is, with soul and body again united. The temporary separation of soul and body, both of unbelievers and believers, must be connected to something quite different. But we
cannot discuss that in detail now. We must first of all establish that
death is inflicted punishment. Sin is disobedience, unrighteousness, rebellion against God, and therefore transgression. And now
through that one transgression of Adam, guilt has come upon all
mankind unto condemnation. The whole world is accursed before
God, that is, worthy of death. And even as transgression is the vi-
olation of God's majesty and the breaking of His law, in which He
demands absolute and unceasing obedience and devotion, in like
manner the bearing of punishment before the face of God must be
without end. In the highest sense, sin is an absolute and unending
evil, also in duration, for he who sins becomes a slave to sin, so
that he cannot and will not do anything but sin.

He may be placed beyond the opportunity to continue on his
sinful way, but he himself does not control that, since his internal

desire is to sin eternally. Therefore, sinners will also bear the wrath of eternal perdition before the face of God.[29] This bearing of wrath brings about separation from God. Thus, the essence of death does not consist in the separation of soul and body, or a severing of that which naturally belongs together, nor even in a local separation, but it is a spiritual disharmony with and spiritual separation from God. The sinner stands at enmity with God, and therefore he does not share in God's favor and friendship, but experiences the fury of His wrath.[30]

This bearing of punishment has an organic character, because mankind exists and lives organically. Adam (this is also Kuyper's view, as we saw above) sinned as the organic head of our race. His sin was a *principle* or *root* sin, from which all other sin develops. Therefore, the bearing of wrath had also to be of an organic character and had to develop organically. Keeping this in mind, we can also understand the language of the Baptism Form when it states, "... that they may, with a comfortable sense of Thy favor, leave this life, which is nothing but a continual death..."[31]

And we can agree with the answer to Question 10 of the Heidelberg Catechism:

> Q. Will God suffer such disobedience and rebellion to go unpunished?
>
> A. By no means; but is terribly displeased with our original as well as actual sins; and will punish them in His just judgment *temporally* and *eternally*, as He hath declared, *"Cursed is every one that continueth not in all things which are written in the book of the law to do them."*

God punishes the sin of the individual, who is a temporal-eternal being, in time and in eternity according to the nature of his temporal and eternal character.

---

29. See Romans 5:18; Romans 3:19; Romans 1:32; 2 Thess. 1:9. See also Bavinck, *Gereformeerde Dogmatiek*, vol. 3, 410; vol. 4, 793.

30. Romans 1:18 and Bavinck, *Gereformeerde Dogmatiek*, vol. 2, 161.

31. Form for the Administration of Baptism, in *The Psalter*, 87 (liturgical section).

That seems to be the idea of Sikkel when he says:

> "In the day *that thou eatest thereof*"; that does not merely mean *on that day*, but it tells us that dying will necessarily be connected to the eating from the tree, and then not merely on the *day* in which the eating took place, but in the *fact*, in the *event*, in the *deed*. "Wilt surely die" is exactly the certainty of dying. However, death is not an immediate giving up the ghost. It is a sinking away of life into death, a dissolution of the bond with God, which ends and reaches its culmination in death. This dissolution of the bond takes place at the time of the fall, in the spiritual violation of fellowship with God, who is the Fountain of Life, and it carries through into all life's relationships. Death is carried out in the fact that Adam and Eve are driven away from the tree of life and live in all spiritual and physical misery, ending up in the eternal bonds of outer darkness.[32]

We can also listen when Dr. B. Wielenga teaches and warns us:

> A delusion of our day, which captivates the world, is that in mankind and in every creature there is a seed of that which is good waiting to be developed unto perfection. The empty lies of liberalism and the loathsome superficiality of the chatter about neutrality belong to that dogma of which evolution is a pitiful sprout. Men are infatuated with their own ignorance! But the church confesses that the child spiritually, in its soul, enters this world as a monster in the sight of God; that already at the time of his birth, the sentence of death awaits the child, the judgment not only of temporal, but of eternal death...He is born to die.[33]

---

32. J. C. [Johannes Cornelis] Sikkel, *Het Woord Gods* (The Word of God) (Amsterdam: Van Schalk, 1906), 233. Sikkel (1856–1920), a Dutch preacher and pioneer of social reform, wrote three commentaries on different Old Testament books, probably under the series title *Het Woord Gods*. As the commentaries were not available to us, we cannot identify which commentary was cited.

33. B. Wielenga, *Ons Doopsformulier* (Our Baptism Form) (Kampen: J. H. Kok, 1921), 26, 27.

And, as a child of wrath,

> he rises out of wrath, is *made* in wrath, lives under wrath, or rather *dies* day by day, and finally will assume the inheritance of the full revelation and outpouring of divine wrath. It is the wrath of God by which sinful mankind appears on the scene and which marks his end. The wrath of God is the horrible capital that awaits him, from which on earth he receives in bitter foretaste only a little interest when he is still in the midst of life's disappointments and opposition, life's cares and life's weariness. Who can even begin to fathom the depth of the gaping abyss of misery! By nature children of wrath are born outside of the *kingdom*, thus *in* the kingdom of the devil. They enter the world through the portal of hell.[34]

We and our children *are*, do not *become*, such children of wrath; that is, by nature we are children of wrath, even as all the children of mankind. Therefore, the wrath of God is revealed from heaven against the wickedness and unrighteousness of men. And this will continue unless a person is born again.

All this does not harmonize with Kuyper's presentation of common grace. We would almost dare to say that if it is true what Wielenga, for example, says about us and our children, namely, that we *are* by nature children of wrath, even as all others, then there simply cannot be any talk about a good development of all things. Then the sinner can never produce good works in the sight of God. No, then we will be compelled to say, with the poet, "By Thy wrath our spirits languish."

But let us first hear Kuyper's position on the death of the sinner as it relates to common grace.

He says:

> Death, considered in connection with the eating of the tree of knowledge, can be understood in a twofold sense: either as a punishment that is threatened, or a punishment that flows from eating. If the

---

34. Ibid., 28, 29.

death penalty is placed upon treason, then this is a threatened punishment, for the act of high treason itself does not result in death. But
if I say, "Do not drink that Prussian blue[35] or you will die," then there
is no mention of punishment; I only mean that this poison is deadly,
and any one who swallows it will die. Even in this latter case, if someone swallows it in spite of the warning, I can still make the attempt to
prevent the fatal consequences with a strong emetic or antidote. Even
then I spoke the truth when I said, "If you swallow that, you will die."
And I am not contradicting myself in the least if I attempt to save the
one who carelessly swallowed the poison.

If this is clear, then one must also grant that this is exactly what is
meant by the words "If thou eatest from the tree of knowledge, thou
wilt die." I take these words to mean nothing more than a declaration,
a warning: "Beware, if you allow yourself to be tempted to eat of that
tree, then you will see that death results." If these words have that
meaning, there is no conflict with the fact that death did not immediately come to Adam with finality and on that very day. The same
God that warned them, immediately after their transgression gave
them something to check the consequences of their evil. We are therefore strongly inclined to give these words that interpretation.[36]

And further:

When God says in paradise, "The day that thou eatest thereof thou
shalt surely die," that by no means implies, "Then I will externally, as
an automatic punishment, lay death upon you," but it is to be taken
in a completely different sense. Sin is a *poison*, and as soon as this poison begins to *take effect* in you, you will feel death coming over you.
Death is not added to sin as a second power, but follows out of sin itself, is a part of it, just as decomposition follows in a corpse and is the
natural consequence of dying. When an individual ventures to oppose
God, as if he himself were God, deciding for himself what is good and
what is evil, instead of accepting in quiet submission the difference
that God placed between good and evil, then, as a natural result, the

35. Prussian blue is a poison.
36. Kuyper, *DGG*, vol. 1, 209, 210.

bond that united his soul to God is broken, and *spiritual* death immediately enters.

When once the bond between God and the soul is torn apart, also the bond between the individual and the world, the mutual bond between the individuals, the bond between soul and body, and the bond that bound together the powers and abilities of the soul, are severed. In all this, death is fully realized.

All this would happen as God predicted. The day man dared to have the audacity to sin, he would not only come into contact with death, but *in the fullest sense of the word would surely die*. Not later, but *on that very day*. Not little by little and gradually, but at *once*.[37]

Further, Kuyper considers the essence of death to be separation from God, and he applies that idea to what God joined together in creation.

He who once understands that the essence of death is a rending of that which God has joined together is also able to understand all this in its natural development. At this point we arrive at that significant moment in which *common grace* enters in and begins to operate. For, it is as clear as the day that what God had spoken is not carried out. That which from God's viewpoint was most justly pointed out to be the natural and immediate result of sin, in fact *does not happen*. Had it happened as God had announced, then the corpse of Adam and the corpse of Eve would necessarily have lain at the foot of the tree of life before the sun set that evening, and decomposition would have begun its destructive work. Trying to find some way out of this does not work. If you say that they did die *spiritually*, and that the seed of death was planted in them physically, you still fail to give any explanation of the explicit and absolute words *surely die*. The expression *surely die* is the strongest and most absolute expression of the full and complete destructive power of death that you find in the Hebrew language. You may not limit it to the spiritual death that entered, nor may you explain it as an implanting of the seed of death. Had God's Word been carried out, that would have been the end of it on that very day for

---

37. Ibid., vol. 1, 206.

Adam and Eve; the curse would have destroyed everything upon the earth, and complete chaos would have resulted. But it did *not* happen in that way, and the very fact that it did *not* happen in that way is because of the entrance and operation of common grace or common favor.[38]

And if one asks, how can this be harmonized with the Word of God, the answer is that every difficulty falls away if one interprets the statement, "On the day that thou eatest thereof thou shalt surely die," not in a way that is deceptive, but rather as a pure prediction. It must be taken in this sense: the eating of that tree will bring you into sin, and *sin* has as its natural consequence *death*, death *immediately*, death fully carried out. But the unspoken understanding is, *"Unless I, your God, should restrain in my mercy the operating consequences of the sin."*[39]

But when one explains things this way, one is playing with God's Word and is speaking a language that departs from the position of Scripture and the confessions. It is a simple fact that Scripture and the confessions do not teach this, and that nothing like it is found anywhere in the Scriptures. According to the Scriptures, the sinner is dead, everlastingly dead, unless he is quickened by the Holy Spirit through regeneration in Christ, who is the resurrection and the life. Also sin is not, according to the Scripture, like taking poison, which would naturally result in death. Sin is disobedience, transgression, unrighteousness, rebellion against God, placing oneself in the place of God. Sin is an offense to God's majesty, and therefore a misdeed that makes guilty. That guilt comes upon all mankind unto condemnation. Therefore, the sinner must suffer the punishment of eternal perdition before the face of God.

The words *In the day that thou eatest thereof thou shalt surely die* must very really be regarded as a threat. It is also clear as well that the essence of death is not, as Kuyper says, a tearing apart of that which God has joined together in creation, as, for example, the

---

38. Kuyper uses both terms here: *gratie* and *genade*.
39. Kuyper, *DGG*, vol. 1, 208, 209.

soul from God. That is impossible, unless you believe that man, and along with him the entire creation, returns to non-existence and is annihilated. Nor can it be a separation of soul and body, or of all individuals mutually, or of all things created. But the essence of death is spiritual disunion with God. As a result, God treats sin as an enemy and brings it under the fury of His wrath. The separation of soul and body is actually such an insignificant element in death that the unbelievers who still remain on the earth in the day of Christ's return will in that sense not even die. In a manner similar to the believers who remain, they will be changed in a moment, in order that then, in body and soul, they may bear the burden of the wrath of God against sin in that everlasting sentence against sin, and according to the nature of that sentence. The suffering of full death in eternity demands the reunion and union of that which temporarily fell apart and ceased operating here in the world, in order that the sinner, in his complete human nature in which he raised his hand against his Creator, may taste the full power of God's anger against his misdeed, even in all the relationships in which his Maker placed him.

Christ also tasted eternal death for His own, not when soul and body were separated, but when they still were united, that is, on the cross. We must accept this as an established fact, as also our Catechism states: "...that sin which is committed against the most high majesty of God, be also punished with extreme, that is, with everlasting punishment of body and soul."[40] This is true for the simple reason that the sinner exists in body and soul, for time and for eternity. As the highest creature standing at the apex of all creation, he offended the majesty of his Creator. Therefore, the wicked will, according to Article 37 of our Confession, become immortal in the day of Christ, also according to their body, which will again be united with the soul.

This is, therefore, the situation: sin does not lead directly, that is, causally, to death in the sense of separation of soul and body,

---

40. Answer 11.

but it makes a person guilty. The punishment of sin is death. That death was threatened by God in paradise before the fall, and applied after the fall. The divine carrying out of that verdict of death was according to the demand of God's law and justice and the principle and character of the sin and guilt of man.

If for a moment we assume Kuyper's position, we would arrive at a very distorted and thoroughly erroneous (we would almost say *deceptive*) conclusion. Supposing we regard God's words *In the day that thou shalt eat of that tree thou shalt surely die* as a prediction or warning. Does it not immediately follow that:

1. Mankind was threatened with an evil that God Himself placed in His good creation.

2. The eating of a natural poison (for something different could hardly have been in that tree) could never have brought about a spiritual and eternal death of the one who ate it.

3. Man would not be guilty before God, but rather God before man.

4. Death at a later date for the one who ate the fruit, after he had taken the antidote of common grace and saved his life for a time, becomes an inconsistency.

5. It is entirely inexplicable how one who takes poison "can become incapable of any good and inclined to all evil." Yet, during the working of the antidote of common grace, whereby the operation of the poison of sin is temporarily restrained, man is able to raise this earthly creation in glorious cosmic development in a way that is pleasing to God. Yet, in a spiritual-moral sense, he does not live a good life before God.

6. Kuyper's own argumentation elsewhere becomes the more incomprehensible. Kuyper sees in the two special trees in paradise—the tree of life and the tree of the knowledge of good and evil—trees of a higher order[41] and ascribes to the eating of the one and the not eating of the other a sacramental character, in the

---

41. Kuyper, *DGG*, vol. 1, 126, 127.

same way as the rainbow in the covenant with Noah is sacramental. The tree of knowledge refers particularly to the spiritual life of the human spirit in distinction from his physical life.

Moreover, Kuyper is of the opinion that eating from the tree is the same as the individual determining for himself what is right and what is wrong and not leaving that to God, and thereby putting himself in the place of God.[42] That would make the sin of paradise a moral offense against the majesty and justice of God, and have nothing whatever in common with the eating of poison.

7. This entire presentation must almost necessarily end in a denial of God's moral world-order. This actually happens in the works of Newton N. Riddell, author of *Vital Christianity, and Other Works and Discourses*. In an "address" given recently, he maintains that

> Spiritual death is the result only of disobedience to a warning...God never condemns any soul; it is not his will that any should perish...Sin makes man subject to spiritual laws, the inevitable consequence of which is spiritual death. If an electrician shall say to his helper, "Don't touch that live wire; if you do, you will be killed," he is warning the man of the inevitable sequence of electrical law. The helper is heedless. He touches the wire and dies. His death in no way represents the arbitrary will of the electrician. Likewise, God's statements, "The soul that sinneth, it shall die" and "Believe on the Lord Jesus Christ, or thou shalt be condemned," are warnings for man's protection.

Naturally, with such a view one makes God dependent upon His own laws, and there is no longer any possibility for an essential spiritual relationship between the Creator and the creature. Then nothing remains but the iron law of necessity, the chance of the Mohammedans, the *fatum* [fate] of the heathen. It is the end of all such concepts as guilt, punishment, justice, justification, judgment, and condemnation. Also it is, in a very special sense, the end of this comfort:

---

42. Ibid., vol. 1, 186–201.

> Jesus! the atonement of Thy death
> Is all my hope while I have breath.
> If I lose everything on earth,
> My spirit still shall know no dearth;
> Thy love abides e'en in my sorrow
> To comfort me through each tomorrow.
> Though eye grows dim and heart should fail,
> And waves of death my flesh assail,
> Yet Thy atoning blood shall be
> My hope—the shield that covers me.[43]

Nor do we entertain such an idea. Kuyper has no right whatever to make God say something different from what He actually said, and then arbitrarily add something to it. Kuyper has God say, "On that very day thou shalt plunge thyself into spiritual, physical, and eternal death,"[44] while, in fact, God is silently thinking to Himself, "...unless I, your God, restrain in my mercy the process of the result of your sin."[45] Naturally, once having thus arbitrarily changed and amplified God's Word, he can go on to add, "And things did not happen in that way." No, of course not! But that was not, in any sense, God's Word. God declared, "The day thou eatest thereof thou shalt surely die." That did happen. Adam and Eve, and with them all their descendants, died and are dead, suffering God's anger against sin temporally and eternally, even as we have shown above from Scripture, the confessions, and the Baptism Form. Only the regenerating operation of the Holy Spirit can bring about any change in our death, and that is by God's grace in Christ.

Some have tried to show that this is not what Kuyper means, but that he wants his presentation to be considered only as an example. Let me once more answer that. There is no possibility

---

43. The versification was made by Thelma Westra of Jenison, Michigan, at the request of the translator. The original Dutch source is not known.

44. Kuyper, *DGG*, vol. 1, 211.

45. Ibid., vol. 1, 209.

whatever that we can attach such meaning to it. Kuyper uses this as the basis for his theory of common grace, and without that view of God's words addressed to mankind in regard to the tree of the knowledge of good and evil, every basis for the theory of common grace falls away. We can choose between two views only: if Kuyper's idea of warning and prediction falls away, then God's Word must be a divine threat, and then, when man sinned, the threat was carried out and man is now dead.

The issue, to our minds, is that Kuyper does not know what to do with the sinner in paradise. He does not dare to let him die, for he is not able, by his common grace, to call him to life again, and still less to have him once more live a good life in the sight of God. If he dies, there is no room left for the theory of common grace, for then the sinner could hardly be alive again and accomplish good deeds through grace in Christ Jesus. Therefore, the sinner has to stay alive. But it is impossible to have the sinner appear unscathed after the fall. That would be full-blown Pelagianism. Then there would be no need whatever for grace.

What is the solution? Well, the solution is that the sinner must die, but not at once. He must die, it is true, in such a manner that he is completely dead and can do no spiritual good in the sight of God. But in the period between the eating of the poison, partly made innocuous by the emetic of common grace, and his final dying, man can still bring cosmic life to a glorious development and can display God's masterpiece in creation in a manner pleasing to God. That becomes his major accomplishment. Man, when he sinned, actually died at once; that is, he died a spiritual death. But since his body and soul were not immediately separated, he could still continue in his earthly existence. What can be gained by this view for the theory of common grace is difficult to see, but we are compelled to regard Kuyper's presentation somewhat in that way. The fact that Adam did not *immediately* die a so-called physical death is, then, the result of common grace.

Considering the matter in this way, we can understand somewhat why Kuyper constantly repeats the contention that if there were no interference of common grace when Adam and Eve sinned, they would have immediately dropped dead before the face of God in paradise. On that very day their corpses would have lain at the foot of the tree of life. In brief, mankind did die, but he did not fully die at once. Through the checking and restraining operation of God's common grace, the principle of death did not immediately develop into complete death. Common grace sustains the sinner for a time between dying and completely dying. The corruption of which God had warned began to work in the one who imbibed poison, which would have caused complete death. But death is restrained, checked, and even for a time forced back, only later to resume and finish its devastating work. In the meantime, all the good that is left in mankind after the fall manifests itself.

One should have, says Kuyper,

> a clear insight into the relationship of all things. The life-center for this whole earth lay in the soul of man. If life in Adam's soul breaks down, the death of his soul would include the death of the *body*, and presently the death of the entire *race*; then the curse would be upon *this entire world*. This is all related like links of the same chain. If, then, this earth was not to be destroyed, and if Adam's body was to continue to live for nine centuries, then in his soul the full operation of death would have to be curtailed. If it were not curtailed, that would be the end of man, of his body, of our race, of the whole world. The fact that it was not the end, that the world continues to exist, that our race comes into existence upon the earth, and that Adam continues to live for nine centuries, is only possible because the last spark of life was not quenched in his soul, but was fanned alive. For at the very moment when the image of God in him was at the point of perishing, divine grace interfered to save the last remnants.
>
> Everyone should clearly understand this. This is true not only in the elect. Common grace does not deal exclusively with them. That which we are explaining here pertains to the entire human race...
>
> Common grace is to be regarded as a separate entity. We must understand the wonder which God performed in the heart of mankind

immediately after the fall when He poured out drops of an antidote to counteract the poison of sin. That wonder of grace was already performed when Adam fled from God. It came before seeking, saving grace had gone forth to call Adam out of his hiding place. If nothing had been done to Adam's heart, death would have immediately worked complete destruction. The fact that death did not at once lead to its termination in eternal death can only be ascribed to the fact that God took hold of Adam's heart and wrought within it the wonder of common grace.

That wonder was *not* regeneration. Regeneration belongs to special grace. Regeneration does not restrain sin, but conquers and destroys it. Regeneration changes the evil into the good, unrighteousness into righteousness, death into life ... But common grace is not like that at all. It smothers, but does not extinguish. It checks the nature, but does not change it. It restrains and reins in, but in such a way that when the reins are loosened, evil spontaneously begins to gallop. It trims off the wild branches, but does not cure the root. It surrenders the inner driving power of the *ego* in man to its own evil, but prevents the full development of evil. It is a binding, delaying, limiting power that restrains and brings to a halt ...

Thus, this common grace[46] is an omnipresent power of divine mercy, which reveals itself wherever human hearts beat, and it spreads its blessing over those hearts ... It is no less than common grace that sustains a human nature in the sinner in order that man can still be an object of compassion. Even though it may happen that sometimes we no longer can discover even the weakest glimmering of this common grace, yet we continue to confess that under the ashes its small spark still continues to glow. Certainly people sometimes can fall unbelievably far, but their fall would be still deeper if they had become *completely* devilish and the last operation of common grace had disappeared out of their lives. Even the fact that they are still alive and that they continue their existence here on earth proves that a power still operates that sustains them. Were they entirely abandoned, that would be the end of their earthly existence; they would sink away into eternal death ...

---

46. Throughout this entire section, Kuyper uses the word *genade*, not *gratie*, yet there is no discernible reason for this.

When speaking of "little sparks" and "small remnants," the church of Christ tries to say that common grace has its basis in the sinner himself...For if one investigates the *nature* of common grace, then the confessions speak of "glimmerings" and of "remnants" that are still present, not as something external, but as something found in the deepest being of man. Life proceeds from the individual *ego* that is in us, and thus enters into our inclinations and thoughts. After the fall, in keeping with the character of sin, evil creeps into us, falsifies our lives, and attempts to force its way into our inclinations and thoughts to arouse us to sinful deeds. If the restraint of sin would take place at precisely that point where, apart from this restraint, the sinful deed would be committed, common grace would be no more than an external restraining power, but that is not the case. It checks internally the progress and penetration of the poison of sin, so that it does not deprive our whole life, nor all our inclinations and all our thoughts of that which God's image had stamped on us. This does not excuse us, for if it depended upon us, we would allow the poison to continue to work in us. It does not remove the devastation brought on our nature, for if common grace would withdraw for a moment, that nature would immediately reveal all its wickedness. But our nature is a point of contact which common grace chose for its operation in our hearts...

God showed this grace to Adam and Eve immediately after the fall. Otherwise immediately after the fall they would have mocked and cursed God. Now they trembled before his holy majesty and fled. This common grace was shown to them, not personally, as was the case with special grace, but as *bearers of our human nature*. This restraining and taming power becomes glorious in a human depraved nature. And when fallen Adam begat sons "according to his image and likeness," he produced corrupt children like himself, but in whom the corrupt human nature displayed the same evidence of common grace...

The definite starting point for *common grace*[47] is now evident. *In a limited sense* it can be found in the fact that when man fell, he did not immediately fall entirely away, but the full operation of death was postponed. In a broader sense, common grace entered so that immediately after sin had crept imperceptibly into the human heart, the direct and

---

47. Kuyper returns to the use of *gratie* instead of *genade*.

complete progress of that sin in the human race was arrested. Or to express it more briefly, and in their relationship to each other, both sin and death as sin's consequences ruled over mankind, his race, and his related world, but with a rule *that was kept in bounds by God,* and that is in principle in *the human heart* itself...

Yet even though the starting point for "common grace" is in mankind as such, it does not limit itself to the human heart in its restraining operation. The individual is not merely a spiritual being, but is also *physical.* And there is a *world* that is related to man's physical being. Soul, body, and world belong together. The soul, still in its original purity, has a body in original perfection that is related to a world, a paradise. Finally, in perfection, the saved soul will possess a glorified body along with a world which is the kingdom of glory. The soul of the wretched, which has become devilish, will exist in an entirely unnatural body, with hell as its world.

A *soul* sunken away in sin, but in which the operation of death has been temporarily restrained, will still need a *body* that is subject to sickness and death, but in which the operation of death is temporarily restrained. And in that soul and with that body, a man will be compelled to live in a *world* that lies under the curse, but without that curse being fully carried out. It is obvious that in that way, and only in that way, do we attain to a proper conception of the relationship and condition of *soul, body,* and *world.*[48]

There we have Kuyper's presentation of the relationship of all things. Man, in whose soul lies the center of life for this entire earth, sinned and ate of the poison of the forbidden tree of which God had warned him not to eat. By that act of eating, destruction came within him, as well as into his world. But God came dripping the antidote of common grace against the poison of sin, so that the destruction of death did not immediately cause him to fall completely into eternal death. He remained hanging by the cord of God's amazing common grace between the principle of destruction and complete eternal death. And through Adam also,

---

48. Kuyper, *DGG,* vol. 1, 249–255.

the entire human race that springs forth from him, and the earthly creation directly connected to him, hangs on that same miraculous rope of common grace. That makes it possible for all things to continue to exist. Common grace is not personal, but is granted to individuals as bearers of the human nature.

Common Grace and the Good Works of the Ungodly

We will not now compare this presentation to the Reformed use of such concepts as sin, guilt, punishment, and the curse; nor to the teaching of Scripture and the confessions; nor even to the lesson of history and experience. Nor do we ask whether the entire creation could not continue to exist far better by God's grace in Christ wrought in the heart of elect humanity, since then indeed we would have a definite starting point. But we wish only to point out that this temporary hanging of the whole earthly creation on the cord of God's common grace, taken by itself, serves no essential advantage whatever. Indeed, if God would, after a short time, release man, who is temporarily sustained by common grace, then according to this view, God would still plunge him, with all that pertains to him, into eternal perdition. There must be something else. The sinner must also be qualified to do works that are good in the sight of God.

That is the next step that Kuyper tries to take with his theory of common grace. Consequently, we ask the question, How does Kuyper achieve, through common grace, a restored capability in the center of the heart of the sinner, who is incapable of any good and inclined to all evil, that which enables him to will and to do what is good in the sight of God? Only when we see that, will we understand Kuyper's idea of the relationship of all creatures to each other and his idea of the proper development of the whole of creation.

This is exactly what Kuyper has in mind. The good development of things happens because of common grace. He says:

> Common grace is given to continue the development of our human race, even in spite of Satan, precisely at that point where sin would have restrained and destroyed that development. In spite of the changes introduced by sin, the great plan of God continues. Man's humanity continues, that humanity has its history, and in that history it goes through a process. This process must unfold that which the creation ordinance hid away in the bud, and common grace is the holy instrument whereby God realizes this process, even in spite of sin.[49]

This is the idea. God's original creation-plan is still carried out through common grace in spite of sin.

The presentation of Scripture is that God from eternity drafted a plan for the creation in which sin also has its place; and that plan is realized not in spite of, but in connection with sin. God's counsel for His world will stand; He will do all His good pleasure. The Reformed presentation is therefore also that the original creation-plan is realized in the plan of redemption. That, and that only, brings us to the doctrine of an eternal predestination with its subpoints of election and reprobation.

But Kuyper wants a realization of the original creation-plan through common grace, in spite of a power of sin and destruction entering in from without. God and sinful mankind set themselves in covenant agreement over against a hostile third power to fight against it. The idea of the covenant which we apply to the relationship between God and His elect in Christ Jesus is transferred by Kuyper to God and sinful mankind. The salvation of the elect is disconnected from the actual development of things and is regarded as purely individualistic and particularistic.

But let us first consider how Kuyper conceives of the possibility

---

49. Ibid., vol. 2, 24.

of a positive, good development of all creation. Naturally he is compelled to relate his common grace to sinful mankind, because they must carry out that development. In their souls, according to Kuyper, lies the center of life for the whole earth. Outside of mankind there is therefore no possibility of development in the whole creation. Each individual is a spiritual-ethical being. Thus his doing good must be of a spiritual-ethical character. If that cannot be realized, then the positively good development of things by common grace, outside of the grace in Christ, must be considered impossible. Then the theory of common grace, the theory of such a development, must fall away.

Kuyper evidently also realizes this. Therefore, he does not let sinful mankind hang endlessly over the gulf of eternal destruction on that cord of common grace, but makes it possible for him to do what is good, to do spiritual-ethical good, even though it be in a limited measure. He says:

> And finally, in the fourth place, we must conclude from Romans 2:13, 14 that this common grace leaves, maintains, and works in the fallen sinner not only an awareness of that which is honorable and dishonorable, right and wrong, good and evil, but this common grace also gives the fallen sinner the ability to do that which is good. Paul states: "The Gentiles, which have not the law (of Sinai), *do by nature the things* contained in the law." Thus they not only *know*, but they also *do* these things. And exactly because they do the works of the law, Paul concludes that they have knowledge of it. That *doing* is therefore the starting point for Paul's statement. If it is established that even a child of God confesses that of himself he is "incapable to think, much less to do anything that is good," then it must necessarily follow from this that the Gentiles cannot do that which is good in their own strength, but only because common grace spurs them on and enables them to do it.[50]

What strange reasoning! Why did Kuyper not refer to Calvin? Usually he is quick to do this. Is it possibly that Calvin holds the

---

50. Ibid., vol. 2, 17.

very opposite view? Evidently so! Calvin cannot be of use here. But we will not dispose of this with a mere appeal to Calvin. The situation is simply this: that Paul does not say what Kuyper puts in his mouth. Paul's purpose is to establish the fact that Jew and Gentile stand accused before God. Whether the individual has the law of Sinai or not, he can do no good, nor can he excuse himself. For even the Gentiles have a law written in their hearts, though they do not possess the written law of the Jews. But do they keep that law of God according to its demand, according to its content? Not at all. No, they do the *things* that are of the law, the work of the law, while they continue to be "a law unto themselves." These formal activities, which are performed in keeping with the idea of a divine law, betray their knowledge of the order and character of all life's situations and of the relationships required by God in which men consciously and willingly live together.

Yet this does not justify them before God; it only deprives them of any excuse. That which justifies before God is the perfect keeping of the actual law of God, according to its content, for God's sake, and in every situation and relationship of life. In that sense man, by nature, does not keep the law, nor does the Gentile; but he transgresses all its commands in thought and word and deed. Anyone who claims that the Gentile, even by means of common grace, does keep the law in a material sense in any respect, is not Reformed. The confession that unless we are regenerated by the Spirit of God, we are incapable of doing any good and inclined to all evil, is Reformed. You would be inclined to say that if Kuyper is right, the Catechism is wrong. And yet the Catechism is exactly what all truly Reformed persons confess.

Kuyper himself is unable to subscribe to that confession and at the same time maintain the idea of a spiritual-moral good in the unregenerate without further explanation. This explanation Kuyper must attempt and does attempt by his theory of common grace in order to clarify the development of things in their underlying relationships.

One of these attempts is found in what follows:

If we should ask, What is the condition of one before regeneration—not the condition of men in general, but specifically of a mature and upright man—we understand that he is "dead in trespasses and sins," but that he nevertheless retains certain "remains" and "glimmerings" of good [You will recall that Kuyper himself, in the quotation we made earlier, explicitly denied that which he now says is true—the authors], and that he, supported and strengthened by common grace, is capable of doing, not saving good, but what is called "civil righteousness." This brings up a number of questions, the most important being how anyone who is dead can still do works, and how the checking of sin by common grace can result in works. This checking not only excludes or reduces the effect of sin, but also enables a man to do positive good, even if such good is only civil righteousness. If a young child, lying in the water, is threatened with drowning, and a completely unconverted man jumps into the water to save the child at great risk to himself, is that man when he does that "inclined to all evil and incapable of doing any good?" You would say, "Definitely not!" Yet it is the confession of all Reformed people that such a man does no good. But one immediately feels that such an idea as the Catechism sets forth, which so clearly contradicts the example of an unconverted man who risks his life, requires further explanation. The Catechism does this when it states that only that is *good* which proceeds from a true faith, is according to God's law, and is done to God's glory. But this, too, requires additional explanation.[51]

Kuyper gives the explanation in what follows.

> Sin is unrighteousness, that is, something that is not in conformity with God's law ... Since saving a child's life is not contrary to, but in conformity with God's ordinance, no other judgment can be made of that deed but that it is *good* ... Thus there may be various manifestations of an essentially *good* deed. When a spider spins its web, it never

---

51. This quotation from Kuyper's *DGG*, vol. 2, 299, 300 was mistakenly ascribed to Danhof and Hoeksema in the material on common grace that the synod adopted: *Acta der Synode van de Christelijke Gereformeerde Kerk 1924* (Acts of the Synod of the Christian Reformed Church 1924), 131.

makes a mistake. The web is always good, because it is spun exactly in harmony with God's ordinance. But there is no merit for that spider, for it did what it was supposed to do... A person can act in the same way, doing what he is supposed to do... This proves that a deed which as such is always *good*, certainly cannot be reckoned to that person's credit... If it would be reckoned to his credit, then he himself must have willed the good, not like an animal that is spurred on by a certain instinct, but as a person who *willed* to do it and *did* it in obedience.

Obedience is the characteristic of every morally good deed. Obedience is conformity to the will of God, living and wanting to live in conformity to His ordinance... Therefore, the question must be raised, not whether a deed *as such* is in conformity to God's law, but is it done, though in conformity with God's law, out of obedience. But even that is not enough. No one can be obedient reluctantly... One who obeys out of fear or under pressure does not intend to obey... Obedience must be rooted in the conviction that God's demand is good, and that He alone has the right to demand; that is *faith* . . . And finally, it is not enough to believe that God's ordinances are good for you. Even more is required.

The ultimate motive for our actions must not be

our personal welfare. Something must be added. It is true, after all, that God's ordinance is that we do not endanger our life. But if your confession of Christ threatens you with persecution, perhaps with the threat of death, it is obvious that the martyr puts himself in danger and is even willing to climb the scaffold, when death is required of him. That is required of us, *because that is best for the cause of the Lord*. From that aspect, what is *good* is only truly *good* in an objective and in a subjective sense, if it is: (1) in conformity to God's law; (2) done in obedience; (3) done out of an obedience rooted in the faith that God's ordinance is best; and (4) not best for our temporal welfare, but best because it is to the glory of God, and thus for our eternal welfare. In that sense the unregenerate is "incapable of any good" and always inclined to pollute that which appears to be good. Yes, he is incapable of doing that which is essentially good, for he is dead in sin. There are no latent powers in him whereby he can once more arouse himself to do good in that high and noble sense of the word. That is not only true at any given moment, but it is always true, so that (unless God interferes) the sinner ends up in everlasting death.

But this cannot possibly mean that the person *no longer lives*. It is very evident to everyone that he is still alive. Even in hell the wretched still live. Because of this it follows that many powers are still operative in the unconverted that are aimed, be it in a limited sense, in the direction of God's ordinances. Sin and death are not inactivities, but rather strong powers . . . If common grace had not entered paradise immediately after the fall, fallen man would have been in the same situation as the fallen angels. He would soon have become completely sinful and beyond deliverance.

Now, however, it is a different matter. The power within them that would have *completely* diverted them from God's ordinances was restrained by God. And His common grace is still active in at least partially steering in the right direction those powers and operations which, if left to themselves, would be diverted completely in the direction of sin. These works do not merit, for the motive of the person doing them is the very opposite, and the motive would have forced these activities in an entirely wrong direction. But God intervenes, and by His common grace He restrains, in part, man's apostasy and brings man's activities, at least to a degree, in conformity to God's will . . . Men's sinful inclinations would normally bring about absolute sin, but common grace checks them, so that they can still end up doing civil righteousness . . .

That which causes sinful mankind to end up doing civil righteousness is *not* the driving power of common grace, but the life that is active in them. Even as the rudder of a ship restrains it and keeps it on its course, so common grace restrains the actions of the sinner from working in the wrong direction and diverts the sinner in the direction of the ordinances of God. But it is the rudder that brings the ship to its destination, and in the same way it is common grace, and not the sinner, that brings about civil righteousness . . .

If we are not mistaken, the difficult question is now answered: how it is possible that if common grace merely restrains sin, it yet can lead to that which is positively good.[52]

---

52. Kuyper, *DGG*, vol. 2, 299–303.

Yet Kuyper is seriously mistaken. He has allowed God to murder mankind in the ethical sense. Such an operation of God's common grace simply does away in the most absolute sense with all man's essential spiritual-moral activity. Kuyper's individual is dead, like his ship. Just as a ship, man is incapable of any self-motivated, independent action. This is confusion of concepts. The concepts *life* and *action* are confused, and likewise *grace* and *ruling*. Nor does Kuyper make the proper distinction between man, the devil, and non-rational-moral creatures. He ends up in determinism of the purest sort. We are considering man from the viewpoint of his morally free deeds. And the morally free deeds of the sinner are, also according to Kuyper, sinful, only sinful. This is also the confession of the Catechism, namely, that man is incapable of any good and inclined to all evil, because "man, by the instigation of the devil, and his own wilful disobedience, deprived himself and all his posterity of those divine gifts" [Heidelberg Catechism, Lord's Day 4, Answer 9]. He can neither will the good nor do it. So now Kuyper must not make an effort to prove that God does something to the sinner. We know that very well, and we readily believe that. But he must show that the sinner, apart from Christ, by common grace, practices that which is good in the sight of God. He has not yet succeeded in doing that, but we should have a bit more patience.

> As far as the unregenerate is concerned, we came to the conclusion: (1) that the same powers are still operative in him which have been given to man and belong to his nature; (2) that the corruption of his nature consists exactly in this, that he, as sinner, always uses these powers to work *in exactly the wrong direction;* (3) hence the effect of those powers would never be other than *completely bad,* as long as no other outside power restrains these wrong inclinations; (4) that common grace introduces this restraint in a gradual way so that these inclinations diverge from their wrong direction. Thanks to this restraint, all sorts of life's activities sometimes result in tender and careful acts of civil righteousness. But (5) no matter how much objective good may still result, the subjective ego *can* never escape the fact that what

happens is contrary to the will of that ego, when the power which proceeds from the nature ends in good...[53]

Consequently, the good that God accomplishes through the
sinner is contrary to the sinner's will, and is therefore not a good
work.

However, Kuyper considers a possible objection to this. Even
the sinner's will does not seem to be so bad. Therefore, Kuyper offers us still another distinction. Distinction must be made, he says,
between ego and ego. He speaks of the *central point* in man:

By that central point we understood our *ego* as the center of our being, and, considered in connection with all the manifestation of our
life, it is a unity. But if we regard that central point as such, then it immediately becomes evident that we must again distinguish, on the one
hand, among our inclinations, our mind, and our will, and, on the
other hand, between our *ego* that operates in these three. "I" am inclined, "I" think, "I" will. The inclination, the mind, and the will find
the point of union in the *ego*. This shows that one must once again
make a distinction in the central point of our essence: (1) the seed of
it in our "I," and (2) the various motions or functions of that "I." If we
thoroughly understand this, then we will also see immediately how
only that "I," as the deepest kernel, remains what it is. But contrary to
that inclination, the activity of thinking and willing undergoes a
change of direction because of the influence of common grace.[54] You
can test this by taking three or four thin copper wires, which you tie
together as one wire, but lay them out in different directions. At the
bottom you turn the point where they are joined with your left hand
to the left, while at the same time you bend them half way with your
right hand to the right. You yourself will feel how the pressure exerted

---

53. Kuyper, *DGG*, vol. 2, 304.

54. The idea is this: Kuyper understands that the will must be involved in all
men's actions; therefore, he distinguishes between the will as such, influenced by
common grace, and the will as it resides in the ego or person. It is a strange distinction and impossible to understand.

by your right hand not only turns the extreme ends of the wires to the right, but also you exert a certain downward pressure on the lower part, and you can also definitely notice the pressure on your left hand. The same thing applies to common grace. If it grasps that line, no matter where, and bends it to the right in its further advancement, a tension is created, a pressure downward, that surely can never affect the kernel of the "I," but it will have influence upon the feeling, the inclination, the consciousness, and the will. This explains how the unconverted can experience the influence of common grace upon his inclinations, his consciousness, and his will.[55]

However, no matter what it accomplishes, the outcome repeatedly shows that it never changes the "I" itself, and that this change of the "I" actually can only be the result of re-creation and regeneration.

In that way Kuyper deems it possible,

on the one hand, to appreciate to the full all the good that is found in this world, and, on the other hand, still maintain strongly and accurately our Confession, that common grace *cannot* accomplish one thing. As far as the "I" as kernel of our being is concerned, the first impulse of the sinner always remains not to direct the activities of his life toward God, but to turn them away from Him. Common grace does not change that. That is exactly what the Catechism means when it says that the "I" is incapable of any good and always inclined to all evil. All that is improved or is outwardly manifested does not result from the "I," but comes from common grace.[56]

---

55. This peculiar illustration means to show how pressure on one strand of intertwined wires will affect all the strands, even though no pressure is applied directly to the other strands. So common grace. If common grace directs only one aspect of man's psychological life, it will also affect the entire man. The reader will quickly see how Kuyper finds these distinctions necessary to hold to his doctrine of common grace. Common grace must be able, according to Kuyper, to affect the whole man in such a way that he does good works. At the same time, this common grace cannot be allowed to regenerate the man.

56. Kuyper, *DGG*, vol. 2, 306, 307.

Here we have a very sharp distinction. We have the following to say about it:

1. That Kuyper himself formerly taught, as we have noted above, that the sinner, who is entirely sinful, is not capable, either intellectually or willingly, of doing anything that is good; in that sense, the light of his original righteousness is turned into darkness.

2. That the Catechism does indeed speak of being inclined by nature to all evil. But this should not be limited to the smallest motions of the kernel of the "I" while the various motions or functions themselves of that same "I" are under the influence of common grace, so that the unconverted is affected in his inclinations, consciousness, and will. This is not the language of the Catechism and finds no support in the Scriptures.

Yet what is the essential difference within the sinner between the first impulse of the "I" as kernel of our essence, and the various motions of that same "I"? Both are plainly motions. However, let us accept for a moment such a fine distinction as Kuyper makes. Is the nature of the sinner (for inclination, will, and mind certainly belong to the nature) indeed capable by common grace of doing good, but then without the person becoming involved, so that it does not become *his* work, but *God's*? Then we have the same thing as before, except for the fact that it is far more detailed and far more broadly expanded. Then almost the entire sinner becomes good through common grace. Only the narrowest actual activity of the "I" is excluded, but then it is God's work, and not that of a sinner.

Or, must we accept the notion that the *person* of the sinner can accomplish all this through common grace? In the first case, the determinism mentioned previously is emphasized even more, and in the second case, the inability of man to do any good and his inclination to all that is evil is reduced to an insignificant minimum. Kuyper seems to want to maintain both ideas. Yet that is impossible.

One link is missing. Kuyper breaks up the organic unity of the life of man. The deepest soul-activity of the innermost kernel of the sinner's "I" (whatever that may be) he causes to arise out of the principle of sin, while that same "I" in the activities of mind, inclination, and will moves in the direction of that which is good through common grace. Such cannot be understood, much less defended—not even by means of an example.

3. Kuyper does not understand his own metaphor, or if he does, he applies it incorrectly. Those copper wires are incapable not only of performing any moral action, but of performing any action whatever. No action at all comes from those wires. All the action is from Kuyper himself, and returns, quite naturally, to Kuyper. And this is the strangest of all and exactly what Kuyper denies and does not want: what defeats his theory of common grace. That which proceeds from Kuyper and returns to him passes exactly through the center, that is, through the innermost essence of the actual kernel of the "I" (forgive this personification) of the copper wires. We leave it to Kuyper to cause his own action through the copper wires to return to himself in some other way.

However, the matter is too serious to make light of it. Therefore, we wish simply to point out that Kuyper's presentation does not harmonize in the least with Scripture and the confessions.

The Catechism speaks specifically of an *inclination* to all evil. Take note: not only inclined to evil in case no common grace should interfere, but actually evil in fact.

The *Kort Begrip* (Compendium) maintains that by nature man is *inclined* to hate God and his neighbor, and to transgress God's commandments in *thought*, *word*, and *deed* (Q&A 7).[57]

---

57. The Compendium, an abridgement of the Heidelberg Catechism meant for teaching young children, was composed by Herman Faukelius and originally printed in 1611. It was adopted in that form by the Synod of Dordt. A copy of it, titled "A Compendium of the Christian Religion," may be found in *The Psalter*, 28, 29 (liturgical section).

According to the Confession of Faith, man through sin is "be-come wicked, perverse, and *corrupt in all his ways*" [Art. 14]. And this corruption of his whole nature is "an hereditary disease, wherewith infants themselves are infected even in their mother's womb, and which produceth in man *all sorts of sin*, being in him as a root thereof" [Art. 15].

Finally, the Canons of Dordt maintain about man that, "revolt-ing from God by the instigation of the devil and abusing the freedom of his own will, he forfeited these excellent gifts, and…entailed on himself blindness of mind, horrible darkness, vanity, and perverse-ness of judgment, became wicked, rebellious, and obdurate in *heart* and *will*, and impure in *his affections*" (III/IV, Art. 1).

Scripture calls us *haters* of God and testifies that there is none that *understandeth*, that seeketh after God; that the *imagination* of man's heart is evil against God; and that those who *are in the flesh* cannot please God. Therefore, Paul can justly say of himself and his fellow believers, "For we ourselves also were sometimes *foolish*, disobedient, deceived, *serving* divers lusts and pleasures, *living* in malice and envy, hateful, and *hating one another*" [Titus 3:3]. There is nothing to show that this might be limited to the deepest root-activity of the innermost kernel of the sinner's actual "I," and there is never any reference in Scripture or the confessions to a change brought about through common grace. All this is pre-sented as virtually an established fact.

But let us once more look at things from Kuyper's viewpoint. If we do this, must not his attempt to find a basis for the good development of all things be regarded as a failure? Does not the innermost kernel of the sinner's "I," also from his viewpoint, continue to act out of the principle of sin and in enmity against God? In spite of common grace, there is no positive and good life-principle for the development of all things in their mutual relationship except by the re-creating grace of God in Christ. Kuyper's common grace is inadequate for the work of re-creation, according to his own admittance. Thus it cannot happen, as our Confession states, that God wills that all creatures are "for the service of mankind, to the end that man may serve his God" (Art. 12). Man does not by nature serve God; and from Kuyper's own viewpoint, this does not even happen by common grace. It therefore does not happen at all. Thus, the totality of all things never answers to its calling and purpose, not even by common grace, assuming that there is such. The principle of destruction works in the creation, destroying it sooner or later. This is true even when looked at from Kuyper's viewpoint: that God checks, restrains, and arrests that destruction by His common grace, or allows it to develop. Even if the whole creation, with the destruction that is within it, should continue to hang on the thread of common grace for thousands of years, it is threatened with eternal destruction, for outside of re-creation in Christ, there is no cure for it. If that thread is let go, which will soon happen, it plunges into full and eternal death, without having left behind any real, good fruit. That is the situation. Man, whom all creatures must serve in order that man may serve his God, lacks the ability, in spite of common grace, to accomplish his purpose. Man hates God. Who can be satisfied with Kuyper's view?

With that, we could conclude this part. The psychological basis is lacking for a good and positive development, with the result that the superstructure is nothing more than a dream castle.

Post-fall Common Grace

However, it is evident to us that Kuyper's view becomes something far worse than that. Therefore, we wish to listen to Kuyper yet for awhile.

In all his reasoning concerning common grace, Kuyper proceeds from the never-proved assumption that Adam and Eve—in case common grace had not interfered immediately after the fall, or at least after a short process of negative development—would have fallen dead in front of God in the sense that on that very day their corpses would have lain at the foot of the tree of life, which would have brought an end to all earthly development. But Kuyper with all his power desires a good and positive cosmic development of all things. He does not grasp the organic idea. He does not reason from God's eternal decree of predestination with its sub-points of election and reprobation. The salvation of the elect through the grace of God in Christ Jesus is set aside as something unrelated, and regarded and explained in a purely individualistic way. Kuyper is busy with the earthly, cosmic development of things in the realization of the original plan of creation, but not in its relation to sin and grace in Christ Jesus. According to him, cosmic development happens in spite of this grace and apart from it. He makes no attempt whatsoever to treat the development of all things as it arises out of God's grace in Christ. On the contrary, the creation continues to exist and develop through common grace. It is true that this development is brought into connection with the saving grace in Christ, but that connection is not organic. Two lines move side by side. The two lines find their unity of origin and purpose in the person of the Mediator, but even in Him they are not essentially and in the organic sense one, but two. It appears as if after the fall, the work of common grace is carried on by the creation-Mediator, and the work of salvation, from beginning to end, by the salvation-Mediator. And the first is actually of greater importance.

Kuyper speaks continually of the organic whole, but always entirely in connection with common grace: the organic whole of all creatures, the elect in their earthly relationship included. This organic whole lives out of common grace. If common grace had not entered, the situation on earth would have become

> a hell, a huge insane asylum, a stupefaction and a brutalization, one physical and spiritual savagery with the most hideous sicknesses and inhuman cruelties, one general destruction of all humanity.[58]

---

58. Kuyper, *DGG*, vol. 1, 441.

In such a society the saints naturally

> could not be of service to God, would not be able to exercise godli-
> ness, and could not have manifested the church on earth. Their life
> would have been mowed down before they came to years of discretion,
> and all the work of particular grace would have remained a hidden
> work of the Spirit in the heart.[59]

In brief,

> Nowhere would historical development have been possible. Neither
> the people of God, nor the church of the Lord would have found room
> for the hollow of its foot.[60]

From such statements it becomes evident that Kuyper does not
understand the actual character of sin. The rich man in hell would
have been able to instruct him. Even the evil spirits would have
been able to enlighten him more perfectly. Although they were
deprived of common grace, there is apparently no evidence, according to Kuyper and Hepp, of stupefaction, brutalization, and
insanity among them.

But Kuyper is determined to concentrate on cosmic development, and cosmic development arises, according to him, out of
common grace. That development is of actual and abiding value,
and the revelation of particular grace is of secondary importance.
With an allusion to the weightier matter of Melchizedek, to which
the book of Hebrews refers, he says:

> It was first of all *De Heraut* [The Herald][61] which felt constrained on
> more than one occasion to call the attention of Reformed Christen-
> dom to what Paul calls "*a going on to perfection*" by declaring that "Par-
> ticular revelation, and therefore also particular grace, has only an

---

59. Ibid.
60. Ibid.
61. *De Heraut* was a weekly paper that Kuyper wrote for many years.

interjected significance, and that not particular revelation, but the creation ordinance, is of enduring and abiding significance."[62]

One must understand that Kuyper speaks in this way in connection with his attempt to explain Melchizedek as an evidence of common grace. Since it was shown earlier that this is in flagrant conflict with all that the Word of God reveals concerning Melchizedek, we will not discuss this matter as such any further. Yet we remain fully convinced that no Reformed person who understands the content of what was quoted above would want to subscribe to such an exegesis, or adopt it as being Reformed. Our present purpose is only to show that Kuyper not only allows the creation to continue to exist by common grace and serve its purpose through its development, but he also makes it of lasting significance, at least in its fruit, into eternity.

Therefore, he is also compelled to reach back behind the world of the children of men to explain the evil that at least for the present is in the world. The devils are really the culprits. Yet fortunately God's common grace is rooted in His government over the world of devils. Kuyper says:

> Therefore, it is evident how the starting point of "common grace" is to be found in the rule of God over the devil and his demons; and how this rule of God rests in omnipotence itself, which omnipotence makes it impossible for the creature to stir or move apart from God's will. The power by which He allows or does not allow demons to move or stir depends on the extent of His common grace. According to the measure that He allows them more freedom, His common grace decreases, and according to the extent that He checks and restrains them, His common grace increases. Yes, providence is so completely dependent upon this "common grace" that in the absence of "common grace" there would be no revelation whatever of the decree of God's providence. Paradise would have been the end of us.[63]

---

62. Kuyper, *DGG*, vol. 1, 329.
63. Ibid., vol. 2, 394.

We regard any commentary on all this to be entirely superfluous. The sin of mankind is the sin of mankind, not that of the devil. We refer merely to the language of the fathers in the Confession (Articles 12, 13, and 37) and in the Catechism (Q&A 1), in which the Catechism allows the child of God, who is pardoned in Christ Jesus, to speak. God also makes the devil, God's archenemy, subservient to the salvation of His child and to the cause of His kingdom. But that the devils work evil in the sinner, and sinners choose to become a party with God against the devils—no, truly that cannot be. Those who are Reformed know nothing about that. The sinner, as sinner, is nothing more than a friend of the devils and an enemy of God.

In the same way Kuyper puts the starting point of common grace in the spirit world:

> You are bound to err if you limit yourself in your interpretation of common grace to human, earthly life. You can understand the essence and operation of common grace only when you put the *starting point* of common grace in the starting point of our *moral corruption*, that is, not in mankind, but in Satan; not on earth, but in the spirit world.[64]

Thus God had to intervene in the demon world in order to restrain evil on earth.

But we have already seen that understanding all this, even from Kuyper's own viewpoint, means that evil is not essentially restrained in the heart of the sinner apart from regeneration. Kuyper never gets what he wants and what he must have.

According to Kuyper, there is no doubt about it

> that the first rustle of common grace is *outside* this world, in the *spirit* world. God, intending to restrain corruption, checks the source out of which the poison flows to us. He does not completely check it, but par-

---

64. Ibid, vol. 2, 414.

tially, that is, only insofar as Satan's spiritual influence upon our lives
is no longer completely corrupting.[65]

Here we meet once more the poison theory, now in its influence
on Satan. The power that restricts it proves to be common grace
for the sinner. Whether this would thereby make Satan a partaker
of common grace is not certain. One could readily reach that conclusion. Many have also accepted it. But Kuyper himself does not
seem to go along with it.[66]

However, we will not discuss this now. For us the presentation
we have here of the source from which the poison of evil flows to
us is of far greater significance. That idea is incorrect and not according to Scripture. Mankind itself transgressed the most high
majesty of God by a free, moral deed, with the result that men
are punished by God with eternal destruction. No checking of de-
monic operations will be of any avail for that. The guilt of mankind must be removed. Men must be reconciled to their God. Life
must be restored to them. The original relationship of friendship
must be restored. Only then will men be capable of doing good and
enjoying salvation in fellowship with God. But if God remains
their enemy, they are destroyed, not with earthly fire and not that
they cease to exist, but by God's wrath against their spiritual opposition to God. Thereby the fellowship with their Creator becomes wretchedness.

However, Kuyper continues to cling to his unspiritual, physical
presentation of things. He takes death to be virtually the same as
non-existence; and continued existence here on earth, according
to him, is the fruit of common grace. The quick-wittedness and
the alertness of mankind in contrast to the beasts of prey is common *grace*;[67] it is a gracious divine arrangement. The same thing

---

65. Ibid., vol. 2, 402.
66. Ibid., vol. 1, 428.
67. Ibid., vol. 1, 35.

applies in a very special way to the development of human life.[68] Its increase is the result of a richer distribution of common grace, without which the world would have speedily plunged into the abyss of destruction.

Mankind continues to advance, not always in the same degree. Common grace operates differently now, in a stronger way than before Noah, and always in a variety of ways in different dispensations, nations, and persons. But it operates. And it preserves the reality of the earthly creation. Specifically, it saves the spiritual treasures of humanity.

Actually, common grace preserves the entire creation for glory.

> If you relate this to *common grace*, you realize at once how "common grace," which is not only related to your soul-life but also to your physical existence as well as to the preservation of this world, maintains this world in order that it can be renewed "in that great and glorious day." Had common grace not entered in, sin, the curse, and death would immediately after the fall have carried through to the very end. This entire world would have become corrupt, and finally nothing would remain but one massive wilderness... Thus the world continues to exist, and even the face of the earth is gradually enriched... How many deserts have been transformed into beautiful landscapes. How many waters are enclosed within their bounds. How many swamps have been dried up and made into fertile fields. How human habitation has everywhere changed formerly wild land into orderly and pleasant dwelling places. Also what treasures have been brought to light out of the depths and holes of the earth. Numerous sleeping powers have been awakened. What amazing wonders the human hand has accomplished everywhere by bringing the form and value of creation to a higher level.[69]

Thus, Kuyper rejoices over the material advances of our day. It is all the fruit of common grace.

---

68. Ibid., vol. 2, 600.
69. Ibid., vol. 1, 490, 491.

Yet he does not want to limit himself to this earthly development. Common grace creates also an environment for special
grace:

> If it is established that this world with its external phenomena would
> certainly not exist . . . without the introduction of common grace, then
> this also proves that particular grace cannot dispense with common
> grace, even for a moment. And it clearly shows how the great work of
> God's grace in Christ presupposes, along with everything else, the fruit
> of common grace.[70]

Moreover, common grace brings the church and the world into
mutual fellowship.

> The very purpose of *common grace* is to maintain the relation between
> God's people and the *world*. It directs itself toward the life of *that world*.
> It upholds the glory of God's work of creation in that world. And it
> cooperates with particular grace to make possible the penetration of
> the Kingdom into that world.[71]

In glory, particular grace and common favor will flow into one.

> Christ will then return, enter into the judgment, and then also the
> hour will come when the period of common grace . . . will be com-
> pletely brought to a close . . . Common grace and particular grace will
> then flow into one and be absorbed in the revelation of the glory of
> the liberty of the children of God.[72]

In sharp contrast to this merger of both, common grace gives
sin a refined form:

> Regardless of how indispensable common grace may be for the exter-
> nal revelation of particular grace, it must be noted, too, how common

70. Ibid., vol. 2, 680.
71. Ibid., vol. 1, 485, 486.
72. Ibid., vol. 1, 428.

grace is the cause by which unrighteousness ultimately reveals itself in such a horrible manner in "the man of sin" or in the "son of perdition." Even though you accept the fact that apart from common grace a monstrous revelation of unrighteousness would not become manifest, yet this terrible mystery would never have revealed itself in the form in which it does, apart from common grace. The form of that revelation as "a great falling away" and as the appearance of the "man of sin" will be occasioned by the operation of common grace. The outcome of unrighteousness would always be terrible, *with* or *without* common grace, but common grace does give it *its refined form*.[73]

One should not ascribe this reasoning to Kuyper. He undoubtedly does not mean what he says. Certainly, we agree wholeheartedly with him when he says:

> It is the artistic thinkers, the sharpest minds, who ponder and reflect on the sin against the first table of the law, and who peddle the product of their wicked efforts in beautiful volumes, and who are accordingly honored, adored, believed, and even praised after they are dead.[74]

How true. But that is not the fruit of God's common grace. It would be wicked even to harbor the thought. Nor does Scripture call the Antichrist "the son of common grace," but "the man of sin" and "son of perdition." When a sinner has many means at his disposal, both in the subjective and objective sense, then he develops in his sin. In time this produces the man of sin. The man of sin stands at the pinnacle of a humanity that has steeped itself in wickedness.

We must also understand that man does not come into possession of all sorts of gifts and talents through common grace, but through his creation. Nevertheless, even with all those gifts of sci-

---

73. Ibid., vol. 1, 442, 443.
74. The source of this quotation from Kuyper was not identified by the authors.

ence, art, and so forth, apart from regeneration the sinner develops in his sin against God.

We have one very obvious example of this in Pontius Pilate, before whom Jesus stood to be tried. According to Kuyper we have
in Jesus' trial by Pontius Pilate a double fruit of common grace:

> The "common grace" in Pontius Pilate demands a further explana-
> tion. His significance lies in the fact that he is a worldly judge. To this
> is added the fact that He (Christ) was to appear before a worldly tri-
> bunal. At that time nowhere in the world could be found a jurispru-
> dence which sought to maintain real justice in a more serious manner
> than the administration of justice as it had been developed by the Ro-
> mans.
>
> Thus we make two remarks by way of explanation: (1) that every
> proper administration of justice on earth is a common grace of God;
> and (2) that the development of jurisprudence by the Romans showed
> this common grace in its richest and fullest form."[75]

But this goes too far. Let us demonstrate this in the concrete
case before us. Pontius Pilate is a worldly judge and is in possession of the highest development of the administration of justice.
The absolutely and perfectly righteous Son of God stands as the
accused before this tribunal. Pilate knows that Jesus is innocent
and even testifies openly of that fact before the whole world. Jesus' innocence is even announced to him in a mystical manner by
his wife. Now he will most certainly acquit the Just One, won't he?
Wrong! He does not do that. He condemns Christ to the accursed
death of the cross, not because he did not know justice, but because his heart was wrong. He, the judge, surrendered Jesus
because he wanted Caesar's favor.

Is that the fruit of common grace, or of sin? Answer just this
once, agreeing with us: Pilate's deed was not the result of common
grace, but of sin. Otherwise we ascribe to God that which is un-

---

75. Kuyper, *DGG*, vol. 2, 157.

worthy of Him. Pilate was a very wicked man of sin who used the gifts and power entrusted to him by God in the service of sin for his own sake and to the condemnation of the Christ.

Those who so eagerly seek justice from a worldly judge, who, in their opinion, can judge better than a spiritual, ecclesiastical judge, as for example, a Reformed synod, can learn from this what their lot would be if they stood on trial in a just cause involving God's kingdom before a judge like Pilate.

Kuyper implies that gifts and abilities are to be regarded as fruits of common grace. They are not that. Gifts and abilities were given by God to man in creation. Along with the family and society, the state and its authority arose out of creation. Before the fall, man not only received lordship over all that was created, but he also received lordship over the woman. And when relationships multiplied, the authority of one person over another took on different forms. Thus, at the time of Noah, when God mentioned the shedding of man's blood, God assumed the authority of the government. Strictly speaking, there is no mention of the institution of government, not even of a death penalty, but government is assumed. Thus it is to be understood that not the sword, but the scepter, is the symbol of the authority of the government. None of that is grace, but *means*. And the means God gives can be used very well in the service of sin. This is what, in fact, happens when the heart is inclined in the direction of sin. That is taught us by Pilate's condemnation of the Christ (Confession of Faith, Art. 12).

Actually, Kuyper teaches that. Let us once again take a brief glance at this. In the end, even Kuyper does not close his eye to the reality of things. He is not so completely blinded by his notion of common grace that he can no longer see that there was still a fearful amount of evil found in the world, and that evil increases. And he knows that the evil increases in the measure that mankind develops and more means are put at his disposal. Therefore, he himself raises the question whether common grace must be regarded as a failure. One would say that it appears as if development must always serve to improve mankind (and there are those who were for

a while under that delusion). But that is not the case. How does
Kuyper solve this difficulty? In the following manner, by saying:

> In the middle of this century [the nineteenth] the leading spirits, es-
> pecially a man like Opzoomer, in good faith made our children believe
> that a better development of the schools would decrease crime. For
> each new school you could close one cell of the prison. On the sur-
> face, there was some truth to this. Broadening of knowledge, when
> properly applied, can restrain the savagery of people. This is the salu-
> tary power of all development in the sphere of common grace. But
> what these clear minds forget is that this same common grace can lend
> its weapons to the service of *wickedness* as well as of *virtue*, simply be-
> cause it operates in a sinful world, and therefore among unconverted
> persons. As a result of this, the outcome was disappointing. The Chris-
> tians profited in their area, but in the haunts of evil, in the circles of
> wantonness, and in the market of dishonesty, this great development,
> knowledge, and skillfulness could and did lead to no more than refined
> abomination, more skilled deception, more venomous performance,
> and more cunning sin. The courts of justice began to show an in-
> creasing helplessness over against more proficient, better armed, more
> cunningly planned evil. Superior power can be set against rough vio-
> lence, but what can be set against ingenuity and cunning, against pro-
> ficiency and trickery that simply laughs at the naiveté of the court of
> law? A nobleman who, dressed in the latest fashions and wearing kid
> gloves in broad daylight, in the highly civilized city of Paris, in a busy
> neighborhood, rang the doorbell of a rich lady, entered into her home,
> drugged her, then choked her, took her money, and quietly disap-
> peared. He was a good example of a type of murderer completely in-
> conceivable apart from the great development of common grace. Only
> when development and civilization have reached such heights, thanks
> to common grace, can this kind of man be possible.[76]

We are of the opinion that we can close the door on such remarks of Kuyper. Here Kuyper's argument is that God's common
grace works successfully on converted Christians who practice

---

76. Ibid., vol. 1, 443, 444.

virtue, but that the unconverted apply it in the direction of wickedness, and they are unable to do anything else. That is the "worse" view of common grace to which we referred before. Kuyper's common grace plan for the development of all things in their mutual relationship is a failure. We suspect that no Reformed person will willingly and consciously ascribe anything to God like that which we have heard from Kuyper.

We also do not believe that Kuyper actually wanted anything like that. As we see it, he made a mistake. What he calls common grace are good gifts that God entrusts to man: means, development, inclinations, and so forth, that man develops out of his own life-principle of sin, or out of grace in Christ, in his own place in the organic totality of all things. It is, to put it in other words, a work-capital. Without that capital he could not carry out his task and attain his purpose.

The situation is simply this. The creature receives gifts and talents and opportunities from the Creator to use in his own place and with his own life-principle, either by sin in the natural man or by grace in the regenerated person in Christ. This brings about the organic development of an organically existing and living humanity in its connection with the sum of all created things. That is what Kuyper actually had in mind, according to his previous writings, as we have already shown. But unhappily, possibly because of a desire for earthly power,[77] he turned to common grace. The sinner does not develop by common grace. That would be an inconsistency. He develops because of the talents entrusted to him.

Proceeding from that position, we can escape the dualism that often confronts Kuyper. According to Kuyper, common grace is the basis for particular grace. Both are united in Christ. But both are to be distinguished: common grace works *in the entire human*

---

77. This is a reference to Kuyper's desire to become prime minister of the Netherlands, something he could attain only in a coalition with the Roman Catholics.

race, even as Adam is the covenant head and Noah the second father of the race; while on the contrary, particular grace operates
only in the congregation of the elect, that is, in the restored and renewed humanity, which possesses Christ as its covenant head.[78]

> Does not the holy apostle write to the church of Colosse that the same
> Christ is at the same time both the root of the creation life and the
> root of re-creation? Paul states first that Christ is "the firstborn of every
> creature: For by him were all things created, that are in heaven, and
> that are in earth," so that "he is before all things, and by him all things
> consist." It could not be declared more clearly and plainly that Christ
> is the root of creation, and thus also of common grace, for common
> grace prevents all things from sinking away into nothing. And it is
> added, that *by Him all things consist*. But now, it immediately follows,
> in the second place, that this same Christ is also "the head of the
> body, . . . the firstborn from the dead" [Col. 1:15–18]. Because of this,
> He is also the root of the re-creation life of particular grace. Both are
> expressed in terms that remind us of each other. He is the root of com-
> mon grace, for he is the firstborn of all creatures, and at the same time
> the root of particular grace, for he is the firstborn from the dead. There
> can therefore be no doubt that since the beginning, common grace
> and particular grace stand in most intimate relationship to each other,
> and this connection is in Christ.[79]

But again, all this reasoning is wrong. The question concerns
who Christ is and what He does, and what God does through Him.
Christ is the Second Person of the Trinity and was present at creation as Mediator. As such He is called the Word, and all things
still exist through Him. This very same Person is appointed of God
from eternity to be the Mediator of the covenant, so that God,
having made peace through the blood of the cross, has reconciled
all things unto Himself, whether they be the things that are on
earth or the things in heaven. This passage [Col. 1:20] deals with

---

78. The authors here refer their readers to Kuyper, *DGG*, vol. 2, 292.
79. Ibid., vol. 2, 641.

God's reconciliation of all things through Christ. There is no reference whatever to common grace.

In connection with Colossians 1:20, Kuyper himself states in his *De Engelen Gods:*

> It was the Father's good pleasure, that through Christ, "having made peace through the blood of the cross, God would reconcile all things unto Himself." Then follows: "both the things which are on earth, and *the things which are in heaven,*" words that when we first read them leave the impression that also the angels had need of "reconciliation." We read the same thing in Ephesians 1:10 that God "hath purposed in himself, that in the dispensation of the fullness of times, He might gather together in one all things in Christ, both which are *in heaven,* and which are on the earth," an expression that sounds even stronger in the original, where *the gathering in one* is a *bringing together again under one head.* Thus the question cannot be avoided, as to how far the mediatorial *reconciliation* of the Son of God refers to the angel world. There can be no objection to the fact that He as the Son, by whom all things are created, is also creation-Mediator of the angels, but there is no reference to that in Ephesians 1:10 or in Colossians 1:19, 20. In both of these passages reference is undoubtedly made to the Mediator, who brought reconciliation through the blood of the cross, as is also expressed in Colossians 1:20.[80]

Biestenveld says:

> Along with Ephesians 1:20–23 and Philippians 2:6–11, these verses form a trio of excellent witnesses concerning the person of the exalted Mediator. If one wishes to make yet sharper distinctions in these verses, then in verses 15–18 Christ is considered according to His eternal Godhead and Sonship; and in the verses 18–20 He is Mediator of the church. We may never separate the two, because of the union between the two natures of the Mediator, and because of the relationship between His work in creation and in redemption. Making a distinction does not separate the two, but permits the distinction to

---

80. Abraham Kuyper, *De Engelen Gods* (The Angels of God), second edition (Kampen: J. H. Kok, 1923), 170, 171.

be made . . . Thus the plan of God is carried out, the curse is taken from
the earth, the debt of heaven is paid, the creation is snatched from Satan, and God's good pleasure in the world, which He once so gloriously formed, is again revealed.[81]

Kuyper confuses creation with common grace. The fact of the
matter is that God redeems His creation in Christ. That is also
what Paul declares in Romans 8. The curse—not common grace,
as Kuyper says—which God brought over the whole creation as
the result of the sin of mankind, will be lifted from it. This will
take place when the entire creation, which is now subjected to the
bondage of vanity and destruction, will be delivered to share in
the freedom of glory, that is, in the freedom connected with and
accompanied by the revelation of the glory of the children of God.

Nor does Kuyper succeed in maintaining his theory of common
grace with this appeal to the Scripture. The same applies to every
other appeal to Holy Scripture, the confessions, and Reformed
writers of importance.

Kuyper never actually appeals to other writers. One finds
among the fathers practically nothing, according to Kuyper himself, about the doctrine of common grace. Kuyper ascribes this to
the struggle which the fathers had with the Anabaptists and the
Arminians. They did oppose the Anabaptists with the doctrine of
common grace, according to Kuyper. However, just a short time
later the Remonstrants laid so much emphasis on the light of nature that they taught that the sinner had no need for God's grace
in Christ. The result was that Reformed people were silent about
common grace and joined their forces to maintain the character
of the new life wrought by God in mankind without the cooperation of the old "I."[82] That explains why we must not expect very
much from the fathers of Dordt, as has already become evident.

---

81. P. Biesterveld, *De Brief van Paulus aan de Colossensen* (Kampen: J. H. Bos,
1908), 129, 165. See also J. Van Andel, *Paulus' Brief aan de Colossensen aan de
Gemeente Verklaard* (Kampen: J. H. Kok, 1907), 23–36.

82. Kuyper, *DGG*, vol. 2, 190.

In his appeal for his theory, Kuyper cannot boast that he has the Reformed confessions on his side, for they do not mention it. Kuyper does not actually make such an appeal, nor does he appeal directly to Calvin. He refers only to the idea of common grace as he imagines that he has found it in Calvin from a few remarks which Calvin made.

> Calvin has expressed the profound idea of common grace the most clearly when he, in his *Institutes*, Book 2, Chapter 3.3, answered the question how we must explain the fact that honesty and decency often are to be found among the heathen and unbelievers. Some thought that they could deduce from this that our nature was not so bad. Calvin answers that "in all this general corruption there is a certain operation of common favor or common grace, which does not purify the evil nature, but prevents it from breaking out." In a somewhat sharper way Calvin says, "By His providence, God checks the depravity of our nature in such a way that it cannot break out into the deed. And this is done without purifying a man internally."[83]

Thus Calvin took note of the phenomenon that not every principle of evil present in the human heart continuously breaks out in evil deeds. He ascribed that to a restraint by God's providence, or grace. But the sinner is not improved by it. Therefore, it follows that no positive good development of things can grow out of it.

We have taken note of that already. We do not find anything so mysterious in all that. God's government very really controls sin. Not every sinful inclination or desire comes to manifestation in an evil deed. Each individual can sin only in his own place and according to his own circumstances and opportunities. This is precisely what follows from the organic idea. But the fact of the matter is this: the sinner never does that which is morally good according to God's will, but he uses God's gifts for his own sake, and to live out of the principle of sin. Calvin does not deny that, but rather admits it, also in connection with the so-called virtues of the heathen.

---

83. Ibid., vol. 1, 6.

Kuyper also gives a brief quotation from Calvin on his view of the covenant with Noah. That covenant, according to Calvin, is common to all nations. We will grant that view in the sense that God's covenant is established with mankind as it is redeemed historically and organically in Christ, represents God's cause here on earth, and is brought into the inheritance of the glory that belongs to the children of the kingdom. But we should understand that Calvin did not build upon this idea of the covenant, which is the framework of Kuyper's theory of common grace. Nor do we consider ourselves bound to every exegetical interpretation of Calvin and Kuyper.

With respect to the Reformed confessions, Kuyper states that the following must be considered:

1. Confession of Faith, Art. 14:

> And being thus become wicked, perverse, and corrupt in all his ways, he [fallen man] hath lost all his excellent gifts which he had received from God, *and retained only a few remains thereof.*

Kuyper forgets to add, as he had done previously, that these remnants are sufficient to deprive mankind of any excuse, and that the light that still remains in the sinner is changed into darkness, as the Confession adds.

2. Confession of Faith, Art. 15:

> Nor is it [original sin] by any means abolished or done away by baptism, since sin always issues forth from this woeful source, as water from a fountain.

3. Canons III/IV, 4:

> There remain, however, in man since the fall the glimmerings of *natural light*, whereby he retains some knowledge of God, of natural things, and of the differences between good and evil, and discovers some regard for virtue, good order in society, and for maintaining an orderly external deportment.

However, in this manner: "So far is this *light of nature* from being sufficient to bring him to a saving knowledge of God and to true conversion, that he is incapable of using it aright even in things natural and civil" [omitted by Kuyper from his quotation of Canons III/IV, 4].

Here Kuyper again leaves out, "Nay further, this light, such as it is, man in various ways renders wholly polluted, and holds it in unrighteousness, by doing which he becomes inexcusable before God."

4. Heidelberg Catechism, Q&A 114:

> But can those who are converted to God perfectly keep these commandments? No; but even the holiest men, while in this life, have only a small beginning of this obedience.

5. Canons V, 4–8, where it is stated that although the believers are preserved, they can still fall into sin.

According to Kuyper, from these quotations it becomes evident: (1) that in the sinner, that is, in fallen mankind, remnants of original glory remain. A certain light of nature is still present; and (2) that even in believers sin continues to work until they die, and that as a result they can still fall into grievous sins.

This brings Kuyper to the conclusion

> that the world exceeds our expectation and the church disappoints . . . Therefore, there is no sharp contrast in our confessions between faith and unbelief, sin and holiness, but our confessions offer an emphatic explanation of how it happens that *a certain good remains* in fallen mankind, and of how it happens that *evil* is still an aftereffect in the believer.[84]

Naturally we do not agree with this conclusion. *Light* and *good* must not be confused. According to the confessions, a certain light

---

84. Ibid., vol. 2, 9, 12. Kuyper's quotations from the creeds, numbered 1–5 above, are found on page 11 of vol. 2.

of nature, of creation, not of common grace, remains in the sinner. He now employs that light; it is a means. But he does not employ it properly, not even in things natural and civil. He even
suppresses it in unrighteousness and completely pollutes it in various ways. And while he does this, every excuse is taken from him
before the face of God.

Can one still speak of a *certain good* that remains in fallen man?
Men only grow worse. We should by all means follow the organic
line, according to which the sinner develops in the wrong direction, while the regenerated child of God, through grace in Christ
Jesus, walks in the right direction in principle. Possibly the two are
not too far apart as far as the mere outward manifestation of life is
concerned. But in the principle of the internal light of the heart,
they form a contrast, the contrast of light and darkness, heaven
and hell. And in the measure that anyone searches in a more fundamental way and learns to know them, one will find that the
world disappoints and the believing church surprises. Let us break
away from such great superficiality and live according to Scripture
and the confessions.

The passages of Scripture which Kuyper particularly wants to
be considered for the study of common grace are Genesis 3, John
1:1–11, Romans 1, and Acts 17:22–37.

Genesis 3 is, according to Kuyper, preeminently the chapter for
common grace. He says:

> It is incomprehensible that many could treat this dreadful history
> without focusing their attention on this *common grace*, which is almost
> exclusively on the foreground. They reckon only with that which God
> said to the serpent and with the *punishment* of Adam and Eve.
>
> *The restraint of sin and its consequences* as the real essence of com-
> mon grace is immediately evident from what we read of Adam and Eve
> after their fall.[85]

---

85. Ibid., vol. 1, 242.

Yet we cannot understand this, for in Genesis 3 we read nothing of what Kuyper states. Mention is made of sin, punishment, and the curse, and furthermore, of the gospel, as the Heidelberg Catechism [Q. 19] correctly states. And mention is made in Genesis of the future development of all things.

In John 1:1–11 we read of the light that shone in the darkness, but the darkness, the sinful world, comprehended it not. That can hardly be called good. The sinful world, wrapped as it is in darkness, did not comprehend the light. It did not even understand the light, much less use it properly. Mere knowledge in the intellectual sense is not sufficient; there must be a sincere practice of the will of God. Also the devils and the accursed, who, according to Dr. V. Hepp have no part in *gratis communis* [common grace], very really have light, knowledge, certainty, and even faith; yet they do not do the will of God. However, for them God's presence is wretchedness. But the unregenerate world does not have that measure of clear, conscious knowledge. It is darkened in its understanding, and that leads it continually farther from God, constantly deeper into perdition.[86]

That is what Romans 1 teaches. God reveals not common grace, but His wrath from heaven against all the unrighteousness and ungodliness of men when they suppress the truth in unrighteousness. The natural man develops in wickedness with the means entrusted to him, and is therefore constantly driven farther from God.

This is also evident from Paul's speech on the Areopagus. The Athenians did possess some knowledge of divine power and glory. But when the apostle spoke of the necessity of conversion because God would soon judge the world through the resurrected Christ, they considered, in their worldly wisdom, the idea of the resurrection such foolishness that they quickly let the ambassador of the cross stand alone, and they rejected the gospel which was preached to them for a witness.

---

86. Valentine Hepp, *Het Testimonium Spiritus Sancti* (The Testimony of the Holy Spirit) (Kampen: J. H. Kok, 1914), 203.

Such an appeal to God's Word is of no help for the theory of common grace. All the passages referred to teach the very opposite.

We are therefore of the opinion that we can bring the matter to its conclusion. In reality there is no communal life of all men, both elect and reprobate, rooted in a third life-principle, that of common grace, as the proponents of this theory contend. This is true even though one limits it to the so-called sphere of natural life, which to our mind is impossible, because organic life is one whole. Psychologically there is no solution. The sinner is an enemy of God, and apart from regeneration, he does not allow himself to be changed into a friend of God. He is also treated by God as an enemy. This truth Kuyper does not bring out clearly, not even in his series of articles on particular grace. For although there he follows the organic-antithetical line, it is especially in his *De Gemeene Gratie* that he has God and sinful mankind in covenant fellowship, working together against evil, which evidently threatens mankind externally. Especially so-called science, which is supposed to be a fruit of common grace, must serve as an example. The Free University, which tried to cultivate science on the basis of "Reformed principles," rests, according to Kuyper, almost completely on the foundation of common grace. Even holy theology, as a science, is one with the positive good in other sciences. God and unregenerated man, by means of common grace and science (whatever that may be), set themselves against the evil powers of sin, death, and destruction in order to bring to full revelation God's works of art found in creation.

Evidently Kuyper is interested in so-called cosmic life and the physical development of the material world. Therefore, sickness, suffering, and death as destructive forces must be eliminated. Sin is quite like imbibing poison, and death, the natural result, consists of the dissolving of that which is joined together in the creation. Carried through, this can only lead to a totally preposterous and pagan presentation. Seemingly Kuyper tries to limit common grace to the external aspects of life and to its development. This not only requires that life be divided into separate spheres, but also that every deed of the unregenerate be likewise divided. In the most intimate and most internal soul-action of the actual essence of his "I," the sinner always continues to oppose God as his enemy, and he is therefore also treated like an enemy by his Creator. Apart from that, through the influence of God's common grace upon his mind, inclination, and will, he carries out the will of His Maker.

This presentation we regard as inconceivable, scientifically indefensible, and in conflict with Scripture and the confessions. But even all this does not give Kuyper what he wants and what he needs to be able to maintain his theory of common grace. It does allow for determinism, but it does not allow for a free, morally good act of the will of man. And that is our concern. All the threads and fibers of the life of creation are, according to Kuyper, joined in the will of man, which was at first good and free, but now, because of sin, is not free in a material sense, but is perverse and moves in a negative direction. Naturally God can now deal with man as a man deals with his boat. By means of the stormy wind and with the rudder to keep it on course, man arrives at the haven of his destination. God does the same. But God does not attain His purpose and goal in this way. According to Article 12 of our Confession of Faith, the purpose and goal of the creation is that it may be "for the service of mankind, to the end that man may serve his God." That is attained only by regenerating grace in Christ, and not by Kuyper's common grace.

Conversely, even according to Kuyper himself, so-called common grace gives the sin of man a refined form, and in this way produces the Antichrist. Kuyper himself admits that the unconverted can use the treasures, gifts, and possibilities of common grace only in the development of what is evil. That settles it. If that is true, the maintenance and development of the totality of created things by so-called common grace has no room for particular grace and the salvation of the elect. Nor does it serve, through its cosmic, physical, and material development, the glory of God and the shaming of Satan. But everything must inexorably rush towards eternal destruction. Surely no one feels the need of common grace for that. In fact, that is exactly what happens through development out of the principle of sin, in contrast to development out of God's grace.

This is certain: the presentation of the defenders of common grace does not follow logically out of the Reformed doctrine of predestination, with its sub-divisions of election and reprobation.

Nor is it logical and organic, but on the contrary, mechanical and dualistic. Nor does it proceed from the moral-spiritual life-principle, but rather from the external, purely physical, and material development of all things. It apparently treats the appearance of things to be reality. It is not theological, but humanistic, and historically it is obviously closely connected to the Pelagian and Remonstrant view of "remnants" and "sparks" of "natural light" and "civil righteousness."

We wish now to take up the defense of the principle of election by grace, and thereby offer for criticism our view of the relationship and development of all created things.

3

Our Viewpoint

⌒∞⌒

Instead of offering a solution to the question which Dr. Kuyper presented to us, we shall try to develop briefly our own viewpoint.

The Organism of the Creation

It should be understood at the very outset that we must think of the development of created things in an organic way. All individual creatures together form one organic whole. God not only makes the entire human race out of one blood, but He binds all creatures together in one whole. This must be understood in such a way that the central point of the life of the creation lies in the heart of man. It is true, obviously, that the angels are also independent, spiritual-moral creatures who are able to make choices, but this does not give them control in the creation. The creation itself grows worse as man becomes more sinful, because it finds its touchstone in man. Man is not only a microcosm, a miniature world; he is also prophet, priest, and king. He causes every creature to know God's will. He dedicates the creation to the Creator. In his relationship to every creature, he exercises God's authority. And according to the choice of his own free will, he performs the basic purpose of God's will for him. In short, man is God's covenant friend-servant.

This is also the meaning of our Confession when in Article 12 it speaks of the creation of all things:

> We believe that the Father, by the Word, that is, by his Son, hath created of nothing the heaven, the earth, and all creatures as it seemed good unto him, giving unto every creature its being, shape, form, and several offices to serve its Creator; that He doth also still uphold and govern them by His eternal providence, and infinite power, for the service of mankind, to the end that man may serve his God.

According to this article, all creatures serve their Creator with their gifts, powers, and offices, yet always through man. That is still the purpose of God. God still upholds and rules them all by His eternal providence and infinite power for the same purpose. All creatures must serve man so that man may serve his God. All things are still bound to that requirement. God still upholds and rules according to the counsel of His providence in order that every creature is able to answer to its calling in its own God-ordained place in the organic unity of all things.

That is precisely our viewpoint. We are of the opinion that each creature is able to attain to the full realization of the original purpose of God in creation, which is its own eternal blessedness. It attains this purpose in its organic interdependence under the uninterrupted control of God's power, which entirely apart from any consideration of sin, upholds, works through, and rules all things. This is the organic idea.

The Effect of Sin

It must, however, be immediately added that in this view of things, sin did not introduce an *essential* change. The life that was in man's heart was turned around to its opposite in the spiritual-moral sense of the word. God's covenant friend became Satan's covenant friend, but this did not touch the essence of things. Sin did not remove the creation, nor did it destroy the original unity of the creation. God continued to work in all creatures by His infinite power and according to the counsel of His providence. Even the formal, covenantal life of the sinner still shows its beginning, essential nature, and original destiny.

Yet man's nature is corrupt, acts negatively, and works wrongly. The final result is that the material and spiritual-moral fruit of the life of the creation has become the opposite of what it ought to be, according to God's original creation ordinance.

Nevertheless, the unity of the life of the creation remains untouched. This can be more clearly seen if one of the basic errors upon which the theory of common grace builds its assertions is exposed. It is well understood that the essence of man as such is not affected by sin, and that man, in spite of sin, remains a man. But what is overlooked is the fact that the same thing was true of *all* that existed. And it is true of the essential and organic relation of things. The changes which sin brought about are never changes in the essence. They are always of a spiritual-ethical nature.

The same is the case when we consider the change brought about through the power of the grace of God in the final spiritual-ethical fruit produced in and by the organic life of the creation. If God destroys the enmity in a man's heart and once again works friendship with God, but does not perform this work of grace in all spiritual-moral creatures, then the antithesis is the result. The life of sin continues to develop in opposition to the life which rises out of the root of regeneration. But even this antithesis does not destroy the original organic unity of things. What happens in life is not the creation of a dualism. Two halves do not emerge from the original unified organism. But the spiritual-moral antithesis of light and darkness, of grace and sin, of life and death, of heaven and hell, comes into existence. All things continue to develop according to their own natures and in an underlying organic relationship to each other. But they develop out of the principles of sin and grace, and in the eternal, spiritual-ethical antithesis of friendship with God, on the one hand, and enmity towards the God of the covenant, on the other.

Just as sin does not affect the essence of things, so grace does not affect the essence of creatures. Nor does sin affect the original relationships and divine ordinances of creation. But it does affect the spiritual-ethical character of man's deeds. The organic unity of the life of the creation is never elevated, nor is it pulled apart into pieces. It is maintained in spite of everything. The spiritual-ethical character of the fruit of the development of the organic life of the creation is determined by sin and grace.

This truth has an important result. The result is not that eternity will present to us the perfect realization of the original purpose of the creation, but that eternity will reveal the one fulfillment of the counsel of God concerning all the works of His hands. It is precisely the antithetical fruit of the organic development of the life of all created things which shall reveal that God does all His good pleasure.

God's Purpose in Christ

We are determined to maintain this organic and unifying idea of the development of the life of all created things.

First of all, then, it seems to us that we can, by taking this viewpoint, understand the revealed mysteries of God's will, determined eternally in Himself according to His own good pleasure, "that in the dispensation of the fulness of times he might gather together in one all things in Christ, both which are in heaven, and which are on earth," both visible and invisible things (Eph.1:10; Col. 1:15–20). God has not only made the entire human race of one blood, but all creatures are united. Paul's words in Acts 17:28 are not only true of men, but apply to all creatures in their basic, mutual relationships and communion of life: In God we live and move and have our being.

When, therefore, Adam sinned in paradise, the fruit of sin was not limited to man, but along with sin in the heart of man, death and the curse came into the creation. On account of man, as cause, or at least in connection with his sin, God cursed the earth. The entire creation was subjected to vanity, not willingly, but by reason of Him who has subjected the same in hope. This subjection took place in the hope that the creature itself also would be freed from the bondage of corruption into the glorious liberty of the children of God. The creation sighs as one in travail, but it cannot develop normally according to its original creation-life. The original creation-life is lost. Everything is filled with and geared for strife. A terrible wrestling takes place between two spiritual powers. God and Satan enter the arena against each other. The struggle is over man and his world. It is in man and through man. Ultimately it is a struggle for man's love, a love which comes from his heart.

Everything takes part in that struggle. The earth bears the burden of the Lord's curse. The animals adjust themselves for a while to the service of corruption. The angels, as willing spirits, go out from the face of God in the service of those who are the heirs of salvation. The dragon and his angels also fight with Michael and his angels, and an ages-long battle over the covenant of God goes on between the holy seed and the people of the world.

Meanwhile, Jehovah, the Lord of hosts, makes all things subject to His purpose and puts them in the service of the salvation of His chosen people and the coming of the kingdom of the Son of His love. He rides on a cherub, makes the heavens drip, divides the sea, and turns the Jordan back again. Fire, hail, stormy wind, darkness, lightning, drought, heat, cold, sun, moon and stars, the heaven and the earth: all are His servants and do His will. He kills His enemies with the sword, with hunger, with pestilence, and with wild beasts. At the same time He creates Adam's offspring. He sends His Son into the world. He gathers His elect church through His Spirit and Word out of every tribe, language, people, and nation.

This all has a place in the work of organic development. Events in the world follow the line of the organic development of the seed of the woman. According to the requirements of this development, God reveals to us His salvation, creates the Holy Scriptures, realizes His covenant, permits His Word to become flesh, and through His Holy Spirit He enables His people to walk in the world, making confession of His name.

The world power also develops organically. It affects, with a certain human power, all tongues, peoples, and world kingdoms until finally Antichrist comes. At last the opposing powers of Gog and Magog lift up their cry against Zion: "Let her be profaned." That all this certainly happens is especially evident from the fact that already at the beginning of history God proclaimed the end. He did not only make known to Israel its future, but even Nebuchadnezzar saw before his very eyes in his image the entire progress and final destiny of the ungodly kingdom of men. The development of all this occupies the whole of this earthly history. God fills up the measure of time. He is very patient with the development of both the good and the evil. Good and bad grow together to the end of the world, according to the parable of the tares of the field. All the historical development of the kingdom of God here on earth is compared to growing seed. When judgment is given in the great day of the Lord, Christ shall send His sickle on the earth to cut and gather the wheat harvest and the grape harvest. And then, when all this has happened, God shall gather together in Christ all things both in heaven and on earth, both visible and invisible. Nothing shall be left out which is not subjected to Christ, except God Himself. Included are all the fruits of all the world's events. All created things develop in an underlying organic unity in the way of an appalling conflict in order that the covenant of the friendship of our God may be realized through the antithesis of love and of wrath.

The Dualism of Common Grace

It is a riddle to us how anyone who has such an understanding of Holy Scripture still dares to maintain an individualistic and par-

ticularistic doctrine of predestination *and* a realization of the original plan of creation through common grace. And yet that is precisely the difference between Bavinck and Kuyper and us. We
want an organic development of all things. They, however, limit
God's eternal predestination to a determination of the eternal destiny of rational and moral creatures, and they permit the organic
unity of the creation to develop according to God's purpose in a
good way through common grace. They end with a dualism; we
want to maintain a unity. We are agreed that our fathers saw predestination almost exclusively as particularistic. But we want the
eternal character of eternal foreordination to be understood correctly as a part of the will of God, which includes the whole organism of created things. They, on the other hand, at least in a
relative sense, continue to speak of predestination as the eternal
intention of God concerning the lot of rational, moral creatures
only. Then, naturally, if they inquire further about the life of other
creatures, they must ask different questions about the will of God.

It is true that they find the answers to their questions in God's
counsel. And they admit that the purpose of the life of all creatures is indeed the honor of God. But that life, though proceeding
from one source, goes in two directions. The mistake is that in this
way the idea of the honor of God is actually without any content,
because they place the life of the creation outside the foreordination of the life of rational and moral creatures. And so they make
a division between that which we insist must be as closely united
as possible. That is, in fact, the one difference between us. In order to make this point as clearly as possible, we will make use of a
series of quotations.

The following quotation is from Bavinck:[1]

> This is the case if one wants to solve successfully the problem of
> supra- vs. infralapsarianism and still do justice to the variety of state-
> ments in Scripture. For one thing, both sides have solved the problem

1. Bavinck, *Gereformeerde Dogmatiek,* vol. 2, 404–410.

only by making themselves guilty of one-sidedness. It is not right, as so many have said, to describe the supreme end of all things as the revelation of God's mercy in the elect and God's righteousness in the reprobate. It is certainly true that the glory of God and the manifestation of his perfections are the purpose of all things. But the double state of salvation and misery is not to be understood as if its proper relation is that of the one serving as the means to the other. It cannot be demonstrated at all that, if God's glory is indeed the purpose of all things, the consequence must be this double state of being. Indeed, God performs his works *ad extra* [outside his own being] in such a way that He cannot do anything else but seek the honor of his own name. But that God seeks the honor of his own name in this way and in no other way depends exclusively on his own free purpose.

Apart from that, however, it is also not true that God's righteousness is revealed only in the misery of the reprobate and his mercy only in the salvation of the elect. Also in heaven his righteousness and holiness shine, and also in hell there is still something of his mercy and compassion.

In the second place, it is incorrect to make the misery of the lost the goal of predestination. It is true that sin can not be reduced to a *nuda praescientia en permissio Dei* [a bare foreknowledge and permission of God]. The fall, sin, and everlasting punishment are included in the determination of God, and in a certain sense they are willed by God. But this is true only in a certain sense and not in the same way as grace and salvation. God finds pleasure in grace and salvation, but his desire and joy are not sin and punishment. When God makes sin serve his glory, He does this through his omnipotence, but it is contrary to his nature. And when He punishes the wicked, He does not rejoice in their suffering itself, but He celebrates the triumph of his virtues (Deut. 28:63; Ps. 2:4; Prov. 1:26; Lam. 3:33).

In the third place, there is another reason, equally important, why *praedestinatio ad mortem aeternam* [predestination to eternal death] may not be made coordinate with, and may not, in the same way, be made the purpose of *praedestinatio ad vitam aeternam* [predestination to eternal life]. The object of election is not merely individual people, as with reprobation, but in election the human race, with its new Head, Christ, is the object. Thus, through grace, not only are some individuals preserved, but also the human race itself with the entire cosmos is preserved. In this preservation of the human race and the entire cosmos, God does not reveal only a few of his attributes, so that an eternal destruction is necessary to reveal his righteousness; but all the perfections and attributes of God are unfolded in the completed kingdom of God: his righteousness and his grace, his holiness and his love, his sovereignty and his mercy. This *status gloriae* [state of glory] is the only direct purpose that God attains with his creation, though that purpose be subordinate to the glory of his name.

In the fourth place, both supra- and infralapsarianism err in that they make all that precedes God's final purpose the means in a mutually subordinate relation. It is true that these means are subordinate to God's final purpose, but not to each other. Creation is not a means for the fall, nor the fall a means for grace and perseverance. Nor do all of these serve as means for salvation and misery. It is sometimes thought that the decrees of God are as equally rich in content as the history of the world, for this latter is the unfolding of the former. Who is in a position to put the history of this world together in a logical scheme of a few ideas? Creation, sin, Christ, faith, unbelief, and so forth are certainly not in a relation in which one serves as means to another, so that the earlier event falls away, as it were, when what follows is completed. They are not mutually subordinate, but also coordinate—as Twisse[2] taught earlier. Creation truly did not have its place only so that the fall could happen, but it gave to the world a certain character that will also continue in the state of glory. The fall did not only happen so that there would be a *creatura miserabilis* [a miserable creature], but it has significance for all the consequences which come from it. Christ has not only become Mediator in order to accomplish what was necessary for atonement of sin, but God has also ordained Him to be Head of the church. The entire history of the world is not a means that falls away when God's purpose is achieved, but history continues to operate and produce fruit for eternity. Election and reprobation do not take place here on earth as two straight lines alongside each other, but in unbelievers is to be found a great deal that does not come from reprobation; and much is present in believers which does not have election to thank for its presence in them.

---

2. William Twisse, who died in 1646, was an early Scottish supralapsarian theologian.

On the one hand, we find among men both sin and sin's works of mercy and righteousness (Rom. 9:15, Eph. 1:4); on the other hand, both are also deeds of divine power and sovereignty (Rom. 9:11, 17, 21). In the same way Adam before the fall was already a type of Christ (1 Cor. 15:47), and yet the incarnation always finds its necessity in Scripture in the fall of the human race (Heb. 2:14). Sometimes Scripture speaks so strongly that reprobation is completely coordinate with election, and everlasting punishment is described as a purpose equally important to God as everlasting blessedness (Luke 2:34; John 3:19–21; 1 Pet. 2:7, 8; Rom. 9:17, 18, 22, and others). But sometimes *mors aeterna* [everlasting death] completely disappears in the description of the future: the final purpose of all things will be the triumph of the kingdom of God, the new heavens and the new earth, the new Jerusalem, where God shall be all in all (1 Cor. 15; Rev. 21, 22). All is subordinate to the church, just as the church is to Christ (1 Cor. 3:21–23). Reprobation is entirely subordinate to election.

Therefore, finally, neither the supra- nor the infralapsarian presentation of predestination is able to express the full and rich truth of Scripture and to satisfy our theological thinking. The truth in supralapsarianism is that all the decrees constitute a unity; that there is a final purpose to which everything is subordinate and which everything serves to attain; that sin did not come into the world apart from God's thought and in a way unexpected by Him, but that it is, in a certain sense, willed and determined by Him; that creation is from the beginning formed for the re-creation of all things, and that it was, before the fall, reckoned as Christ's through Adam.

But the truth in infralapsarianism is that the decrees, although one, are also distinct from each other when considering their object; that not only a theological but also a causal order in the decrees must be noticed; that creation and the fall do not have their only purpose in serving as means to a final purpose; that sin is above all and in the first place a disturbance of the creation and that it can never be willed by God for its own sake.

In general, the formula that the final purpose of all things is the revelation of God's righteousness in reprobation and the revelation of his mercy in election is too one-sided and sober. The *status gloriae* shall be indescribably rich and glorious. We expect a new heaven and a new earth, a new humanity, a re-created creation, a continuous development which shall never be disturbed by sin. And to that end, creation and the fall, Adam and Christ, nature and grace, faith and unbelief, election and reprobation, work together and each in its own way, not only after, but also alongside of and with each other.

Yes, the present world with its history is also, by itself, already a continuous revelation of God's virtues. It is not only the means for a higher and richer revelation which comes in the future, but it has worth and value in itself. It is not only a means to attain the higher and richer revelation which shall come; it has importance in its own right. It continues to operate even in the future dispensation, and it shall produce continuous benefits to the new humanity for the worship and glory of God.

Therefore, there is not only a causal and a teleological, but also an organic order in the decrees of God just as there is in the facts of world history. We can only, with our limitations, see things either from the one viewpoint or the other, so that, on the one hand, the advocates of a causal conception and, on the other hand, the advocates of a teleological world-and-life-view are at every point opposed to each other. But it is entirely different with God. He oversees everything. Everything is eternally present in his consciousness. His counsel is a unified conception. And in that counsel every distinct decree stands in the same relationships in which the facts of history, considered *aposteriori* [after the fact], appear only partially to us and shall be seen fully only later. This relationship is so rich and complicated that it cannot be described in one word such as infra- or supralapsarianism. It is both causal and teleological. That which has already taken place works on that which follows; but the future is already fixed in the past and in the present. There is a rich, many-sided *wechselwirkung* [interaction].

Predestination, in the usual sense of the word, is a foredetermination of the eternal state of rational creatures and of the means to that state. But it is not the one, all-embracing and all-inclusive decree of God. It is an important part of the counsel of God, but it is not an integral part of that counsel. The counsel of God is the chief idea, because it is the all-inclusive idea. It includes everything without exception: heaven and earth, spirit and matter, visible and invisible things, lifeless and living creatures. It is the one will of God for the whole cosmos, past, present, and future. But predestination deals with the eternal state of rational creatures and the means which attain that state. But one cannot fit under those means everything that is and happens in the world. Therefore, providence must be discussed separately from the decree of God, though not divorced from predestination.

Much more than formerly, common grace has properly been given its rightful place in the counsel of God, and it has been given its own proper worth. In one word, the counsel of God, and the history of the world which answers to it, is not to be described exclusively as one straight line with various other lines before and after which are related as cause and effect, means and purpose, as infra- and supralapsarianism want to describe it. But they are a whole, in which things stand *alongside* each other and work *with* each other towards what always was and is and shall be the deepest ground of all things that exist, the glory of God.

Just as in an organism all the members are dependent on each other and, in turn, influence each other, so the world is an artistic production of God in which all things are bound together in organic relationships. And the counsel of God is the eternal idea of that world both in its length and in its breadth.

We are not going to raise a lot of objections to this view. It is, for example, very strange that Bavinck sees operations of some aspects of God's mercy and compassion even in hell. Kuyper as well as Hepp wanted nothing of this. With respect to this point, neither Rev. Tuuk nor Rev. Manni can appeal to Bavinck in support of their sentiments.[3]

It sounds still stranger to us when Bavinck contends that we expect a new heaven and a new earth, a new humanity, a re-created world, a continuous development without sin and without death. And that to this end, creation and the fall, Adam and Christ, na-

---

3. Dr. Valentine Hepp was a professor in the Free University, Amsterdam. Rev. Edward J. Tuuk, a CRC minister and Janssen supporter, wrote against Herman Hoeksema and Henry Danhof at the time of the controversy over common grace. Rev. J. Manni was also a CRC minister who opposed Herman Hoeksema and even filed a protest against him, which was treated by the Synod of 1924. Rev. Manni had earlier served with Rev. Hoeksema on the committee that investigated the teachings of Dr. Ralph Janssen.

ture and grace, faith and unbelief, election and reprobation, work together and each in its own way, not alone but also cooperating alongside each other.

We cannot form, in the light of Scripture, any plausible conception of such a view. Apart from the fact that this reasoning, which joins nature and grace, rests in part on a false antithesis, it also joins the things which, following God's Word, cancel and exclude each other, as faith and unbelief. And this reasoning permits things to stand alongside of each other, things which, according to revelation, follow upon each other, such as Adam and Christ. With the coming of Christ, Adam disappears. It is indeed true that this representative of men and all those included in him lie in the midst of death apart from redemption. And it is also true that Adam, in the earthly life which he possessed, was the image of God in heaven and possessed a life of glory. Yet that in no way suggests that he could remain such alongside of and outside of Christ. The Scriptures know nothing of this. Whatever is and remains outside of Christ goes lost. And the entire creation, as a unity, is ushered into blessed glory.

The Scriptures know only one organic unity of things, which, however, develops out of the spiritual-moral principles of sin and grace as cause. It develops in an eternal, antithetical fellowship with the Creator, of love and hate, life and death. It is impossible for Bavinck to arrive at such an organic conception of things on the basis of his viewpoint. He ends up with a conglomeration of things and not an organic unity. The individual creatures and groups of creatures surely are related according to God's counsel and have their life and existence for the honor of God. In Bavinck's conception, however, they do not develop out of one common life-principle. That is also our chief objection. Bavinck, just as our fathers, applies predestination and the means of it to the everlasting state of rational creatures. But he denies that *everything* that is in the world and happens in the world can be included under these means. He does not connect all things to man, as Article 12 of our Confession does.

And whatever, according to Bavinck, cannot be included under those means and cannot, therefore, be connected to man, he allows to develop according to God's counsel and for God's honor all right, but he does not join the two in an organic relationship. In his world-view he does not have a truly organic unity. According to him, all things are surely to be included in the idea of the counsel of God, and the honor of God is the purpose of everything, but the counsel and honor of God remain empty ideas. He clearly fails to explain how the counsel of God is realized, or could possibly be realized, in the way of the development of all things to God's honor. In fact, Bavinck really makes that impossible by separating a part of what happens in the world from the everlasting destination of man. The relation, then, in every case is not organic, but mechanical, and he fails to give an explanation of all things. Bavinck is willing to make a broad place for his treatment of the counsel of God only in connection with so-called common grace. Obviously, therefore, what is in the world and what happens in the world are not related to the spiritual-moral development of the rational creature, according to eternal predestination. The things in the world and the things that happen must develop according to God's counsel and to God's honor through common grace.

This creates a breach in the organic unity of the life of creation and does not succeed in solving any difficulties. Bavinck stays hanging in the one-sided, faulty conception of the fathers concerning the theological idea of eternal, divine predestination. He does not carry through the biblical idea of the will of God. What Bavinck fails to understand concerning predestination and the counsel of God with respect to all things is bound up in God's Word in such words as *will, counsel, foreknowledge,* and *foreordination*. But Bavinck, just as Kuyper, wants a one-sided separate cosmic development of the creation through common grace, which development is neither rational, spiritual, nor normal. Bavinck appeals in support of his opinion to Kuyper. Therefore, we now give a quotation from Kuyper through Bavinck.[4]

---

4. The quotation is from Kuyper's *DGG*, vol. 2, 95, 96.

The question of infra and supra is a very weighty question, but the way in which it was explained neither helped nor led to a solution. Each one who considered this question from *man's perspective, had* to take election, as did Walaeus,[5] as an election out of the fallen human race. On the other hand, he who considered the matter from God's perspective understood the matter of election, as Gomarus[6] did, as a decision taken before the foundations of the world that included the creation ordinance. All the controversy which raged between parties over this question did not bring the church one step closer to a realization of the simple fact that both parties were proceeding from opposite standpoints. The one side stood foursquare on the ground; the other looked at the difference from the top of the mountains. And so neither one could understand the other. It is therefore absurd to say that one theologian in our time is a "before-the-fall proponent," while over against him is to be placed an "after-the-fall proponent."[7] This is simply unthinkable, because this profound question has taken on an entirely different form in our day.

Further, in the same work[8] Dr. Kuyper asks the question whether our Reformed dogmatics are not in a one-sided way in conflict with Holy Scripture, because foreordination has been considered almost exclusively as a decree of God concerning the eternal well-being and eternal woe of his rational creatures. And he answers this question thus:

In earlier times theologians, although properly placing man in the foreground of the decree, yet applied the decree in a one-sided way to

---

5. Antonius Walaeus was a Dutch Reformed theologian and professor at Middelburg who was present at the Synod of Dordt and served on the committee which drew up the concept Canons.

6. Franciscus Gomarus was a Dutch Reformed theologian, a professor at Leiden, and a delegate to the Synod of Dordt. Gomarus represented the supralapsarian position.

7. "Before the fall" and "after the fall" are literal translations of the terms supralapsarian and infralapsarian.

8. Kuyper, *DGG*, vol. 2, 91–93

men and angels. Thus, they lost from sight the overall creation of God and made no use of common grace in the development of the doctrine of predestination.[9]

We have repeatedly seen how Kuyper allows the creation after the fall to continue to exist and to develop cosmically through common grace. We have also seen how he makes provision for the working of particular grace in election to eternal life. In Bavinck and Kuyper, even though there are some slight differences, we meet with the same duality in the life of the creation in its mutual relationships. They have discovered that the fathers, also the ones at Dordt, considered saving grace in an individualistic and particularistic way. This discovery agrees with our opinion, which we expressed earlier. The fathers at Dordt spoke of a certain crowd of people which God had from eternity elected unto eternal life and a reprobation of the rest unto eternal death. And now Bavinck and Kuyper want to retain this imperfect theological development of the doctrine of eternal predestination, even though they could have known that the fathers in no sense wanted to maintain election and reprobation in a particularistic way. But the fathers could not express the doctrine differently over against the Remonstrants, because the Remonstrants denied personal predestination. The fathers set over against this view the idea of a will of God, included in the counsel, which concerned the rational-moral creature, but they did not establish a truly organic connection between these two parts of God's will. They did not agree with Article 12 of our Confession of Faith,[10] which connects all things to man as means in the eternal predestination of God. Some things they separated from the "all things" of Article 12. These things exist and develop

---

9. See Bavinck, *Gereformeerde Dogmatiek*, vol. 2, 407. Kuyper is being quoted by Bavinck.

10. The meaning is not that the fathers at Dordt disagreed with Article 12, but that they did not include in the Canons the organic conception expressed in Article 12.

in a cosmic development, according to God's counsel and to God's honor, through common grace.

This latter is inadequate, however, as is the whole conception. No attempt was made to understand the opinion of the fathers in the context of their practical handling of the Arminian error, and to relate this opinion organically to the truth which runs through the entire Confession of Faith; or, if not that, at least to correct it.

On the other hand, theologians have connected these ideas to such things as natural light, remnants, and civil righteousness: things which Pelagians and Remonstrants had pushed to the foreground but which had not been completely thought out by our fathers, nor carefully defined. Over against these theologians, we want to push into the foreground the organic character of divine predestination. This is, after all, in harmony with the positive line of thought in the fathers, and it is clearly perceptible in our confessions. All things are related to each other, and especially to man as the head, and thus are to be considered as an organic unity.

It is also true, in a relative way, that a distinction must be made between God's counsel in the broadest sense of the word, and predestination with particular application to rational-moral creatures. But that idea does not negate the fact that God's counsel must be thought of as including all created things in their underlying relationships. And it is against the background of that real and actual object, that God, according to the counsel of His will and in incomprehensible ways, loves and is filled with wrath, elects and reprobates, blesses and curses.

Nor must we think of a second line, parallel to this purpose of God, which is, for example, the line of man's accountability. This is what some propose. God's will and man's accountability do not run parallel to each other. God deals with man in organic relation to all things, so that man acts with a will and with accountability before God. That is, neither one can be denied, but both are to be maintained in agreement with each other.

The Biblical Concept of Grace

To arrive at an accurate conception of the operation of the will of God, we cannot proceed from the meaning of the word *grace* in our everyday usage of the term, nor even from its usage in Holy Scripture. We must study specific terms and the use of words, but it must be done with great care. We always run into the danger of arguing from something in man to what is in God. That is the reverse order. We must work theologically. God Himself determines the character of His will, grace, love, hate, wrath, and so forth. But it is also true that we know nothing definite about God apart from God's revelation in Scripture. And so we must have a clearly defined idea of God and the operation of His will, which we get from God's self-revelation, before we say anything at all. Such submission to the same Word of God's revelation must also be present when we consider election by His grace, and the accompanying reprobation of His wrath, because both are the operation of His eternal will.

The word *grace* in Scripture has the meaning of beauty, pleasantness, goodness, benevolence, favor, helpfulness. It also means bowing down, giving of thanks, and showing unrestrained guilt-forgiving love for the unworthy. These meanings are found in the ancient and modern languages that come into consideration in our present study. The last meaning of the word for grace, showing unrestrained guilt-forgiving love for the unworthy, does not actually have that meaning outside of the New Testament, but in Scripture that meaning stands on the foreground, especially in the epistles of Paul. It is then contrasted with such concepts as law, work, duty, and reward.

The word sometimes has similar meanings in our modern languages. The Latin word *gratia*, from *gratus* (gratifying), and likely related to the Greek *charis* (in the sense of "glad," or "favor," or "gracious"), has approximately the same meaning. In Psalm 45, according to the metrical version, we sing this in regard to Israel's king: "Supremely fair Thou art, / Thy lips with grace o'erflow; / His richest blessings evermore/doth God on Thee bestow." It refers to the appealing appearance of this King, given by God in His grace. According to Ephesians 2:8, we are saved by grace, and not by our works of the law.

Also the Dutch language speaks of a gracious figure, of being in the favor of some one, of being king by the grace of God, or of being an artist by the grace of God. It refers to asking favor, granting, making grace available, as well as gratifying or gratification. In the English we also speak of *grace* as gratitude; in the Dutch we use *gaarne* (willingly), *graag* (gladly), and *begeeren* (desirable); in the German *gerne;* and in the Italian *grazia* (thanks). All of these translations can be used for the Greek *charis* (grace). These various meanings of the word tell us that *grace* is rich in content.

But this is by no means sufficient to reach an accurate concept of the grace of God. Indeed, we are not dealing with the use of the *word* grace, but with the *idea* of grace—grace as it is in God. Regardless of that, in determining the concept of grace we must emphatically take note of the use that is made of the word in Holy Scripture, the translations of God's Word, the confessions, the liturgical forms, the metrical version of the Psalms, the works of Reformed theologians, and our own usage; and we must take note of many related words, such as benevolence, mercy, compassion, patience, kindness, pity, and (though the word is rarely used) endurance. (Compare, for example, Hos. 2:22; Rom. 9:23, 25; 1 Pet. 2:10; 2 Pet. 3:9, 15; James 5:7, 11; Rom. 3:25; and the metrical version of the Psalms: 6 verse 1; 24 verse 3; 25 verses 3–6, 8, 9; 36 verse 2; 51 verse 1; 77 verses 5–7; 79 verse 4; 86 verse 3; 89; 95; 99; and 103;[11] and the Baptism Form. This comparative study will enable us to see that the same concrete idea is expressed by all these words, and many others, even though it is true that each of these words, some with interchangeable meanings, usually shows

---

11. The reference is to the Dutch Psalm book. In *The Psalter,* the numbers and verses would be these: 12:1; 59:3; 67:2, 3, 5; 94:1, 2; 140:1; 212:5, 6; 216:3; 233:3; 242; 254; 265; and 278:3.

us the rich grace of God from a particular viewpoint and in a special relationship.

A study of all sorts of words, terms, and figures that deal with reprobation, such as hate, wrath, anger, and rage, must obviously still be added. This twofold revelation of God's will (electing grace and reprobating wrath) must be carried through in regard to their object, their historical development, and their eternal result.

God's Eternal Counsel

Even at that we are not finished. All of this must be elucidated and interpreted in connection with God's counsel and eternal purpose. We are dealing here with what God wills. That will cannot be explained by something *apart from* God. The main reason for God's will must be sought *in God Himself*. God's will reveals itself in connection with man's sin. That sin did not take God by surprise, did not occur in creation apart from His counsel and will. Thus, we are concerned with the study of God's will of electing grace and reprobating wrath as works which, in the end, must be ascribed to God. God's grace and disfavor are not determined by one or another attribute in God, but by God Himself—or if we may express ourselves in this manner—by the fullness of God. We must even diligently guard ourselves against separating the attributes of God. God's attributes are in a certain sense to be distinguished, but are not essentially different from the essence of God, neither individually nor collectively.

We are dealing with God Himself: God's grace and disfavor, His love and His hatred. Election and reprobation are His—God's. He finds reasons in Himself for His will. This is true whether we understand it or not, whether we will it or not.

The Reformed usually designate *God's glory* as the purpose of this will. Formerly we have sought to define this more accurately by speaking of covenant fellowship or friendship. The concept *God's glory* is very abstract and has no content for our thinking. This becomes somewhat different when we consider that God is the fully Blessed One in Himself. He is fully blessed as one who lives His life of love as the triune, covenant God. God is the God of the covenant. He is that not only according to the counsel of His will in relation to the creature, but He is that, first of all, in Himself, by virtue of His nature. The family life of God is a covenant of friendship between Father, Son, and Holy Spirit. Indeed, God is one in essence, three in persons. The three persons all possess alike the same divine essence. In their individual independency they are also alike. But in their individual, personal attributes they are different. Their oneness of essence gives them harmony; the equality of persons requires agreement, while the possibility for most intimate fellowship and cooperation lies in the diversity of their individual personal attributes. Oneness and diversity give harmony. The love-life of God, welling up from the unsearchable depths of His being, willed by Father, Son, and Holy Spirit, and streaming forth in the many forms of the individual attributes, reveals in a glorious, variegated display the full riches of the eternal friendship of the Trinity.

That divine love-life in God has become, as we see it, the basis for the fellowship and covenant relationship between the Creator and the creature, and between the creatures mutually. That covenant idea is willed by God. He seeks a reflection of His life of friendship in the creature. That is not a cold concept. Nor is there any evidence of insensibility or hardness in it. It is truly an essentially free and sovereign act of God's will. Its essential character is glorious. The life of love and friendship in the family of God is divinely good and beautiful. To cause His creature to share in it is good and beautiful. This sovereign will of the God of the covenant is the will to reveal and glorify that which is divinely good and glorious. The life and friendship of the Trinity is thus completely enveloped in the glow of love and grace.

God's Counsel and Grace

All of this becomes incredibly more amazing and profound when it is related to man's fall into sin and his redemption by and in Christ Jesus. The song of re-creation has far greater depth of tone than the song of creation. We can find good reasons for this most exalted self-revelation and self-glorification of God, even though we are humans of limited understanding. Although we cannot answer all the questions that arise, yet, as we see it, we must seek the solution to the problems in the direction we indicated.

Speaking of grace, we must therefore consider that we are dealing with the God of grace. God is gracious. He is beautiful, appealing, glorious, amiable, completely desirable, and worthy of praise. This does not apply merely to His external appearance, but also to His inner being. God is as good as He is great. His goodness is higher than the heavens. He only is good. This exalted God lives with the lowly. He stoops down to them with the fullness of His goodness to cause them to share in the fellowship of His friendship. He does this most eagerly. He persists therein even when man, as far as he is concerned, turns this friendship into enmity through sin. Then it becomes fully evident that God is gracious, merciful, patient, and of great compassion. He justifies the ungodly and causes His mercy to extend to the sinner, in Christ, whom He eternally anointed to be the covenant Mediator. He does not forsake the work of His hands. He reveals that His thoughts surpass those of the creatures, even as His ways prove to be higher than their ways.

He has reckoned with sin. Sin serves Him according to the counsel of His will. It is over against sin that grace scintillates in all its glory, according to His good pleasure which He has determined in Himself. More gloriously, He now impresses His own divine virtue-image upon the consciousness of the person who is fallen in sin but has been enriched with grace in Christ Jesus. He does that in such a manner that this person, filled with the grace of thanksgiving, now bows before Him in praise and adoration and causes the song of the re-created creation to echo through the heavenly throne-chamber throughout all eternity. Man will even increase God's praise, because God provides for all man's need, grants all the means, and makes everything serve His praise.

That is the positive line. With an eternal, unchangeable purpose of irresistible love in Christ His beloved, and through His work of reconciliation and reunion by the Holy Spirit of regeneration and qualification, He turns to His elect people. He brings that people to faith in Christ, makes them worthy of suffering for Christ, and allows them to experience in Christ the covenant of His friendship. The end result is that the tabernacle of God is with men, and God shines forth gloriously in Zion in the perfection of beauty. The grace of God has triumphed.

God's Counsel and the Antithesis

But parallel to that runs the negative line. At the same time and in the same manner[12] as the work of God's elective love delivers, saves, and exalts to a fellowship of friendship, there is a separating, banishing, rejecting, humiliating action of God's aversion, hate, wrath, anger, and great displeasure in regard to the non-elect, along the line of reprobation. This also takes place according to the immutability of God's will. This must be emphasized, for this is often the issue. Here is where the denial of God's revealed truth begins. Many eagerly make the possibility of salvation dependent upon the sinner. We have shown this previously

---

12. Hoeksema was later to pay more attention to the conclusion of the Canons in his development of sovereign reprobation, especially the rejection of the Arminian charge that "in the same manner in which the election is the fountain and the cause of faith and good works, reprobation is the cause of unbelief and impiety." He never denied these earlier statements concerning reprobation, but he clarified the way in which reprobation is subservient to election. In this passage he refers to the fact that election and reprobation are equally sovereign decrees of God.

from history, and the Reformed fathers always opposed it. Emphasis must be laid upon the twofold operation of God's will: from the will of God's eternal good pleasure proceeds not only the operation of love, election, and saving grace, but also the operation of hate, rejection, wretchedness, and banishment. Scripture speaks of life and death, of blessing and curse, of light and darkness, struggle, victory, rest, salvation, and the joy of the Lord, but also of increase in unrighteousness, hardening in that which is evil, perishing, condemnation, suffering, punishment, and everlasting fire. Living out of the principles of sin and grace, humanity is divided into friendship and enmity toward God and toward one another. The development of all things takes place along antithetical lines.

This is almost so obvious, as we see it, that in the light of Scripture, history, and experience, no one can have any other impression. We are therefore of the opinion that we must emphatically warn, not only against maintaining a false antithesis, as, for example, between nature and grace, as is done repeatedly by Kuyper and Bavinck, but especially against a false mixture of spiritually similar elements and the resulting separation of various parts of the same life according to definite, specific areas of life. One essential antithesis exists between God's people and the people of the world in the spiritual-ethical sense of the word: the antithesis of sin and grace. That is the antithesis which Scripture establishes and we must establish. The children of Adam have all things in common, except grace.

The fact of the matter is that God's grace is not general. According to God's witness, humanity is split spiritually into wheat and chaff, into church and world, into bride and harlot, into children of light and children of darkness. But this occurs while both maintain their natural relationship and organic unity. If that were not the case, there would be no essential conflict possible along the entire line of human activity. All creatures in their organic fellowship, according to the counsel of God's providence, experience moment by moment God's sustaining, cooperating, and governing power. By this power they can develop according to their essence, capacity, and place in the organism and according to their eternal destination. Because of this, a conflict is carried on in the very bosom of creation as two parts of it live out of two mutually exclusive principles.

But these principles are of a spiritual-ethical nature, so that natural fellowship as such is not disrupted. Each party makes use of all that belongs to life in this present dispensation in an effort to crowd out the life that proceeds from the opposite principle and to cause its own principle to triumph. Therefore, the regenerated and the unregenerated experience the same influences of divine power. They live in mutual, natural, organic fellowship. This fellowship is according to each one's inclination and need, according to the demand of their natural relationship and original destiny. Although their life here on earth is amazingly interwoven in all sorts of ways, Adam's children, because of their differing spiritual relationship to God, still separate in principle always and everywhere and form a contrast along the entire line of human activity. This contrast keeps pace with the natural organic development of the human race and of all cosmic life, according to the nature of each dispensation and in harmony with the various circumstances of time and place, of life-sphere and relationship. The wedge of God's grace separates them.

That is the fearfulness of God's free grace. If grace were general, there would soon be, even though this was preceded by a period of bitter suffering, a general restoration of all the creatures, and sorrow and crying would flee away forever. Purely from the aspect of principle, there would then be no real conflict. But since God shows mercy to whom He will show mercy, and hardens whom He will, there will surely presently be eternal light but also outer darkness and eternal fire, weeping and gnashing of teeth.

Therefore, it must not surprise us at all that throughout the ages it is precisely the doctrine of grace that has been contradicted. If we have learned from experience to taste that eternal election is meant for us, that we are God's children, and that God wills to be our Friend; if we have learned that the bonds of God's covenantal mercy have drawn us out of the estrangement and the bondage of sin and out of all the power of the enemy; then we have discovered indeed that the mystery of election is great. Then the humbled heart praises God's mercies, and the mouth rejoices: "I am once again the possession of the Lord." Then the Pelagian in us dies, and we, as far as we are concerned, desire to be saved only by grace. Then we understand men like David, Paul, Augustine, Luther, Ursinus, the Reformers in general, and the true martyrs. Then the doctrine of grace is indispensable for us, but also gloriously pleasant.

Denials of Grace

But as soon as we lack only a little of that rich, conscious knowledge of the mercies of God, the situation changes. As beautiful as the doctrine of grace may be, and how seemingly easy it is to grasp it, it is extremely difficult to live out of the principle of grace. The sinner wants no grace, and the one on whom grace is bestowed wants only as much as has been bestowed. It is not difficult to see the reason for this. Sin is putting oneself in God's place. When the sovereign God comes with the irresistibly powerful work of His grace in absolute independence from the creature, He clashes with the enmity of the sinner. By nature the sinner refuses to subject himself to this irresistible power. He is willing to be saved, but with a salvation invented and realized by himself. He does not want God's grace. As long as God's irresistible grace has not caused the sinful individual to lay aside all enmity against the Creator and has not made him understand and love God's sovereign good pleasure down into the very deepest imaginations of his heart and desires of his soul, he will continue to detract from the work of God's grace. Man's sin and God's grace are mutually exclusive of each other.

Thus it is to be explained that not only all unbelievers, but also a great mass of Christians, do not want the doctrine of God's free grace. That God's grace is made dependent upon sinful man is a common error. Men are not opposed to God's grace if the disposal of it pleases man. Naturally, if this latter were true, man would, by grace, triumph over God. Therefore, men try to change God's grace into a work of man. They make all kinds of distinctions and speak especially of conditions. They speak of baptismal grace, preparatory grace, helping grace, covenant grace, and lastly now also of a common grace that our human race enjoys, and whereby in the so-called sphere of natural life, men are enabled to live a life that is pleasing to God, although only particular grace is saving. Mostly they speak of an objective grace, of which the subjective application is dependent upon sinful man.

All these distinctions have actually no other purpose than to maintain something in the sinner over against God—a certain capability for natural or spiritual good, or a certain claim upon something in God, even though that be nothing more than God's compassion.

But that is impossible. Such a vain, basically wicked attempt must fail. In the bestowal of mercy, it is the sinner in man that is put down. Irresistibly, God forces His grace upon the person who is at enmity with Him and makes him a partaker of grace. The naturally hostile inclination of the sinner is turned to friendship. The sinner who receives mercy begins to will what God wills, and because God wills it. Henceforth he finds his knowledge in God's Word and His pleasure in God's will. If his heart becomes afraid when he sees that God's freely sovereign grace is not common, but that it sets apart the human race and tears asunder the organic bonds of our natural fellowship; and if he is frightened by an eternal hell for the reprobate, then he does not set a false sympathy for sinful man over against that divine good pleasure, but he works out his own salvation with fear and trembling and declares among the people that the Lord is just. In no way whatever does he try to justify sinful man over against the sovereign God. But out of friendship toward his Father in Christ, he holds high the good pleasure of the Lord in the midst of a crooked and perverse generation, as revealed in the holy gospel. In this way the idea of God's covenant is realized in him in principle. God's love in Christ finds an echo in his heart and vibrates through his deeds. He is once again friend of God.

God's friendship is a specific aspect of God's favor toward His people. By the wonder of God's grace, the enmity of sin between God and His chosen people in Christ is abolished, the relationship of friendship is restored, and henceforth God and His people, in fellowship together, go up in battle against sin, Satan, and the whole realm of darkness. That is the language of our confessions and liturgical forms. The historical realization of this relationship of friendship begins at the very moment when in the earthly paradise God put enmity between Satan and the woman. Its complete accomplishment is in the great day of the Lord. In the meantime, it is the history of salvation, the realization of the covenant of grace. By the wonder of grace, God lifts the creation in Christ out of its fall and brings it to its eternal destination while organically separating the reprobate. The course is not back to the paradise that was lost, nor is there a history running parallel to this history of redemption, a development of the life of creation that at the beginning made itself manifest only in kernel form and later would enter as a double fruit into glory. No, after the fall, the bond that bound us in Adam is broken, but the bond that binds us in Christ remains; and what is now bound together in Christ enters into the glory of the re-creation in and by Christ. That which is not eternally bound up in that Mediator and Redeemer is separated and dashed down into destruction as the organic totality of election is lifted up.

After the fall, the course of events is not essentially different, but it is deeper. There is no actual restoration of the old, but God's creation-plan for the creature is realized according to the purpose of His eternal counsel in a much deeper manner. All history is included in that plan. God's eternal purpose is realized in the development of all creation, in mutual organic relationships, natural fellowship, spiritual separation, and all this in relation to Christ.

Organic Development
of the Human Race

This historical development proceeds along organic lines. It is bound to the organic existence, life, and development of Adam's natural descendants. God created us organically and placed us in an organic relationship, so that our life can develop itself only organically. This must be borne in mind. Adam is not merely our moral representative, our juridical head, so that the guilt of his first sin is reckoned to all human beings, and they are reckoned as worthy of condemnation before God. This does not explain history. Adam was also the principle or seed of the organism of mankind. From him all human individuals are partakers of the human nature. And now, through the sin of Adam as organic head, that general human nature is corrupted. At our birth we all share in that corrupted nature, and in our own individual ways we develop the sin of our generation. Thus, in the course of the ages, the sin of the human race is fully realized in the sum total of the sins of each human individual. In this way we can understand that we also daily increase our guilt. And we can also understand that, as our Catechism states, by the fall of Adam and Eve our nature became so corrupt that we are conceived and born in sin. The disobedience of Adam involves us, because he is the father of us all, and we all have sinned in him.

In and by Adam, man sinned. Man was the friend of God; therefore, sin is breach of covenant. He was king of creation, and as such he dragged the entire creation along with him into the fall. In paradise mankind existed only in its juridical head and organic principle; therefore, that first sin was reckoned to all human beings, and that sin was further developed by various human individuals. This latter takes place along the lines of the natural development of our generation and the development of the totality of creation.

All human individuals in their organic solidarity are connected to the root sin of their organic head, and by their individual sins they bring the sin of the human race to its complete development. We found that thought also in Kuyper in his *Uit het Woord,* in his *E Voto,* and in his *Dictaten Dogmatiek.* This idea is also emphatically on the foreground in our Catechism.

But our Reformed theology has not done full justice to it. An attempt was made to explain our actual sins by our inherited pollution, as punishment of our original guilt, that is, the guilt of Adam reckoned to us. However, this is impossible, since guilt, pollution, and sin are completely dissimilar concepts. Sin implies guilt, and guilt is punished by death. The principle of that death we already have in our pollution. But the actual sins or sinful deeds of the individual children of men grow out of the root of the one principle sin of the human race. This is due to man's organic relationship to the head of the race, Adam. Mankind is an organism. The various members thereof are both individual and independent persons who share in Adam's guilt. But they are also related to each other in a thousand ways and are connected organically to the principle sin of the head of the race, Adam. Thus the sin of the human race has an organic character. As a result of this, it also applies to everything: to our life of sin, but also to the operation of the curse, death, destruction, and the temptation of the devil. It applies to the work of the Holy Spirit, the incarnation of the Word, the gathering of the elect, and the reprobation of the non-elect. It applies to the life of grace in the human race, its spiritual development, its application of principles, and the course of the spiritual battle. It applies to all the world events in this present dispensation.

This is the way we understand the course of history. In paradise we have the kernel; at the end of the ages, we have the ripened fruit. Immediately after the fall, God puts the principle of enmity between the devil and the woman and between the spiritual seed of both. At the return of the Lord, the enmity is complete. Between these two points lies actual history. Adam and Eve, having received the grace of God, desire to bring forth the spiritual seed. But according to God's will, they also bring forth the children of the devil. They share their corrupt nature with both kinds of children. But God works in His elect the principle of regeneration. Thereby the development of the human race is antithetical. Mankind lives out of two principles which separate. Enmity and conflict arise. The children of men cannot understand each other. The one loves God; the other hates Him. Those who are born according to the flesh persecute those who are born according to the Spirit. Cain kills Abel. The conflict broadens as time goes on. All available means are used. There is no possibility of neutrality. Before the flood, an attempt of both parties to create a fellowship in their natural life only led to an amalgamation of those who were spiritually dissimilar, and it dashed the first world into a watery grave, in which it was kept unto the eternal fire. But Noah found grace in the eyes of the Lord. He walked with God, his Friend.

The history of the second world is similar to that of the first. Very soon the new kernel begins to show agreement with the old shell. In his son Canaan, Ham becomes the bearer of the curse over against Shem, who is privileged to call himself according to the name of the Lord. Again there are giants on the earth. Mankind plots violence against heaven. God disrupts the work of the children of men. The principle of the kingdom of Babel is laid: the principle of a human world-power. God places His people who arise from Abraham over against that world-power. This people shows us in typical form the church of the new dispensation and the eternal kingdom of Christ. More particularly it also allows us to see in this history the spiritual conflict between the people of God and the world-powers that are opposed to God. However, it is saved only in its spiritual remnant. The distinction between flesh and spirit runs also through these people, as is also the case in the church in its historical existence here on earth.

The history of the kingdom of mankind is that of the principle of evil. Nebuchadnezzar's dream-image teaches us that. It is thoroughly ground to powder by the Stone out of God's mountain. Its development is certainly regressive. It returns to the earth, and no place is found in the eternal kingdom of Christ for its final fruit.

Therefore, the lines of the historical development of the enmity set by God in the life of our race run, on the one hand, along the line of Cain, Lamech, Nimrod, Pharaoh, Sennacherib, Nebuchadnezzar, Antiochus Epiphanes, Judas, Nero, the Antichrist, and Gog and Magog with their confederates; on the other hand, it runs along the line of Abel, Enoch, Noah, Abraham, Moses, David, Daniel, Mattathias, Stephen, and the church of witnesses and martyrs. The battle is spiritual. Scripture does not speak of a complete cosmic development, of which some so eagerly dream. World events are suddenly cut off by a catastrophe: the solving of the world-riddle by King Jesus. Then follows judgment upon the acquired fruit of men's works, upon what was done in the body, whether good or evil. The antithesis of eternity is that of friendship and enmity.

We must even now judge and evaluate all things according to that standard. The question is, In what spiritual-moral relationship do we stand toward God? Everything else is subordinate to that. Nothing has real value unless we possess it, enjoy it, and use it in God's favor in Christ and in His fellowship and service.

That is impossible apart from regeneration. God's Word absolutely condemns the sinner from the viewpoint of his life-principle. Out of that principle, only evil can develop to its full manifestation. Even if, in our opinion, sin has not at the moment fully developed (which, if circumstances were different, could very well happen), it does not in the least detract from the reality of man's guilt in Adam. The fact remains that the sinner is able to develop only out of a wrong life-principle. Things can get worse, but things can never get better. The sinner sins in every relationship of life, with every talent he possesses, and with all the means at his disposal.

But all is turned about in principle in the life of the regenerate. Naturally, sin still works in such a one, and he is also bound to his own place in the organic totality of things; but he is born of God with a spiritual life-principle, detached from the sinful life-principle. And so he is *in* this world, but not *of* this world.

The Principle of Regeneration

We must determine our place in the community in harmony with that principle. First of all, we must bear in mind that the principle of regeneration is the beginning of eternal life. It is not a mere restoration of that which perished in sin. We do not stand once more where Adam stood before the fall. By virtue of that new principle, we cannot live anew the same creation life so that we would be able to show to the unregenerate a way to life in the things of this world. The fact is that the original life is not lived anymore. The sinner lives perversely, and in his blindness he attempts to make this earth a paradise, an effort in which he will never succeed. But God's child possesses a life which simply is not found here in this world. That life is foreign here. It is at home in heaven.

For that very reason God's child is a stranger here on earth. In life-principle he differs completely from the unregenerate. There is no possibility whatever for a communal cooperation aimed at the advancement of the so-called creation-life, or general human life, both because that life does not exist, and because development occurs in two mutually exclusive directions.

What both can do is to make use of the things of creation. But even as they do this out of different principles, they also do it with a different goal in mind. Neither one can end in the created things as such. Man is inclined to be religious; therefore, with all that he is and owns, he will always bow down in worship, praise, and thanksgiving, either before the true God or before that which he has set up in God's stead.

But something very important must be added. Here on earth the Christian represents the cause of the Lord. His task is not to subject this creation to himself, but to support the cause of Christ. In the cause of Christ, it is indeed given to him by grace not only to believe in Christ, but also to suffer for Him. That should be understood. Otherwise we will, without being aware of it, turn back to live again out of the original creation-life. That is not possible, nor is it permissible. The earthly paradise is closed to us forever.

Through sin we are estranged from all true life and stand damnable before God. But we are shown favor in Christ. He restores life to us: not the old life, but resurrection life. Christ was dead and is alive again, and now He lives unto all eternity. He is the resurrection and the life; He gives us resurrection life. We enter into His victory, and thereby into His rest. Furthermore, we are made worthy to suffer for Him in order that we may also be glorified with Him. We are thereby made God's party.

It will certainly be evident to everyone that in this way we are kept from setting up a false antithesis. We do not want an antithesis between nature and grace, between the material and spiritual terrain and sphere. The creation is God's, stolen by Satan or abandoned by the sinner, but regained by Christ, and in fellowship with Christ it is again our possession in spiritual principle. However, during this dispensation Christ's kingdom does not come in an external form. Nor do we possess the typical bounties of Israel of old. We live and die in the world as far as our physical existence is concerned. Only later will we be changed. Thus, as Christians we do not have our own land, kingdom, king, city, house, school, state, and the like, as did Israel of the past. We do not even have a "home rule," as the Jews in the time of Christ. We are in the dispersion. We are strangers upon the earth, and our captivity lasts until Christ returns.

We place the antithesis between the life-principle of sin and that of grace. We do that because Scripture demands it. Paul thanks God that we formerly were servants of sin, but now, having been made free from sin, we are made servants of righteousness (Rom. 6:17, 18). We have not received the spirit of the world but the Spirit that is from God, in order that we should know the things that are given to us of God (1 Cor. 2:12). In fellowship with Christ, who is God's, Paul, Apollos, Cephas, the world, life, death, and present and future things are ours (1 Cor. 3:22, 23). But now we must also suffer with Christ, and not regard the things that men see. To these also belongs our light affliction, which swiftly passes away. We must regard the things that men do not see, which are eternal. We must no more walk as the Gentiles walk, in the vanity of their minds, darkened in their understanding, alienated from the life of God through the ignorance that is in them because of the blindness of their hearts. They are past feeling. They have given themselves over to lasciviousness, to work all uncleanness with greediness (Eph. 4:17–19). We must not think it strange concerning the fiery trial that tries us, nor complain to each other because of social injustice, nor love this present world or the things in the world. But as pilgrims and strangers, we must withhold ourselves from the carnal lusts that war against the soul.

We do not go out of the world, because we are placed here by God, not because this world is not good enough for us or because we must associate with and raise to a higher level its so-called world-life. Our task is to cause the revelation of the true life of God in Christ to shine forth in this world. That life must be placed over against the life of sin. The antithesis between that twofold life must be brought out. Everything must be directed toward that end: energy, gifts, talents, terrains, spheres, institutions, capital, ability to work, knowledge, and power, with all else that may stand at our service. All must be employed by us as means to the full development of ourselves from the principle of grace. This entire earthly creation is a means for man and must therefore be used by us against the work of unrighteousness. In that way we can reveal ourselves as God's participants in the covenant. He who fails in this is, in principle, a friend of the world. It must also be understood that there is no other way in which we can cooperate with the world. This is the only line of action that can be followed.

Naturally, by doing this we stir up a battle in the world. The world does not so readily allow us to condemn it and its life-principle. On the contrary, the world will attempt to convince us of the correctness of its viewpoint, or force us to be silent. Now if both parties continue to carry on the conflict along the line of human deliberation, inclination, expression, and effort to the very extreme, with the weapons of defense and assault, then it will become evident that the human race is like the house that is divided against itself. Then it will also become evident that one cannot, strictly speaking, draw a definite line of separation anywhere, not even between church and state. The principles simply divide our entire human society. There is then no possibility of a solution to the world-problem. On the contrary, the division and the confusion increase. Our society reaches a dead end. Everything cries for the return of Christ.

But this should not deter us. We must be on our guard that we do not, as Kuyper does with his common grace doctrine and as happens all around us, allow God and sinful man to arrange themselves in an alliance against physical evil. Evil is of a spiritual-ethical nature, and is in man. Therefore, only God and those who have received His grace can fight against sin, Satan, and the kingdom of darkness; and then only with spiritual weapons. It must be clearly understood that the conflict of the ages centers in the name of the Lord and the covenant of our God. Attacking a few external results of sin is of no avail; the real evil only thrives the more profusely. To know the actual struggle, we must go to Gethsemane and Golgotha. Also history itself teaches plainly that no people, however highly civilized they may be, has ever known, apart from God's regenerating grace, how to develop an actual higher moral life before God. The various spiritual attitudes toward God have always divided the children of men.

Principles must carry through. That will cause the conflict to intensify and become more extensive, and especially become more fearful if the enemy turns the steel sword of the magistrate against us. But that may not be reason for us to give up the conflict, nor may we put our trust in unlawful weapons. For that matter, they would be of no advantage to us. The battle is the Lord's. He brings it about. He withdraws all disguises from us at the right time. If we truly confess the name of the Lord, sooner or later we will certainly come into conflict. After all, we cannot remain standing in a neutral position. There is no possibility of an armistice, nor even of giving quarter. Nor can we expect aid from any earthly means or from our own strength. Trusting only in the name of the Lord, we must defend the cause of the Lord. His cause will triumph. And God will cause us to see His salvation.

4

Answer to Opponents

⌐∞⌐

Answer to Rev. Wierenga

It certainly cannot be considered out of place to devote a few pages
to our opinion of the criticism offered by a few brothers to our last
writing.[1]

We begin with what was written by Rev. H. Wierenga in an article entitled "The Light of Nature in the Light of Dordt."[2] He has
not yet finished his views on Calvin, and what has appeared up to
now concerning that subject is of minor importance.[3] We will
therefore limit ourselves to what the brother wrote under the
above-mentioned title.

We want to call the attention of the brother and of the general
public to the method that the brother follows in his essay.

The title is gripping and draws our attention: "The Light of Nature in the Light of Dordt." Upon reading the title, one's atten-

---

1. It is not certain what writing of the authors is referred to in this sentence.
It might have been Danhof and Hoeksema's 33-page booklet "Niet Doopersch
maar Gereformeerd" (Not Anabaptistic but Reformed), which was their answer
to a Van Baalen book.

2. H. [Henry] Wierenga, "The Light of Nature in the Light of Dordt," *Religion and Culture* (Feb. 1923): 133–136. The author was the CRC pastor in
Jamestown, Michigan.

3. Rev. Wierenga was writing a series of articles on Calvin.

tion is immediately aroused. What we expect is that the brother will show how, according to the pure light of Dordt, the doctrine of common grace should be adopted and maintained by all who desire to be called Reformed.

However, we were disappointed. The light that the brother lets shine upon the light of nature is not the actual light of the Synod of Dordt as that continues to shine in our Canons and confessions. Rather, he quotes that which the various delegates at Dordt brought up in the course of the lengthy discussion on this question of the light of nature. Not the established conclusions of the synod, but the personal opinions of individual delegates or groups of delegates, are called in this essay "The Light of Nature in the Light of Dordt."

Naturally, this would have been possible if the brother had distinguished carefully. There is no room for criticism of what the Synod of Dordt officially adopted. We have the sure light of Dordt in the Canons. Yet if the brother did not desire to quote from the confessions, but instead from the individual opinions of the delegates, he certainly should have distinguished and investigated critically before he put everything under the title "The Light of Dordt."

However, the brother does not do this in his essay. He proceeds from the assumption that all the delegates at the renowned Synod of Dordt were equally Reformed, and that everything they wrote or said may be presented as "Light of Dordt." He quotes helterskelter. You find no historical research in his essay. This lack of critical study explains why the article of Rev. Wierenga casts a wrong light on the "Light of Dordt."

We will try to clarify and prove this.

As the reader knows, the Synod of Dordt, 1618–1619, was composed of delegates from various regions. There were delegates from the Reformed Churches in the Netherlands and from the various provinces. Many foreign theologians were seated, and the professors from the Netherlands were also present.

In order to understand Rev. Wierenga's essay and to grasp the error in his method, we should understand how the Synod of Dordt worked. Before the delegates formulated and adopted a final judgment on the various propositions of the Remonstrants, the different groups of delegates deliberated together and put their opinions in writing. These opinions of the delegates were presented to the synod. And these different studies were printed in the *Acta of Handelingen der Nationale Synode* [Acts of the National Synod]. Rev. Wierenga quotes from these *Acta*.

One would expect that the brother, as a knowledgeable man, would distinguish carefully between the Reformed character of the various delegates. It was to be expected that not all who met in 1618–1619 at Dordt were equally Reformed. To mention an example, suppose that Rev. Wierenga and I had both been at the Synod of 1922. Suppose, moreover, that in the discussion of the Janssen case, both Rev. Wierenga and I had handed in our written personal opinion of the instruction of Dr. Janssen. And suppose, finally, that a century later someone cited from the synodical *Acts* the written opinion of Rev. Wierenga under the title "The Instruction of Dr. Janssen in the Light of the Synod of 1922." You would immediately remark that such a writer had bungled badly. The same thing is true in the case of the delegates of 1618–1619. They did not all see the issues with equal clarity. They did not all take the same positive stand. Some were very definitely opposed to the Remonstrants, but there were also those who were rather favorably inclined toward Arminius and his following. If this is understood, one can also see the obvious error of Rev. Wierenga, who cites helter-skelter out of private opinions and then chooses as a title "The Light of Dordt." This is not a case of a wrong motive, but this does show a great lack of care. Rev. Wierenga does not give us a scientific piece of work in this essay.

As a result, the brother sometimes holds before us as the light of Dordt what is actually nothing more than Arminian darkness. The brother has simply not been able to realize that all that shone upon the floor of the Synod of Dordt was not Reformed gold.

We will give a very striking example to show this.

The brother quotes in his essay from the opinion of the theologians from Bremen, and, first of all, from Matthias Martinius. He cites this opinion and agrees with it completely. There is not a word of criticism. That which he quotes is for Rev. Wierenga the pure light of Dordt. This is the quotation:

> There is a certain common love of God to people, according to which He has loved the entire fallen human race and has earnestly willed the salvation of all.
>
> This is carried out without distinction between the elect and reprobate. This certain execution of grace depends upon some general divine love, which all the most eminent and upright theologians also acknowledge and which is revealed by all the Scriptures.

We say again that the brother quotes this with approval. He is completely of one spirit with the Bremers and, first of all, with Matthias Martinius. That is painful to us. Rev. Wierenga is, after all, a minister in one of our Reformed churches. It may surely be expected that his Reformed antennae are somewhat sensitive. He is certainly also responsible as a Reformed minister to give guidance in doctrine. And yet his antennae were in this instance so insensitive that he did not even notice that the quotation was simply Arminian. The brother should have felt this, even if the sources from which he could have come to know these Bremers better had not been available. It is painful for us that the brother did not feel this. When one has become so insensitive to that which is the very heart of our Reformed confessions, what, we ask, is to be expected of our churches!

But despite the fact that his Reformed antennae should have put him on his guard, he still could have known the character of these Bremers whom he regards and cites as light-bearers of Dordt, and he could have learned how far they knew and loved Reformed principles. Rev. Wagenaar in his *Van Strijd en Overwinning*[4] describes them as follows:

---

4. Wagenaar, *Van Strijd en Overwinning*, 133, 134.

What a contrast: the Genevans and the Bremers! Those, fiery Calvinists; these, almost Arminians...

We learn to know Professor Martinius' opinion when he gives his written advice on Article 3. We can then understand that he, although finally swept along with the synod, thought he saw here at Dordt *quaedam divina, quaedam humana, et quaedam diabolos* [something divine, something human, and something devilish].

Everyone knows Martinius as a scholar, but a powerful thinker he was not. His standard for judging doctrinal views is mere edification. In his dogmatics he places a *Christus pro omnibus* [Christ for all] on the foreground. The heavy cares of life and the warning written by Willem Lodewijk[5] seem to have tamed him at Dordt.

Martinius visited Arminius in 1609 at his sick bed, and after his death Martinius wrote to Vorstius,[6] "He [Arminius] was in truth a God-fearing scholar, capable of composing theological questions, mighty in the Scriptures, very careful, and a man with an acute mind when it came to applying philosophical and technical terms to theology. I have not yet been able to detect whether and in how far he erred from the truth. God only knows the truth of that."

Rev. Wierenga declares himself to be of one spirit with that man. He belonged with the almost-Arminians. He counted Arminius and even Vorstius among his friends. He could not see that Arminius had erred, that Arminius proceeded in his dogmatics from a purely Remonstrant principle, a "Christ for all." He saw something human and something devilish in the Synod of Dordt and was finally only drawn along by the pull of the synod. The brother quoted the opinions of this scholar—and all under the title "The Light of Dordt"!

---

5. Willem Lodewijk, the Count of Nassau and governor of Friesland, was a member of the Dutch royalty at the time of the Synod of Dordt.

6. Conradus Vorstius was a German theologian who received the appointment to occupy the chair of theology at the University of Leiden at the death of Arminius. His appointment was revoked when the orthodox leaders in the Netherlands objected strenuously on the grounds that he was Arminian and Socinian.

Where will things end when our Reformed ministers give such leadership?

Shabby from the viewpoint of scientific investigation.

Questionable from the aspect of Reformed sensitivity!

It is enough to make one discouraged.

A second error that Rev. Wierenga makes in his essay, and that is more difficult to explain than the first, is that he quotes very imperfectly and partially. Especially because of his method, the brother should have quoted more fully.

Instead of quoting the confessions, he lets the Reformed fathers speak personally and separately.

But as far as the main content is concerned, it would have been more reasonable had Wierenga put in its proper light what he permits them to express so fully. However, the brother does not do this. What he does boils down to this: he quotes a few isolated sections that appeared to him to favor his view and to be against our view. Thus, the reader does not get to see things in the correct light.

That is the way Rev. Wierenga quotes, for example, from the opinions of the theologians of the Palatinate:

> We both acknowledge and confess with one mouth one general incli-nation of the love of God, whereby He loves all His creatures, but especially the human race. Also, after the fall, the heavenly Father mercifully spreads the same love upon man, giving us life, breath and all things (Acts 17:25), causing His sun to shine on the evil and the good and sending rain to the just and on the unjust (Matt. 5:45). Even in man's continual sinning, God bears the sinners with great patience, that He may at last break wickedness with goodness (Rom. 2:4). And when He punishes and destroys the stiff-necked and unconvertible, He does not have pleasure in the destruction of the creature, but rather in the execution of His just judgment (Is. 1:24).

Rev. Wierenga continues to quote:

> For He still preserves all in His common mercy, as in Psalm 36:6, but He preserves believers by a special goodness and grace in Christ, which

was prepared for them before the foundation of the earth (2 Tim. 1:19).

That is as far as Rev. Wierenga quotes from the theologians of the Palatinate.

It must be remarked that the above-mentioned citations do not deal with the light of nature, but simply with the gifts of natural life which God gives to all men. Yet the subject of Rev. Wierenga is "The Light of Nature in the Light of Dordt." Now it seems strange that Rev. Wierenga does not quote the theologians of the Palatinate on the subject of this light of nature. Did the brother overlook that? Or was it less to his liking? If the first, we are dealing with a lack of thorough and basic research. If the second, we confront a deliberate one-sidedness, something we do not wish to ascribe to the brother. In any case, there is certainly a lack of basic research.

The theologians of the Palatinate did present their opinion in regard to this "natural light." Of that they said the following:

> Desiring to adorn nature with the title or the drapery of grace is a Pelagian error. For the Pelagians, in order that they would not appear to deny grace, gave the name of grace to nature. Yes, they changed grace in nature; but Scripture regards no natural powers, such as reason, will, free will, as worthy of having this title.[7]

This is plain language, especially when we read this expression in its proper context. It is made over against the proposition of the Remonstrants, who said, "The first grace of God is found in the light of nature or in the remnants of the image of God." Now we are fully aware that the Remonstrants built this "first grace" as a bridge to saving grace. Yet it cannot be denied that the theologians of the Palatinate repudiated the entire idea that the light of nature can be labeled "grace." According to their opinion, Scripture never does this. And they called this a Pelagian error. If Rev. Wierenga wishes to call the opinion of the delegates of Dordt "The Light of Dordt," he could have found here the light of Dordt as it

---

7. *Acta of Handelingen der Nationale Synode*, 480.

shines directly upon the light of nature. Naturally, such a citation would prove the brother wrong, or at least have shown that among the Reformed fathers there were those who had a different view of the light of nature than the common grace theory he presents to us. It is a fact that, according to the idea of common grace, the light of nature is indeed ascribed to the work of God's grace in the heart of the depraved sinner, whereby he is somewhat improved. Man would be dead in trespasses and sins, incapable of any good and inclined to all evil, if God had not intervened with His common grace. Well then, we call every effort to explain the remnants of the image of God in the light of common grace a Pelagian error, even as the theologians of the Palatinate did.

In the meantime, everyone will see that a quotation as given above confirms what we said in our booklet "Niet Doopersch maar Gereformeerd." There we expressed as our opinion that the fathers deliberately left out of the Canons and the Confession the term *common grace* and spoke rather of *remnants of natural light*. The Remonstrants spoke of these remnants and this light of nature as *grace*. Therefore, the fathers avoided the term in drawing up their Canons. Their judgment was, "To decorate nature with a drapery or title of grace is a Pelagian error."

We recognize the same weakness in what the brother cites from "The Judgment of the Brethren of North Holland." His citation follows.

> Even though it is true that after the fall there are a few small embers or sparks whereby man can acknowledge and do some civil good or some good as far as morals is concerned; likewise, that man can acknowledge that there is a God and that men should love and honor Him; nevertheless, in the unregenerate man there is no principle left to know or to do any spiritual good.

Thus far Rev. Wierenga. We have no criticism of the quotation above. It is, however, not impossible that Rev. Wierenga would give an explanation of "civil good, or some good as far as morals are concerned" that would not appeal to us and would not be in harmony with our confessions and with the view of our Reformed fathers. If only we both establish that this civil good always remains sin in the sight of God, we can subscribe to the statement as cited above. But that is exactly what the common grace theory does not do. It regards this civil good as the fruit of a work of grace in the heart whereby wickedness is restrained and is somewhat removed. That the brethren of North Holland did not want or intend that becomes evident when we place the above-mentioned citation in its proper light. That we can do only if we place it in contrast to the proposition of the Remonstrants. The following quotation gives us the Remonstrant view:

> In regard to the following, they [the Remonstrants] say that such wickedness as they acknowledge is improved and somewhat removed by a certain common grace in all and every person. Therefore, they write that God calls all men with one and the same calling unto salvation. He announces to every one sufficiently and powerfully the means that are necessary unto conversion. He gives them the ability properly to employ the announced means. By the proper use of these means, they may obtain more grace, and may even receive the preaching of the gospel.
>
> Uitenboogaert, in his response, says that a certain sufficient grace is given to each individual who has received the use of reason. It is a principle by which the course of human depravity is greatly restrained, and by which the individual, if he uses it properly, does not stand in his own way and can obtain more grace."[8]

These are the views of the Remonstrants. Over against this we read, "The brethren of North Holland consider these views to be unorthodox, and declare over against this the truth to be: 'even though there remain in man after the fall some small embers and sparks...,'"[9] etc., as we said earlier.

---

8. Ibid, 788, 789.
9. Ibid., 789.

One must not misunderstand our intention. We understand with absolute clarity that at the Synod of Dordt the issue was not common grace as it is being discussed among us—at least not formally. The issue there was more particularly whether the small embers and remnants were sufficient to lead one to saving grace. That is evident. But that does not detract from the fact that in this judgment of the brethren of North Holland, Rev. Wierenga could have found considerable "light of Dordt" concerning the matter of natural light, if only he had quoted it in the right connection.

What is that right connection? The Remonstrants stated:[10]

1. There is a certain common grace of God, working as a principle in the wicked individual, whereby the course of human depravity is greatly restrained, and evil somewhat taken away and improved.

(Compare this proposition with Kuyper's presentation: "The unconverted can experience the influence of common grace even in his inclinations, in his consciousness, and in his will.")[11]

2. There is a willingness of God to save all, wherefore He also powerfully offers to all men the means unto salvation and gives the ability to use the means properly.

(Note: The Remonstrants are speaking of all men, whether under the gospel or outside the preaching of it.)

3. There is the possibility of obtaining more grace by the proper use of the means.

---

10. The authors did not supply page numbers in the *Acta of Handelingen der National Synode* for the following three points made by the Remonstrants. These may be a summation of the Synod regarding the Remonstrant position.

11. Kuyper, *DGG*, vol. 2, 306.

The brethren of North Holland oppose points two and three in their answer. They do not say, "Although there does exist such a general operation of God's grace whereby He greatly restrains wickedness in its course, which we accept, we deny that the individual can thereby attain to salvation." Not at all. They simply declare the entire proposition of the Remonstrants to be unorthodox, and instead of that general operation of God's grace which restrains and arrests wickedness, they speak just of embers and sparks that still remain. You see, all this would have changed considerably the impression that Rev. Wierenga intended to make in his essay, and only in that way could the brother have done justice to his subject: "The Light of Nature in the Light of Dordt."

The brother could even have gained some insight into the questions of what the fathers actually understood by civil and natural good. It is true that you do not find much clear light on this problem in the *Acta of Handelingen der Nationale Synode*. Our fathers did not directly face how this *good as far as morals are concerned* may be called good. Yet in this one phrase *good as far as morals are concerned*, we may see how carefully they tried to express themselves. But the problem they never subjected to sharp inquiry. It is probable that this can be ascribed partially to the fact that they were not dealing directly with natural good as such, but rather with its connection to grace. However that may be, Rev. Wierenga could have found something and should have quoted that in his essay if he wished to do justice to his subject.

The brother also cites the theologians from Hesse as follows:

> As far as the will is concerned, man in the state of depravity is so bad and corrupt that, although he can desire the good things of this life, and can will and do the works that are all sound and good in the civil sphere, and also can show an external obedience . . .

This is as far as Rev. Wierenga's citation goes.

Had the brother continued to read a bit more, he would also have been able to find what we have previously stated, for on

that very page the theologians of Hesse express themselves as follows:

> Therefore, all that man in the state of sin, before the grace of regen-
> eration, either thinks with his mind or chooses with his will or desires
> with his heart, even though it is good as far as the essence of the deed
> is concerned, is nevertheless so contaminated with sin that if one
> would compare it with the rule of the divine law, it is indeed more sin
> than good and of no such value that it could be said of it that it pleased
> God: Gen. 6:5 and 8:21, "All the imagination..."; Matt. 7:18: "A cor-
> rupt tree cannot bring forth good fruit"; Rom. 14:23: "Whatsoever is
> not of faith is sin"; and Heb. 11:6: "Without faith it is impossible to
> please God."[12]

In any case, this much is evident: the Reformed fathers called
civil good *sin* in the sight of God. The natural man never brings
forth any good by which he is able to please God. The meaning is
clear in the above citation, especially from the quotations from
Scripture. The imaginations of man's heart always remain evil.
Apart from regeneration, he continues to be a corrupt tree which
always brings forth corrupt fruit. Without faith, man never does
anything but sin, and it is impossible for him to please God. All
this can also be said of the civil good that he does. It, too, is corrupt fruit before God, not pleasing to Him. It is only the evil imaginations of his heart.

Rev. Wierenga does not give us a positive explanation as to
what this natural and civil good actually is. We would explain it
as follows. Man has natural light. The work of the law is written
in his heart. He does see that God is and that He must be served
and praised. However, he does not do that. His thoughts turn
against God and are at enmity with God. Although he knows
God, he refuses to honor and fear Him as God. Thus he turns himself in enmity against God. He does not do this merely in his personal life, but also in the life he lives as a part of the organism of

---

12. *Acta of Handelingen der Nationale Synode,* 486.

mankind. He does this in his family, in the state, and in the community. He does this in science and in art, in business and industry. Does this imply that he turns against his fellow man and murders, steals, and plunders at every turn? As such, not. God can lead sin into that direction and, according to Romans 1, He sometimes does that. Then the sinner is surrendered to all debauchery and evil. But it should be understood that this is not always the result of sin. Nor is this the intent of the devil. The devil does not wish to destroy all relationships in society or state, for then he would overthrow his own kingdom. That is certainly not his purpose. He wants to maintain life and cause it to develop fully in its mutual relationships, but apart from and against God. What does happen, then? With natural light sinful man sees the advantages of the second table of the law. He certainly sees that for a well-arranged life, it is better—better for himself and his relationships to others—not to steal, murder, live in debauchery, and so forth.

If he had no natural light, he could not acknowledge or do this. Now he can. The good elements that he sees in God's ordinances, for his own advantage and that of others, he applies to his life in connection with the life of his fellow man. But he always does this in such a way that his personal and communal life is separated from and opposed to God. He has no use for God. He hates God. He loves himself and mankind as they live apart from God with a love that is at enmity with God. He really says, "That which I would never want to do for God, I do for my own sake in connection with my community." And that is pure humanism.

Many examples could be cited to prove this; we will give only one. An employer has twenty-five employees in his shop. He cares nothing about God and His commandments. As far as God's law is concerned, the employer would allow his employees to work seven days a week. But someone tells him that this is not to the advantage of his business. In six days he will obtain as much work from his employees as if they worked seven, and for less wages. With that in mind, he gives his employees Sunday off, and in effect he says to God, "That which I would never do for Thee, I do for myself."

He does this not only in his own personal interest, but also for the life of the community in general. In a society of murdering and stealing, a man is not safe for a single moment; he cannot survive. A world at war works his ruin. Suffering, sickness, and temporal death, also drunkenness and debauchery, work against him. He realizes this very well. Therefore, he must counteract all these things for the welfare of the community. Man, also sinful man, wants to live in fellowship with others, wants to develop that life to its highest possible manifestation and development. He wants these things because of his covenant relationship with the ruler of the world, the prince of darkness. Therefore, he is always against God. There is no restraint of sin, but a developing of all life in enmity against God. Man is capable of this by his natural light and by means of all the gifts and talents that God gives to each one.

Quite obviously, natural light never remains uncorrupted. Despite original righteousness, which man completely lost, this natural light is also corrupted. Man cannot use it properly, not even in civil affairs. Moreover, the wrath of God is revealed from heaven against all ungodliness and unrighteousness of men as they suppress the truth in unrighteousness. It is through the influence of the wrath of God that the development of sin runs in entirely different channels from those man has imagined in his humanistic idealism. No matter to what extent man dreams of world peace, outside of and against God, wars repeat themselves, to the total despair of men. Also debauchery and drunkenness continue, as well as murder. But this does not detract from the fact that by his natural light, man is able to see the advantage of the ordinances of God's law and is also able to apply them to communal life in the state and society; thus he can practice civil righteousness, a righteousness of man against man, of nation in relation to nation.

This is the attractive delusion that arises from an appealing humanism and in principle draws many of God's people off the right track. It also explains how our fathers, who never developed this idea but did realize some of it, speak in one breath of totally depraved man *and* civil good, the good that applies to morals and of man who is totally depraved. He is as a dead tree that never produces good fruit but still does that civil good in the evil imaginations of his heart.

If Rev. Wierenga desires to give another interpretation of this civil and moral good, that is up to him. Yet he must remain within the confines of the plain teaching of our confessions, which without reservation declare that man is totally depraved, incapable of any good, and inclined to all evil. Man is like that—not until common grace improves or restrains him—but as he actually lives in the world in all his existence and in all relationships except he be born again by the Spirit of God. Kuyper's solution to this problem conflicts with Scripture and the confessions.

A failure to see this conflict is the danger of our time. This is the error of men like Rev. J. Groen, Rev. Q. Breen, Rev. E. J. Tuuk, Dr. Kuizenga, Prof. H. Van Andel,[13] and others. Our view of the brethren is not that they deliberately want to lead the church of the Lord into the world, but since they do not clearly see and properly understand the antithesis—the spiritual contrast between God's people and the world—they can come to no other conclusion than this: On the common ground of common grace, light and darkness, Christ and Belial, go hand in hand. In this way humanism is regarded as Christianity, and movements like prohibition, the brotherhood of all mankind, world peace, woman suffrage, the rejuvenation of society, and the like are all judged to be a striving for the kingdom of God.

With that misunderstanding Rev. Q. Breen wrote:

> It is said on good authority that the death of Bavinck was hastened by overwork. And if we regard the task to which he had apparently set himself, and bear in mind his devotion to the same, we can easily un-

---

13. Rev. Johannes Groen, a minister at Eastern Avenue CRC prior to Herman Hoeksema's pastorate there, was strongly in favor of Kuyper's views. Rev. Quirinus Breen was a CRC minister and a supporter of Dr. Ralph Janssen. He resigned from the ministry when Janssen was condemned by the Synod of the CRC in 1922. Rev. Edward J. Tuuk edited the periodical *Religion and Culture* and also opposed the authors. Professor Henry J. Van Andel of Calvin College, mentioned before, was an outspoken defender of Kuyperian common grace.

derstand that he literally sacrificed his life for his work. And what was his object? Nothing less than to show how the chasm that yawns between the church and the world could be bridged. One who has never entered into this field of thought can little realize how tremendous a task that is. A great many Christian people shrink from such a thing from the sheer fear that it must result in a church made worldly. On the other hand, many men of the "world" rejoice in such attempts as made by Bavinck, because they think that the church shall now have to give up her pretensions. Both are wrong, however. The Bavincks, meanwhile, plod courageously on. They are men of faith. For they know that a church that understands not that "the earth and its fulness, the world and they that dwell therein" must perish; just as well as the world that knows not the church, is ruined. That the chasm between church and world, thus understood, is wide, almost immeasurably so, is plain. That it must be bridged is plain also, at least to greater minds. The sincere effort to do this is limited to a very few. And generally they are misunderstood. Usually they stand alone. They come to their own, but their own receive them not.[14]

Certainly, we feel that the brother did not give account to himself of what he wrote. If he had to define his terms and give a clear presentation of church and world with that immeasurable gap between them, he certainly would not repeat what he had written. But the sad fact remains that one of our ministers openly defines the great task of the church as the joining of the church and world, the bridging of the gulf that separates both! But would you ever find such a view defended in Scripture?

It should be understood, therefore, that people are not speaking and writing in the spirit of the Reformed fathers of Dordt when they boast of this natural light, even though such boasting is common in our day. With all the seriousness we can muster, we wish to warn the churches of this tendency. This leads—this must lead—to world conformity. Our Reformed fathers most certainly spoke of natural light. They confessed that man by natural light

---

14. No source reference for this quotation from Breen is given by the authors.

can do civil good, but always in such a way that civil good remains sin in the sight of God. All that does not proceed from faith, all that arises out of the imagination of the natural heart, is always and only evil.

This answers the main thought of Rev. Wierenga's essay. He does give a few more citations, but they add nothing. For example, what connection is there between what Rev. Wierenga quotes from the "Judgment of the Brethren of Drenthe"[15] and the issue that has risen among us? Simply none. It does not deal with common grace as the term is used among us. This should have been evident to the brother from what he quotes. In the quotation the brethren at Dordt write:

> By this common grace, carnal people who are not yet regenerated (we are speaking mainly of those who are called, whether they are reprobate or chosen) are said to be partakers of the Holy Spirit, are enlightened in their understanding, and are moved in their hearts...

Even his own quotation should have prevented the brother from giving the impression that it was related to the issue of common grace. The men of Drenthe did not speak of those outside of the church, but of those who are called: of men, for example, like those who are mentioned in Hebrews 6. But in case the quotation did not offer the brother sufficient light, he could have recognized it by the context in which the quotation appears. The paragraph from which Rev. Wierenga quotes begins as follows:

> Having focused our attention thus far on man outside of God's grace, it now remains that we deal somewhat with this grace itself, by which man is supplied with new strength. This grace is common, that is, it belongs solely to the elect.[16]

---

15. Delegates were present at the Synod of Dordt from Drenthe, a province of the Netherlands. Their opinion was also included in the *Acta of Handelingen der Nationale Synode*.

16. *Acta of Handelingen der Nationale Synode*. The authors did not provide the page number.

Thus the brethren of Drenthe distinguished saving grace as common and as particular. They were not dealing with the light of nature when they spoke of common grace, but with the operations of grace within the sphere of God's covenant and church in the world, that is, a grace by which some reprobates are also partakers of the Holy Spirit. Naturally, this too could be criticized. But at present this is beyond our scope. It is apparent that Rev. Wierenga went by the sound of the word and failed to make a critical distinction.

We could also criticize a few other citations in the same manner, but this is enough. The foregoing examples are sufficient. In general it may be said that the view of common grace as offered by Dr. A. Kuyper was far from the minds of our fathers at Dordt.

Nor does Rev. Wierenga's essay change this in the least. He gathered much in his reading. He aroused the expectation of many people with his striking title. When regarded superficially, his essay does make an impression upon those who are not in a position to look up the articles quoted and to place them in their context and historical framework. But when viewed carefully, it becomes evident that he did poor work. Lines are not drawn; criticism is not applied. Arminian darkness is held before us as the light of Dordt. When all is said and done, nothing is left of the "Light of Nature in the Light of Dordt."

Answer to Dr. V. Hepp

As is known, Dr. V. Hepp, who was appointed in the place of Bavinck as professor at the Free University in Amsterdam, the Netherlands, has written a long series of articles in *De Reformatie* [The Reformation], which later appeared in a booklet under the title "Het Misverstand in zake de Leer der Algemeene Genade" [Misunderstanding in Regard to the Doctrine of Common Grace].

Dr. Hepp is not a stranger to us. The earliest that we learned to know him was through his *Testimonium Spiritus Sancti* [The Testi-

mony of the Holy Spirit], and we are still eagerly awaiting the publication of the second volume. Later we obtained from his hand
De Antichrist [The Antichrist].[17] We also learned to know him
from his articles in *De Reformatie,* a periodical which we read at
first with great interest, but which later became too irenic to suit
us. We also read with interest the biography of Dr. Bavinck that
came to us from Dr. Hepp. We had nothing but the highest regard
for Dr. Hepp and could agree quite well with his trend of thought,
at least at first. This gives us the more reason to write that we mar-
veled at the poor way a professor like Dr. Hepp involved himself
in our differences and acquitted himself of his task.

One should not misunderstand us. We are not speaking of the
general tenor of the brother's writing. That remains brotherly and
beyond all criticism. We can expect that of him. Nor do we blame
him for involving himself in our dispute. We certainly do not deny
that the esteemed writer has that right, although we do question
the wisdom of it. It would have been wiser, to our minds, if the
brother on the other side of the ocean had kept from involving
himself for the present. In the first place, he was informed concerning us, as we learned from a dependable source, by someone
who certainly was not capable of forming an opinion or of fur-
nishing information concerning our views. But even more, the
brother himself realized, and showed in a very clear way in his
booklet, that it is extremely difficult for those in our fatherland to
work themselves into our American ecclesiastical situations and
to pass judgment on them. Even when such a great man as
Dr. Kuyper paid us a visit and saw our affairs with his own eyes, his
opinion in regard to America meant so little that we had to smile
when we read it. One need but consider *Varia Americana.*[18] How

---

17. The authors mention two books by Hepp. The former was published in
1914, the latter in a second revised edition in 1920, both in Kampen by J. H.
Kok.

18. *Varia Americana* (Amsterdam: Höveker & Wormser, [1899]) is a book in
which Kuyper describes a visit he paid to America.

much more this applies when one has never become acquainted at close hand with our life and our circumstances. Regardless of the wisdom of Dr. Hepp's writing, we do not deny him the right to do so. When the brother wrote, as might be expected, we also followed him with interest.

However, what amazed us was the manner in which Dr. Hepp involved himself in our dispute. His articles were written only through the inducement of the book of Dr. Van Baalen. That was not our fault. We would surely have given our answer to Dr. Hepp, to whom the pamphlet of Dr. Van Baalen was sent. Then the esteemed writer could have thought through and judged the issue from both sides. That we did not do this was simply because Dr. Hepp was already writing before our booklet was published. That caused us to wonder about Dr. Hepp. We considered that unworthy of him. It was extremely reckless. It was one-sided work. We place here our protest against it.

The content of the booklet also gives abundant evidence of all this. Ignorance concerning us and our life here quickly led Dr. Hepp to draw the conclusion that we must be regarded as holding a "misunderstanding."

We are informed by Dr. Hepp that Rev. Van Baalen had studied in the Netherlands and that he was, therefore, thoroughly acquainted with the Netherlands and with Reformed theology as developed there. He knew the mind of the spirits and was well qualified to judge the issues regarding the Reformed truth.

But, says Dr. Hepp, it is different with us. We do not accept so readily the ideas of Kuyper and Bavinck. We are a little behind the times, and so Van Baalen is urged to have a bit of patience with us; others are not as far advanced as Van Baalen, nor must he expect that. Therefore, Van Baalen must not immediately regard us as heretical. Dr. Hepp cannot believe that at heart we are such great heretics; there must still be Reformed blood in our veins. Therefore, Dr. Hepp advises Rev. Van Baalen, "Do not be too hasty! Have a bit of patience." If Rev. Van Baalen exercises a bit of patience and instructs us more charitably, Dr. Hepp hopes that all will turn out well with us.[19]

Dr. Hepp should not take offense if we openly admit that when we read all this, we could not suppress a smile. He himself would not have been able to keep a straight face if he had been in our position.

Naturally, Dr. Hepp does not know us. He is not acquainted with the fact that we were not reared on the American prairie, but in the Netherlands. No, we did not study in the Netherlands, but as young men we did share in the religious life of the Netherlands according to our capacity and circumstances. We did join a society and the League of Societies. And we will freely admit that when we were in the Netherlands, and still for some time after we had left our fatherland, we were strongly Kuyper-minded. We learned about the life of the Netherlands firsthand, not from the higher class but the lower; not from school but from experience. We had the pleasure of hearing men like Kuyper and Bavinck. No, Dr. Hepp did not know that. He could *not* know that. We do not take offense that he did not know. But that does not in the least change the fact that Dr. Hepp writes about and judges things that he does not and could not know. And when this product of his pen comes under our eyes, the brother should not take offense that when we read it, we have an urge to scoff.

But there is something that Dr. Hepp *could* have known; at least he could have guessed it. It was very likely that we here in America could read the leading papers and periodicals appearing in the Reformed ecclesiastical world and could also obtain the works of most, if not all, of the prominent theologians of the Netherlands.

---

19. The authors are reporting on the views of V. [Valentine] Hepp in "Het Misverstand in Zake de Leer der Algemeene Genade" (A Misunderstanding of the Doctrine of Common Grace) (Grand Rapids, Mich.: Eerdmans-Sevensma Co., [1923]), page 11 of a 32-page pamphlet that reproduces Hepp's articles as they appeared in *De Reformatie*.

This is true even more so regarding the works of Calvin. And yet
the esteemed brother seems to have the idea that this is not the
case. According to him, that explains our backwardness and our
inability to assimilate readily the thoughts of Kuyper and Bavinck.
As a result, the brother writes:

> The doctrine of common grace belongs to the fundamentals of Cal-
> vinism. One cannot systematically reject this doctrine and remain a
> Calvinist. There is an inseparable connection between the two. As
> soon as our brethren on the other side of the ocean understand this,
> they will undoubtedly withdraw their denial. But to understand this,
> it is necessary to study Calvin's works, particularly his *Institutes*.[20]

This is based upon the idea that to those on this side of the
ocean, at least among us emigrants from the Netherlands, Calvin
is not known or is barely known. The brother could have known
better. We dare to say without hesitation that we are just as thoroughly acquainted with the world of thought of Kuyper and
Bavinck as, for example, Rev. Van Baalen is, who never studied
under either one of these men, if we are correctly informed. And
if Rev. Van Baalen received the doctrine of common grace from
Dr. [Gerhardus] Vos of Princeton, as we suspect, then Van Baalen
never even had Dr. Kuyper's *De Gemeene Gratie* in his possession.
Then we are many years ahead of him, not only in possessing, but
also in studying that work. Truly, it is a "misunderstanding" on the
part of Dr. Hepp, even in the double sense of that word.

However that may be, the booklet of Dr. Hepp has appeared,
and the brother will expect an answer. On this side of the ocean,
we are not accustomed to making someone who throws the ball
wait very long for its return. We will also supply an answer in a
most brotherly manner.

This is made easier for us because we were always more or less
of one mind with Dr. Hepp, had learned to esteem him highly, and

---

20. Ibid., 15.

are indeed sorry that at a time like this, he should have allowed himself to be persuaded to write this booklet. We shall follow the brother step-by-step.

First if all, we consider his chapter dealing with the term *common grace*.[21] Briefly summarized, it comes down to this: Dr. Hepp grants that the term *grace* is actually not correct in this context. Dr. Kuyper also felt this, which was the reason why he spoke of common "favor" (*gratie*).[22] He did this to emphasize the essential difference between particular and special grace.[23] *Long-suffering* would probably be a better term, according to Dr. Hepp. *Forbearance* would be less fitting, because this term is usually employed in connection with God's people:

> He [Kuyper] could also have written, instead of "common favor," the long-suffering of God. That long-suffering, according to Scripture, includes also "the vessels of wrath," those who are not elect. Thus we read, for example, in Romans 9:22: "What if God, willing to shew his wrath, and to make his power known, endured with much longsuffering the vessels of wrath fitted to destruction." "Forbearance" is less fitting, because in Scripture, when it refers to God's relationship to man, it is used with believers. But long-suffering has something in its favor.[24]

Then the brother continues by saying that in spite of these objections, the use of the term *favor* or *grace* is better, and should be kept.

Here Dr. Hepp ascribes the origin of the misunderstanding to

---

21. The chapter is entitled "De Oorsprong van het Misverstand" (The Origin of the Misunderstanding), and it is found on pages 12–14 of Ibid.

22. The reader will recall that Kuyper used the term *gratie* in distinction from *genade*, though both terms mean "grace."

23. The meaning of the authors is not clear. This is a literal translation of the Dutch, but it seems as if the authors *meant* to say, "He did this to emphasize the essential difference between particular and *common* grace."

24. Hepp, "Het Misverstand," 13.

the use of a word. Hepp thinks that we do not understand the use of the word *favor* or *grace* in the term *common favor* (*gratie*), which accounts for our objection.

We sincerely hope that when our book makes its appearance, this idea is completely eliminated. We are not concerned about a word; our battle is not over words. What we oppose is a life-view such as the one Dr. Kuyper offers to us in his *De Gemeene Gratie*. That view itself is not correct; it is not Reformed. This is true not only in the sense that it departs from what is emphatically expressed in our confessions concerning the sinner, namely, that he is dead in trespasses and sins, but it also departs from the fundamental line of the historic Reformed faith. Even though it is true that *common grace* was spoken of in a loose sense of the word, the view of Dr. Kuyper departs from the historical line. That is our position. We also maintain that position in this small work.

Moreover, Dr. Hepp's distinction between *long-suffering* and *forbearance* is not according to Scripture. It could never be maintained on exegetical grounds. *Forbearance* would then be employed in Scripture to signify God's attitude over against His people; *long-suffering* would refer to a more general relationship or attitude, also toward the reprobate. This is not the way in which Scripture uses these terms. The text which the professor cites from Romans 9 already clearly proves this. There we have an instance in which both words are employed with application to the same objects. The text says, "endured with much longsuffering." It is true that in the Greek, another word is used for *endured* than, for example, in Romans 3:25, but this does not change the concept. The same is true of Romans 2:4: "Or despisest thou the riches of his goodness and forbearance and longsuffering; not knowing that the goodness of God leadeth thee to repentance?" Here again we have both words in one and the same sentence. Hepp's distinction—that the words refer to different objects, and that their meaning must be determined by their objects—does not work out.

Still, despite all this, even though Dr. Hepp wished to make such a distinction from the viewpoint of the objects, the words should be applied in exactly the opposite way from the way the writer applies them. *Long-suffering* would be the word that is used with respect to God's people, while, though in an entirely different sense than for God's people, the term *forbearance* is applied to the wicked. That is how it is, for example, in Luke 18:7: "And shall not God avenge his own elect, which cry day and night unto him, though he bear long with them?" These words are spoken by the Savior in connection with the parable of the unjust judge. The meaning is clear. The parable deals with justice. The judge in the parable, in his attitude toward the widow, is a figure of God. The parable describes His people's view of God's attitude toward them in the world. The judge delayed justice. He did not want to offer the widow any justice. Only after a long delay, and after she had caused the judge's head to spin with her continual demand for justice, did she receive a verdict.

God is not like that judge; the very opposite is true. Indeed, "I tell you that he will avenge them speedily." He causes His justice to come as fast as possible. It cannot be faster. But in the meantime, God's people are being persecuted in the world. They sigh, they plead, they call day and night for justice. This lasts for years and centuries; therefore, the hour will come when it will seem to the people of God as if God delays justice. That is not the case, but because of the long period of time and the hard and bitter oppression, it will leave this impression upon God's people. Therefore, the Savior says, "though he bear long with them." God shows Himself to be long-suffering towards the people of His choice, who suffer oppression in the world and who must wait to the very end for justice.

One finds the same idea in 2 Peter 3:9: "The Lord is not slack concerning his promise, as some men count slackness; but is long-suffering to us-ward, not willing that any should perish, but that all should come to repentance." Also here the reference is to the church of the Lord as it is oppressed in the world, and as it seeks justice and complete deliverance. However, God waits until everything is ready. As a farmer waits for the ripening of the corn in the ear and is long-suffering toward the grain in the field, God is long-suffering toward His people. Some regard this as slackness, says Peter. But this is by no means slackness. It is simply a waiting until the right moment has come, until all have come to repentance and the world is ripe for judgment. The harvest will come only when the grain is fully ripe in the field of the world. But now God's people suffer injustice in the world. From that aspect, one would expect God to make an end of it at once, but God is long-suffering in regard to His people. It is the same idea as in the parable of the widow and the unjust judge. The same idea is in 2 Peter 3:15: "And account that the longsuffering of our Lord is salvation."

As is always the case in Scripture, so also here, God's people must know and reveal the life of God. They also must be long-suffering. In James 5:7, 8 we find this same thought, even using the same example that we used of the farmer and his corn: "Be patient therefore, brethren, unto the coming of the Lord. Behold, the husbandman waiteth for the precious fruit of the earth, and hath long patience for it, until he receive the early and latter rain. Be ye also patient; stablish your hearts: for the coming of the Lord draweth nigh." Hebrews 6:12 reads, "That ye be not slothful, but followers of them who through faith and patience inherit the promises."

In one word, you have the same idea throughout. God waits until everything is ripe, even as the farmer waits for the ripening of the corn in the ear. In connection with the oppression of His people in the world, this is long-suffering. And when His people sigh that God is slow in fulfilling His promises, then the Word of God assures us that this is not true. Everything is completely normal. Even as the waiting for the ripening of the grain may not be considered slackness on the part of the farmer, so also God's long-suffering cannot be considered slackness. Things are developing as fast as they can; the end comes as soon as possible.

The speedy return of the Lord already conflicts with the idea of common grace, especially the idea that God restrains the development of all things. He does not restrain. He prevents no development, not in regard to His people, or in regard to the evil world.

He comes speedily and will speedily do justice, for when He comes, His reward is with Him! Dr. Hepp's exegesis of the long-suffering of God can never be maintained.

When you consider that same waiting of God for the ripening of all things from the aspect of sin, Scripture calls it *patience*. Long-suffering is the completely normal waiting in connection with oppression and the final justification of God's people. But patience, as the word already plainly shows, refers not so much to oppression but to sin, yet not in the sense that you can speak in one breath of a general patience in regard to both the elect and the reprobate without distinction. No, the following is the situation:

1. God proves Himself patient with respect to the sin of His people in connection with their reconciliation in Christ Jesus and the final perfection of the believers. At least that is how we would interpret Romans 3:25. There we read, "Whom God hath set forth to be a propitiation through faith in his blood, to declare his righteousness for the remission of sins that are past, through the forbearance of God." It is impossible, as we see it, to give an accurate, not to speak of a Reformed, interpretation of this text on the basis of a *general* patience. The meaning is clear. In the Old Testament the sins of all the saints were forgiven. At the time, it seemed like an unrighteousness of God, for reconciliation in the blood of Christ was not yet a historical reality. Therefore, forgiveness of sins in the old dispensation was designated with a word that in the original actually means "passing by." In the old dispensation, from a historical point of view, God passed by the sins of His people. He did forgive them, but before reconciliation was realized in the blood of Christ, it had the character of passing by. How could God do that? Only with a view to the reconciliation that He had eternally conceived of by Himself through the blood of Christ Jesus. Therefore, Golgotha justified this patience in regard to sin in the old dispensation, thus passing by and forgiving. It was all based on the blood of reconciliation which was to come.

2. But there is also mention of patience with respect to the ves-

sels of wrath, and that is always with a view to the coming final judgment. Even as God can be patient in regard to the sins of His people, looking ahead to their justification through Christ Jesus, so He can also be patient in connection with the sins of the godless with a view to the coming judgment. It is not as if God is slack. It is the same as with long-suffering. The two are indeed also inseparably related. Long-suffering lasts as long as the patience. But from a historical point of view, the end waits, and God is both long-suffering and patient until everything is fulfilled. In that light we can also understand the use of both words in Romans 9:22. God bears the vessels of wrath with much long-suffering. In the example that the apostle uses in the immediate context, both elements are included. Pharaoh oppresses the people of the Lord so that they cry to Jehovah. But God bears all with great patience until exactly the right time comes to deliver His people. Thus, according to Scripture, God's people are always oppressed by the vessels of wrath, and God is patient, with long-suffering.

The manner in which Dr. Hepp continues to defend the use of the word *favor* or *grace* simply cannot be maintained. The professor writes:

> Although particular and common grace differ in principle, they still have something in common.
> The similarity is this, that both words emphasize how completely man lacks the right to both these gifts.
> In both cases, grace forms a contrast with justice.[25]

It is obvious, however, that one cannot speak in that manner. In the first place, this idea is not included in the word *grace*. Grace, the good favor of God, does become more sharply and gloriously manifested in the work of salvation, but as such that idea is not included in the word.

---

25. Ibid.

Despite that, it is not correct to say that God's people have no right to the grace of God. This is true of the wicked, and we continue to wait for it to be explained to us how the justice of God can be harmonized with the granting of grace to those who, not only in themselves, but also in the most absolute sense, are guilty before God.

Kuyper asserts that the covenant with Noah is a covenant of common grace. And in the same connection, Kuyper says that the drawing up of a covenant is an act of friendship. How does one harmonize the justice of God with God's covenant? And how is it that God establishes a bond of friendship between Himself and those for whom there is no juridical basis for that friendship, either in time or in eternity? One cannot ignore this question, nor has it ever been answered; yet it touches on an important principle of our Reformed faith.

Although there is no juridical basis for grace to the wicked, there *is* such a basis for the grace that God's people receive. It is true that in themselves, apart from Christ, they have no juridical basis to plead for grace. But they are not separate from Christ, and in Christ they have the right to grace. Therefore, even though Dr. Hepp has spoken, we continue to protest against making the word *grace* common.

That the wicked receive gifts is evident—gifts related to this natural life. They even receive more than the child of God. If gifts as such were grace, this grace would still not be very common, for the wicked are fatter than the people of the Lord. But the whole idea is wrong. Grace is not in things, but purely in the good favor of God. Even as suffering and grief and adversity as such are not wrath and curse, so also gold and silver, rain and sunshine, gifts and talents, are not grace as such. Grace can very well work in all things, yet it always remains particular and is granted only to His people.

We can be brief in our discussion of the chapter which the esteemed professor devotes to the concept *grace* as used by Calvin. The brother claims:

> The doctrine of common grace belongs to the foundations of Calvinism. One cannot systematically reject this doctrine and remain a Calvinist.[26]

These are strong assertions, which require strong argumentation; yet the latter is entirely lacking. What is shown in the rest of the chapter is that Calvin does speak in a fourfold sense of grace. He speaks of a *common common*, of a *particular common*, of a *common particular*, and of a *particular particular* grace. We agree with this; that is, we agree that Calvin does speak in that manner.

But does all this belong to the foundations of Calvinism? Must one who wishes to remain a Calvinist speak likewise of four kinds of grace? As far as we are concerned, we would want to make some very sharp criticism of this fourfold grace of Calvin. Nor are we aware that this view has ever been adopted as fundamental Calvinism. But if this fourfold view of grace does not belong to the foundations of Calvinism, why then is common grace, as it is presently described, taught among us? The esteemed brother fails to answer. He has merely asserted, not proved.

We do indeed have regard for the aristocracy of the spirit.[27] The commonplace, the breaking down of everything by a false democracy, still does not appeal to us, although we have lived for years in America. But Dr. Hepp must realize, in order to think into and understand our views, that we are completely delivered from all money or class aristocracy. We bow before proof, not before assertions, no matter who makes them. For the rest, it is sufficient that we refer to what we have already written on this subject in our booklet "Niet Doopersch maar Gereformeerd" [Not Anabaptist, but Reformed].

---

26. Ibid., 15.

27. The authors refer here to the class system as practiced in the Netherlands at this time. The educated were in a higher class, and the common people were expected to accept their pronouncements as views to be received without question.

Nor is it necessary, after all we have written, to consider at length the chapter on "'Grace' in the Holy Scripture."[28] We can pass by the examples that the professor offers to prove that *grace* is sometimes used in a very loose sense to refer to the relationship of man to man. No one denies this, but it has no connection with the subject. What we must know is whether the word is employed as referring to God's grace in relation to both the righteous and the wicked. For this, Dr. Hepp can actually offer only two passages, namely, Jonah 4:2 and Isaiah 26:10. That in itself is already a strange thing. Regardless of whether the passages that are offered actually do say what Dr. Hepp asserts, it is still strange that for such a fundamental doctrine, one can appeal to only two passages that mention grace by name. An Arminian can cite many more passages to prove that Scripture literally teaches a universal atonement. The use of two passages is especially strange because there are many passages that can be quoted in which the very opposite is said of what Dr. Hepp thinks he sees in Jonah 4:2 and Isaiah 26:10.

Allow us to cite and explain a few passages. In Proverbs 3:33 we read, "The curse of the LORD is in the house of the wicked: but he blesseth the habitation of the just." Here you have a contrast. On the one hand, you have the house of the wicked; on the other, the habitation of the just. Thus, this deals with temporal life; both just and wicked are living in the world. And now Scripture says in general, and without exception, that the curse of the Lord rests on the temporal life and dwells in the house of the wicked, while the blessing of the Lord remains in the habitation of the just.

The same contrast we have once more in the following verse: "Surely he scorneth the scorners: but he giveth grace unto the lowly" [Prov. 3:34]. Is not this the same as saying, "God giveth no grace to the scorner"? The contrast implies this. You have the same contrast in 1 Peter 5:5: "For God resisteth the proud, and giveth grace to the humble." Also here, there is no possibility of a misunderstanding. He gives no grace to the proud.

---

28. Hepp, "Het Misverstand," 17–19.

We could continue in that strain, quoting clear statements from Scripture that offer the exact opposite of what Hepp teaches. But where are there statements in which Scripture says that the wicked do receive grace, that the proud and the scorners are the objects of God's good favor—favor not through Christ, but to men as wicked, proud, scornful, and so forth?

Dr. Hepp says that there are two such passages. The first is Jonah 4:2. Here Jonah says, "LORD, ... I knew that thou art a gracious God." As such, that word says nothing. It does not say that God shows grace to the wicked apart from Christ, but only that God is gracious. No one would question that. In this instance the meaning of the word must be taken from Jonah's application of it to the city of Nineveh. Jonah grumbles. He is dissatisfied. He cannot understand the history of this wicked world-city. In that condition he explains the history in the words "I knew that thou art a gracious God." But now the citation also loses all its importance. The word of the grumbling Jonah cannot very well serve as proof for a common grace, even if Jonah meant it in the sense that he knew that God shows favor to all men.

We do have a stronger expression, if it is taken as it appears in Isaiah 26:10: "Let favour be shewed to the wicked, yet will he not learn righteousness: in the land of uprightness will he deal unjustly, and will not behold the majesty of the LORD." First of all, we wish to direct attention to the fact that if this text must serve as proof for the doctrine of common grace, it proves far too much. If this is common grace, then it must be viewed in the sense in which we use it. We do not wish to emphasize the fact that the prophet does not state that the wicked are shown grace, but that this is mentioned conditionally. Dr. Hepp denies that, but we maintain it. The meaning is obviously this: If the godless man is shown grace, he shall not learn righteousness. We underscore for the moment what has the emphasis in the text, namely, that the godless man learns no righteousness. The prophet does not say he is spiritually improved by it and his sinful deed is restrained. No, the text says he *deals* unjustly. He carries out the deed, even if he is shown grace. Sin is not restrained by the evidence of grace. But this is, according to Kuyper's repeated presentation, the power of common grace. Sin is restrained by common grace in the consciousness, the will, and the inclinations of the sinner, according to Kuyper. Well now, that is something quite different from Isaiah 26:10. For there the emphasis falls on the fact that the godless one does not improve, that sin is not restrained, that the godless man will continue to deal unjustly in the land of uprightness. This is not an incidental thought in the text while the prophet actually wants to emphasize that the godless are shown grace. It is just the opposite. Isaiah's main thought is exactly that the godless man does not improve, not in his heart or will or inclination, nor in his deed. He deals unjustly in the land of uprightness. If this is the proper text (according to Rev. Zwier,[29] the *only* text) in which the word *grace* appears in that sense, the common grace theory will have to be radically reviewed. For here that view is explicitly opposed.

It is not difficult to grasp the thought of the prophet. The wicked one, as usually is true in the prophets, is the wicked Israelite, the child of the covenant who forsakes the path of the covenant and loves and performs unrighteousness. He lives among God's people, the righteous, in a land of uprightness. In that land of uprightness, Jehovah shows His grace. There He blesses His people Israel. He dwells there with His ordinances. It lies in the nature of the case that the wicked one who lives among the righteous would also enjoy the gifts of God to His people. When that people prosper, he also prospers. In that sense God proves and reveals His grace also to him. Yet unless God actually gives His grace in a subjective sense, grips him in his heart and saves him, all those external evidences, revelations, proofs, and gifts of grace to God's people do not help that wicked one in the least. They do not

---

29. Rev. D. Zwier was a minister of the CRC church in Holland, Michigan, who wrote a series of articles in *De Wachter* under the title "Gods Algemeene Goedheid" in defense of common grace.

change him. He continues to deal unjustly in the land of uprightness. He does not behold the majesty of the Lord.

If you object to this by saying that God, as far as He is concerned, intends it to be different, but that it is entirely the fault of
the wicked one that he receives no grace, then you have forsaken
the position of our fathers and our Confession and have stepped
over to the view of Arminianism. Proof for the use of the word
grace, in the sense of common grace, cannot be found here.

In the following chapter,[30] the misunderstanding of Dr. Hepp
is fully revealed as a misunderstanding. He claims we are guilty of
four errors, which he himself knows are an abomination to us. At
least in regard to the most fundamental error, he writes, "Now
I know very well that our brethren regard this error as an abomination." But the esteemed brother is of the opinion that he can
and must deduce these four errors directly from our view of grace.
We do not go that far, he says; that is our inconsistency. But if we
want to remain consistent, then sooner or later we must reach the
point where we consciously and openly teach all these errors.
They are inherent in our conception of grace.

The four errors referred to are briefly these:

1. We accept a certain change in the idea of grace, a sort of
transubstantiation, for at one time we had spoken of an overflowing of grace.

2. We regard particular grace qualitatively. This follows from
the same expression: *overflow of grace*.

3. We exclude the preparation of the heart from particular
grace. We had asserted that there is no receptivity for grace in the
world.

4. Therefore, we deny the time-tried confession that grace is
irresistible and never lost.

It actually makes us shudder! We should cherish such abomi-

---

30. Hepp, "Het Misverstand," 19–22.

nations? And that, without knowing about it? We shudder when we even consider the possibility that in the future we will consciously accept all these abominations! And yet, in principle they are already hidden in us; they are implied in our view. We shudder at the thought. Everyone will agree that if our situation is that bad, it is high time that we cease teaching our people, even though it is a thousand times a misunderstanding. In fact, however, we continue to preach and to instruct a host of young people. Even though it may be that as far as we personally are concerned, these errors remain hidden in the shell, and the fourfold fruit of our root-error may never become evident, the consequence cannot be avoided in the lives of those who are taught by us.

However, it is a peculiar phenomenon that everyone who knows us will be able to say that these four errors mentioned by Dr. Hepp certainly do make us shudder, and that we put forth every effort to cause the congregation to shudder as well. In our area some accuse us of the very opposite, namely, that we are not sufficiently universalistically inclined in our preaching and teaching, and that we place too much emphasis on God's free election and reprobation and are not broad enough in the preaching of the gospel. But we have never heard anything of what Dr. Hepp writes. When this article of Dr. Hepp in *De Reformatie* reached us, we were wide-eyed and utterly amazed.

We asked ourselves, "How can that be? Could what Dr. Hepp writes actually be true? Is it actually possible that the deepest root of our view still rests in a despised Arminianism, which we so inexpressibly hate with all our conscious faith? As our only faith, we confess from the bottom of our hearts that we despise beyond words the Arminianism described by Hepp. We have never yet been able to detect even the smallest speck of that abominable error in our preaching.

But extremes do sometimes meet! Could that be the case? Or could it possibly be that Dr. Hepp's misunderstanding is entirely his?

The latter is fortunately the case. Dr. Hepp rejoices over it with us.

The occasion for this misunderstanding of Dr. Hepp is an expression which flowed a few times from my pen and from my lips. We have struggled at times to give an accurate expression to the same idea about which Dr. Kuyper wrote in three large volumes. We were not always successful, however. At that time we occasionally used the figurative expression *overflow of grace*. We were never satisfied with that expression; it was faulty. It is true that various wrong conclusions could be drawn from it.[31]

But Dr. Hepp's mistake is that he did not consider the explanation that we almost always gave to the expression. He reasons from the one expression, and from it he deduces four errors and lays them at our door, accusing *us* of them. That is not proper. Dr. Hepp has no right to do that. He knows better. That method almost always leads to a misunderstanding. Even if we had never given an explanation of that expression, it would have been dangerous to draw conclusions from one phrase, even more dangerous because the writer is aware of the horror that we have for the errors he ascribes to us. But Dr. Hepp could also have known from our writings that the expression *overflow of grace*, as he interprets it, is not what we intended by it. The result is that he does not reason from our view anymore, but from the faulty expression. We freely cast far from us not only the errors, but also the notion that these errors follow from our view.

What is the meaning of the expression *overflow of grace*?

Grace itself does not *flow over*. How could we teach that from our viewpoint and at the same time teach that the wicked receive no grace? That would lead to a *contradictio in terminis*, an absurdity. Moreover, how would that be possible unless it was presented in such a way that grace was in things as such, things earthly? That

---

31. Apparently Herman Hoeksema wrote this section, because he refers here to the fact that earlier, in his articles in *The Banner*, he had spoken of an "overflow of grace." The elect receive the grace of God in rich and overflowing measure. That overflow comes to all who live within the boundaries of the visible church. Hoeksema apologizes here for using such loose language, but insists that he did not mean by that expression what Hepp says it means.

was also exactly what we fought with all our might. No, our intention was to teach that even though the external gifts which God gives to His people in His grace come also upon the unrighteous, they come on them without grace. When the manna lies in the wilderness, all the Israelites partake; yet not one outside of spiritual Israel receives grace. When the water flows from the rock, they all drink; but all do not thereby receive grace to drink out of the spiritual Rock, which is Christ. This is still true. It applies to all things in the world. The external gifts are indeed common, but grace is always particular and never *flows over* as grace. Thus, Dr. Hepp's concern that we become involved in denying that grace is irresistible rests entirely upon a misunderstanding.

The esteemed writer draws this conclusion from our statement that the wicked possess no receptivity for grace. Therefore, as Dr. Hepp reasons, our intention is turned into its very opposite: God's grace is dependent upon the will of man. For only if he possesses receptivity does he receive grace, and only then. However, had Dr. Hepp worked himself somewhat into our view, he could have known that this is an entirely wrong presentation of it. Reasoning along that line, we would be compelled to come to the conclusion that no man ever receives grace because all are wicked by nature and there is no receptivity for grace among the wicked. But the situation is somewhat different. Surely God's grace is irresistible. We understand that very well. But they in whose hearts God works the grace of regeneration and faith are certainly made receptive for grace in the sense of gifts of grace; for them all things can work together for good. However, if this work of regeneration is not wrought in the heart, then a person may receive ever so many external gifts, but he is not receptive to grace. By his sin he turns everything to a curse. And that was exactly the point at issue. It was not a question of whether man would be able to resist the operation of God's grace in his heart. That is certainly impossible. But the question was whether anything could be a blessing or grace to a sinner without the first grace of regeneration, without the power of God's grace that makes one receptive to the gospel. That is exactly what we deny. To express it more clearly, apart from regeneration there is no power that makes one receptive to the gospel, and apart from receptive-making grace there is no possibility that anything can be grace for us. We hope that hereby the misunderstanding is cleared up.

"Ten Besluite" [In Conclusion], the last chapter in Dr. Hepp's booklet,[32] deals with the question whether or not God's grace ever changes into a curse. To this the professor answers that the proper use of common grace does not, but the misuse of that grace does change it into a curse, and judgment is made the heavier.

It is extremely difficult for us to pass judgment on this chapter. In the first place, this chapter is not directed against us. We surely would never say that common grace changes into a curse. Grace never changes into a curse. It is possible that one can live under the external revelation of grace and that this living under grace, in that sense, can increase a man's judgment. The Word is also a savor of death unto death. But in the full and true sense of the word, when God actually and powerfully gives His grace, this never changes into a curse. Grace is favor, the friendship of God, blessing. Anyone who shares in that grace is surely kept by that grace, and grace never changes into a curse. But even apart from that, we would never be able to say that man turns common grace into a curse, for the simple reason that we do not believe in common grace.

Placing ourselves in the position of Dr. Hepp, it is also incomprehensible to us how one can speak of a *misuse* of common grace. That statement is objective and subjective, is it not? Does not the theory of common grace mean not only that God still gives gifts to his creatures in general, causing His sun to shine on the evil and on the good, but also that God restrains sin in the heart, improving man in his will and consciousness and inclinations so that he can make proper use of those gifts? The latter meaning is actually common grace in its real essence. If we take that position in our

---

32. Hepp, "Het Misverstand," 30–32.

thinking, we ask ourselves, "How can sinful man make misuse of common grace?" There is but one answer: common grace is a resistible grace. God, from His side, desires to restrain sin in man's heart, so that man can make proper use of natural gifts, but the sinner does not allow God to do so.

As strange as that may seem, Dr. Kuyper says literally that such is true. "Common grace", he writes, "is present, but we push it away."[33] It is therefore a resistible grace. God desires to give light, desires to restrain sin, tries also to do that, but man simply will not allow it, so that God's attempts fail. God's common grace yields because man pushes it from him. Here, once again, we have the position of Arminius and Pelagius in principle. That which Dr. Hepp laid at our door as heresy, namely, that we taught a resistible grace, now lands at the door of the esteemed brother. We know very well this does not apply to *special grace*, but to *common*. Yet it makes no essential difference. God becomes dependent upon the free will of man. That is the position of Arminius and Pelagius applied to so-called common grace.

However, we are willing to accept that Dr. Hepp did not mean that, and that he meant the sinner cannot misuse *grace* but misuses the *gifts of grace*, a misuse that is not associated with the restraint of sin in the heart. But even if he thinks in this way, he cannot possibly speak anymore of *misuse*. Sin is simply restrained, and then natural man always properly uses the gifts that he receives. We are discussing the gifts of common grace in an objective sense. So be it. Our position, then, is that the natural man always misuses God's gifts, that is, always turns them against God. Even though natural man receives those things that are for the welfare of mankind, he still always uses them against the living God, and thus misuses them. It is simply impossible for him to use gifts properly. Is that not also the position of the confession in Canons III/IV, 4: that man in various ways renders it [rational

33. The source of this quotation in Kuyper's works was not provided by the authors.

light] wholly polluted and suppresses it in unrighteousness? Take note: this is not presented as a possibility, but as a fact. Man always does that. He never uses the light of nature properly. That is the position of our churches. Therefore, we stand before three possibilities:

1. Sin is irresistibly restrained by the operation of common grace. But then we can no longer speak of a misuse of common grace. In addition, this is opposed to the position of our confession [Canons of Dordt], which declares that natural man always renders natural light wholly polluted and suppresses it in unrighteousness.

2. God's restraining operation in the heart of natural man is resistible, so that it depends upon the free will of man whether he will accept common grace or will push it from him, use it or misuse it. But this is the position of Pelagius and Arminius.

3. Natural man always suppresses the light of nature in unrighteousness and entirely pollutes it, whereby all innocence before God is taken from him. Then, and only then, do we stand on the position of the confession.

The appeal that Dr. Hepp makes here to Romans 1 is exegetically impossible, but since Dr. Kuyper also appeals to Romans 1, we prefer to treat this passage in a separate chapter.

At the end, Dr. Hepp still gives ten propositions, and he thinks that from both sides we could sign these to remove the misunderstanding.[34] The intention of Dr. Hepp is good. We say this out of appreciation. He wishes to preserve or restore unity in the Reformed churches in America, or at least he offers his assistance. And we express our sincere appreciation for the brother's attempt. Yet the esteemed brother could have readily surmised that this was expecting too much from us. Our answer is in all brotherly love, but at the same time we intend to maintain our own life as Re-

34. Hepp, "Het Misverstand," 32.

formed churches in America. We allow no one, no matter who he is, to prescribe propositions for our signature. Our signature is under the confessions, which we want to maintain and defend. In conclusion, we also wish to present a few propositions, not to ask whether Dr. Hepp is willing to sign them, but briefly to sum up our views:

1. The elect and the reprobate have, from a natural point of view, all things in common, because they belong together to the organism of the human race and exist and develop in the same world.

2. This natural life in all its significance, with natural light, natural knowledge, talents, gifts, and powers, forms the terrain upon which the principles of sin and grace develop.

3. Sin is not restrained in its natural process but develops out of the one root-sin of Adam, along the lines of the organic development of our human race.

4. Darkness is not the lack of natural light, but the antithesis of light in the spiritual sense. Natural light as such is spiritual darkness.

5. Though God gives gifts to all, grace still always remains particular.

6. Apart from the grace of regeneration, the sinner is dead in trespasses and sins, incapable of any good and inclined to all evil.

7. This spiritually dead sinner develops in wickedness according to the measure of his gifts and according to the place he occupies in the organism of humanity.

5

Exegesis

❦

It certainly cannot be considered useless to devote a separate chapter to the interpretation of a few passages of Scripture which are commonly produced as proof for the doctrine of common grace. The passages to which we call attention are:

- A few verses from Genesis 2 and Genesis 3
- The section concerning the covenant with Noah (Gen. 9)
- The prologue of John's gospel (John 1:1–3)
- Romans 1
- Acts 14:16, 17

Genesis 2:17 and Genesis 3

First of all, we want to discuss the interpretation that is given to Genesis 2:17 to prove common grace. The text reads, "But of the tree of the knowledge of good and evil, thou shalt not eat of it: for in the day that thou eatest thereof thou shalt surely die."

Dr. Kuyper sees the first proof of God's common grace in the fact that this threat was not carried out on the day that Adam and Eve ate the fruit. The sentence of death was postponed. Adam and Eve did not die on that very day, for then their bodies would immediately, on that very day, have fallen at the foot of the tree of life.

However, because this did not happen, we now come to that weighty moment when *common grace* entered in and began its operation. It is as clear as day that what God said was not carried out in the way He said it would be. As far as God is concerned, what was completely just, and the natural and immediate result of sin, did not happen. It was prophesied that *the day*, that is, on that very day that they ate thereof, they would die a complete death. But they did not die that day. It is beneath the worthiness of the Word of God to try to glaze over this contradiction. When human prophecy is only partially fulfilled, you may try to find something to justify this failure. But when God has spoken, it is not right or proper to do this. That which God speaks is spoken with perfect insight and clear knowledge of the course of things, and for that reason you lose every right to reason away the words "the day," or to minimize the absolute character of the dying that is implied in the expression "Thou shalt surely die." If it had happened as God had announced, then before the sun went down, the corpse of Adam and the corpse of Eve would have lain before the tree of life, and decomposition would have begun its destructive work.[1]

Here Dr. Kuyper seems to find the reality of death in the separation of soul and body, and to hold to the idea that Adam and Eve would have died a temporal death on that day if common grace had not intervened. Also, the idea seems to be that although spiritual death should have been carried out in paradise, that did not happen either.

This becomes evident from what we read later. Not only was temporal death not carried out, but spiritual death was restrained in its immediate operation.

One should by all means clearly see the connection between the facts. In the soul of man lay the center of life for the whole earth. If life succumbed in Adam's soul, then the death of his *soul* would result in the death of his body and the death of the whole human race, and along with that, the curse over *this entire creation*. All of this hung to-

---

1. Kuyper, *DGG*, vol. 1, 208.

gether as a series of links in one and the same chain. Thus, if that world did not completely sink away under the curse, if our human race was not annihilated, and if Adam's body continued to live another nine hundred years, then the complete operation of death in his soul had to be broken. If that operation of death were not broken, that would have been the end of him, of his body, of our race, and of the whole creation...

You must understand the wonder that God wrought in the heart of man immediately after the fall. God dripped into it an antidote to counteract the poison of sin... If nothing had been done to Adam's heart, death would have immediately wrought complete destruction. That the fall did not immediately lead to eternal death is only owing to the fact that God grasped Adam in his heart and brought about the wonder of common grace... Thus this common grace is the omnipresent operation of divine mercy, which reveals itself in every way wherever the heart of man beats, and spreads its blessing over those human hearts...

But if the restraint of sin had happened at precisely that point where, if there was no restraint, the sinful deed would have occurred, common grace would be nothing more than an externally restraining power. But that is not the case. Common grace restrains the progress and the penetration of the poison of sin within us, so that it does not rob us of our life, of all our inclinations, all our abilities, nor of all God's image which had been stamped upon it.[2]

Thus Kuyper virtually teaches that death was not executed in paradise in any sense. Adam did not become a corpse, nor did he sink away into spiritual death, much less into eternal death.

If you ask how this can be harmonized with the Word of God which says, "The day that thou eatest thereof thou shalt surely die," Kuyper has the following explanation. In the first place, this word must not be understood as a threat that would be carried out by God, but rather as a prediction of that which could happen to man if he ate from the tree. Thus, if I see someone at the point of

---

2. Ibid., vol. 1, 249 ff.

drinking poison, I can predict that if he drinks that poison, he will die. In the second place, God had something else than death in mind. He was thinking to Himself that death would happen only if He did not restrain the result of eating that poison. "The eating from that tree will bring you into sin, and sin has as its necessary result death, death at once, death carrying through to the end." But at the same time, God silently thinks to himself, "...unless I, your God, restrain in my mercy the resulting effects of sin."[3]

Well now, let the following be noted concerning that explanation:

1. Death, as punishment for sin, was certainly carried out by God Himself. It may not be presented as if God did not carry out His own sentence. That death did not naturally follow from the eating of the tree is the implication of Kuyper's view. Exactly for that reason the words *The day thou eatest thereof thou shalt surely die* are not to be regarded as a mere prediction, but very definitely as the announcement of threatened punishment.

2. Dr. Kuyper reasons away the words *the day*, and in his mind reads it as if it said, "If you eat thereof, some day you will die." We do not read this. The words "the day" are certainly a reference to a specific time.

3. Dr. Kuyper explains the text to mean that the very day Adam ate, he would suffer temporal death and also immediately go to hell. That is the interpretation Dr. Kuyper wants to give to the text in order to be able to show later that this did not happen. However, the text does not say that. Temporal death is not the real death, because if Adam and Eve had immediately gone to hell, they would not even have suffered temporal death but immediately suffered the full curse both in body and soul.

4. The explanation is much simpler if we are not compelled to believe that God had some silent thought in mind. There is no exegetical ground for this anyway. We must simply proceed from the

---

3. Ibid. vol. 1, 209.

truth of Scripture that man by nature is dead in sin and trespasses, but not as if he later became a little bit alive again. He is entirely dead and at enmity with God. Then the words *The day thou eatest thereof thou shalt surely die* stand, and God's judgment was actually carried out on that very day and at that very moment, so that only the grace of regeneration could make Adam alive again.

But naturally if another interpretation is given of Genesis 2:17—namely, if Adam and Eve would have suffered temporal, spiritual, and eternal death in paradise had not God restrained the operation of death; and if the situation is such that Adam and Eve then, and their seed later, were not completely dead, but sparks of life remained in them by the grace of God that restrains death— if all these things are true, then it lies in the nature of the case that one must interpret Genesis 3 almost entirely from the viewpoint of common grace.

> Had we in our foolishness been able to come to the aid of Adam and Eve, we would undoubtedly have measured out very broadly the way of salvation and would have spoken of their ordinary, earthly life as of minor importance. But God does not do that. He does not say a single word about salvation in Christ to Adam and Eve personally. That which He says about the Serpent-destroyer who comes in the person of Christ, He does not say to Adam, nor to Eve, but to the serpent. It is incomprehensible that many can treat the appalling history of Genesis 3 time and again without fixing their attention on the *common grace* that is almost exclusively on the foreground. People reckon only with what God said to the serpent and with what He said concerning Adam and Eve's punishment.[4]

Dr. Kuyper finds the following proofs for this common grace:

1. *The shame of Adam and Eve before God and before each other.* Had sin carried through to its bitter end, shame would not have

---

4. Ibid., vol. 1, 242.

been possible. A hardened sinner does not feel shame and does not tremble anymore before God. The devil "lifts up his proud head defiantly against the thrice holy God." Adam and Eve did not do this. They were ashamed. They feared. They were sorry—a sorrow maybe like that of an Esau or Judas, but a real sorrow for all that. Therein lies a proof for the restraining common grace of God.[5]

2. *They make an attempt to excuse themselves.* The man tries to lay the guilt on the woman, and the woman on the serpent. Anyone who has given himself over completely to sin, who has become completely entangled in sin, does not do that. With Satan that is simply unthinkable. Without common grace, when the last small spark is quenched in the soul, when the last small remnant of the image of God falls away, and when sin's entanglement reaches its end, then all excuses cease and nothing remains but haughtiness over the evil that was committed. It is no longer called evil but is defended as good. But even the slightest evidence of haughtiness cannot be found in Adam and Eve. On the contrary, their whole attitude speaks the very opposite, and thus this becomes a perfect proof of what the restraint of sin has already accomplished in them, and that they spoke already then by the power of common grace.[6]

3. *That God sought Adam and Eve and spoke to them* proves that there is still a point of contact for divine influence with the fallen sinner.

> The very fact that God does not cast Adam away, but turns to him, calls him, and seeks him, proves that already then sin was restrained in him by grace, and that the revelation of grace through the Word of the Lord followed upon a hidden common grace.[7]

4. Moreover, *the fact that Eve would become a mother* is unthinkable without common grace, as well as that Adam would eat bread.

---

5. Ibid., vol. 1, 242–244.
6. Ibid., vol. 1, 244, 245.
7. Ibid., vol. 1, 245, 246.

Now read what was said to Eve, and you see life coming into existence and being born. And then read what is said to Adam, and you see how that newly existing life is supported and fed. Had death immediately and fully carried through, the sentence would have had to read, "You die, and the mother in you dies, and no child will ever be born from you." That would be the mother-curse; that would have been the judgment of death…It is no different with the sentence that passes over Adam. Hunger brings death; bread sustains life. To him who is appointed to death, it would have to be said, "Bread is taken from you, and hunger will be your death." But now it is the very opposite: "You will eat bread."[8]

The basic error of this view of Genesis 3 is the assumption that apart from grace, everything in paradise would immediately have become a hell. True, this is not always clear in Kuyper's writings. Sometimes Kuyper says that on the day they sinned, Adam and Eve would have been lying dead at the foot of the tree of life. Sometimes Kuyper says that they would have immediately gone to hell. But that paradise would become hell seems to be the assumption from which Dr. Kuyper proceeds. If there had been no restraint, then Adam would have become a devil, the world would have become a hell, and sin would have revealed itself in all its horror at the very moment of the fall. Well, even without grace, that would have been impossible.

There is an interpretation of Genesis 3 that is far more in harmony with Scripture than Kuyper gives in this chapter, in which we read of almost nothing but common grace. We refer to the following:

1. Adam and Eve died on the day that they ate of the tree. Their death was not temporal, but spiritual death. At that very moment they became entirely incapable of any good and inclined to all evil, haters of God, friends of the prince of darkness, cove-

---

8. Kuyper, *DGG*, vol. 1, 226.

nant breakers. At that moment they were so dead that only the grace of regeneration could bring any change. This is in harmony with Genesis 2:17, and with the teaching of Scripture throughout, which tells us that we are by nature born in death and lie in the midst of death. Adam died in paradise, and it is impossible for him to bring forth anything but a dead race. Not once do we read that God restrained sin and that where death is restrained, life is present. Nowhere does Scripture teach that the natural man is alive.

2. Adam stood at the root of our race. Dr. Kuyper forgets this in his entire explanation. A fallen angel can sink into total destruction. He is connected with no organism that would proceed from him and of which he is the root. But sin, the curse, and death could be revealed only in harmony with Adam's position as root. Sin could never have produced its full fruit in Adam. At that moment Adam could commit very little actual sin. He could not steal; he could not commit adultery. One simply cannot speak of all the bursting forth of sin in which the sin of paradise would reveal itself and bear its fruit at a later time in the organically developed life of society and the state, of business and industry, of art and science. The fact that man did not become a devil and that he is not immediately like the man of sin and the son of perdition at the end of the ages is not to be ascribed to any restraint of sin, but rather to the fact that Adam was the root of the organism and committed the root-sin. Sin and spiritual death would develop organically. Therefore, the corpse of Adam could not lie at the foot of the tree of life. Therefore also, the mother in Eve could not die. The whole race had sinned in Adam and had to be brought forth regardless of grace. It is not true that apart from grace, no human race would have been brought forth; a race was born under the curse, developing organically in sin and death and preparing itself for hell.

3. Grace does enter immediately—not restraining grace, but delivering grace. According to God's eternal good pleasure, Christ stood behind Adam, in whom a new organism according to the election of grace receives a new life-root. The new bond works im-

mediately. At the very moment that man is dead in sin and breaks the bond of fellowship with God, the other bond in Christ works according to God's eternal good pleasure.

From that aspect there is nothing strange in Genesis 3, nothing that can be explained only by common grace.

3-a. Much is revealed in this chapter concerning what is certainly delivering and saving grace: regenerating, convicting grace leading to sorrow and guilt, seeking, forgiving, saving, and covering grace—all this you can readily find in Genesis 3. Convicting grace is in verse 7: "And the eyes of them both were opened, and they knew that they were naked." Who opened the eyes of both of them? Certainly not the devil, nor sin. God alone opened their eyes, and in such a manner that they felt a need for a covering for their sin. This is evident especially if we read this in connection with verse 21: "Unto Adam also and to his wife did the Lord God make coats of skins, and clothed them." The grace of God first opens the eyes of Adam and Eve, so that they are aware of their guilt and impurity, admit their nakedness, and seek a covering for their sin. Then the Lord teaches them to understand that He Himself will cover their sins by means of sacrifice. He does this by preparing a covering for Adam and Eve by way of death (skins suggest the slaughter of animals). Adam's fear when he hears God's voice in the garden can also be explained from that convicting grace. He hides himself with his wife among the trees of the garden. And when God with seeking love approaches him and calls him, Adam says, "I heard thy voice in the garden, and I was afraid, because I was naked; and I hid myself" [3:10]. Thus on God's part, saving grace is revealed.

When He comes into the garden and calls Adam, He is seeking His people in Christ. This becomes evident from what the Lord further reveals and does. For certainly verse 15 remains the heart of the entire chapter: "And I will put enmity between thee and the woman, and between thy seed and her seed; it shall bruise thy head, and thou shalt bruise his heel." Here you have the very heart of Genesis 3, around which, finally, everything revolves: an announcement of regenerating grace taking hold of the seed of the woman, breaking the friendship of sin with Satan, and predicting the final victory of the seed of the woman. Common grace is not mentioned in this chapter. But there is an abundant proof of grace, convicting and covering, leading to an awareness of guilt, and forgiving, regenerating, and promising the victory, seeking and saving.

3-b. Moreover, as far as the development of this present life is concerned, it is announced to Adam and Eve that life lies under the curse because of sin. The emphasis does not fall upon the fact that life will continue to develop, that there will arise a human race, and that Adam shall eat bread. The emphasis is on the fact that this entire temporal life shall henceforth be subjected to the curse of the Lord.

> Unto the woman he said, I will greatly multiply thy sorrow and thy conception; in sorrow thou shalt bring forth children; and thy desire shall be to thy husband, and he shall rule over thee. And unto Adam he said, Because thou hast hearkened unto the voice of thy wife, and hast eaten of the tree, of which I commanded thee, saying, Thou shalt not eat of it: cursed is the ground for thy sake; in sorrow shalt thou eat of it all the days of thy life; Thorns also and thistles shall it bring forth to thee; and thou shalt eat the herb of the field; In the sweat of thy face shalt thou eat bread, till thou return unto the ground; for out of it wast thou taken: for dust thou art, and unto dust shalt thou return" (Gen. 3:16–19).

Thus there is indeed nothing in Genesis 3 that speaks of restraining or delaying. Everything continues, only organically. God could not have attained His goal in Adam alone, because God created Adam as the root of the human race, which he had to bring forth. Only when life begins to develop organically will it become evident how dreadfully the first sin of Adam bears its fruit. But in paradise God announced the operation of His grace and began that work by which sin would not be restrained, but completely wiped out. And God will have a seed in this world that He prepares by the wonder of His grace out of a race which by nature lies in the midst of death. The first principles of all this are found in Genesis 3.

Concerning the Covenant with Noah

We can be brief in our discussion of that portion of Scripture that deals with the covenant with Noah [Gen. 9:9ff.], because in our latest booklet[9] we also criticized, on exegetical grounds, the interpretation that in the covenant of nature we are compelled to find a general covenant of common grace. We will once more briefly examine in the light of Scripture the grounds on which Dr. Kuyper thinks he must accept this.

First of all, there is the argument that is forged out of the difference between the names *God* and *Jehovah* and their use in connection with the covenant that is established with Noah—a completely untenable argument. Dr. Kuyper writes:

> Even the use of the name, by which the highest being who seals the covenant is called, prohibits us from regarding the matter in any other way. When reference is made to the saving covenant of particular grace, the name Jehovah is used. Also, when Shem receives the blessing of the Messiah in Genesis 9:26, the name Jehovah is found. On the contrary, here, in connection with the covenant with Noah, just as with the blessing of Japheth in verse 27, the name of Jehovah is omitted, and only the name God appears. Here it is not Jehovah, but the God of all flesh who enters into a covenant with all flesh and in that covenant swears a promise which certainly reaches out equally to all flesh, to all that has breath.[10]

This argument would hold if it were true that throughout Scripture the names *God* and *Jehovah* are used with that distinction in mind. But, as we have shown before, this is not the case. See, for example, Genesis 4:6, 9, 13, 15; Genesis 6:3, 5, 6, 8; and Genesis

---

9. The writing referred to was probably Danhof and Hoeksema's booklet "Niet Doopersch maar Gereformeerd" (Not Anabaptistic, but Reformed).

10. Kuyper, *DGG*, vol. 1, 18. Kuyper's argument is that Scripture refers to the covenant of saving grace when the name *Jehovah* is used, but refers to the covenant of common grace when the name *God* is used.

7:1, 5. In Genesis 17, where mention is made of the covenant that God makes with Abraham, we read throughout the name *God*, while if the distinction Dr. Kuyper makes were valid, especially there we would expect the name *Jehovah* (See Gen. 17:3, 9, and others). Thus, nothing can be built upon the use of names of God with a view to the generality or limitation of the covenant.

His second argument is that this covenant of nature is established with Noah and his sons and their seed.

> If it had been a covenant established only with Noah, one could say that the words "and with your seed after you" referred only to Noah's spiritual descendants. But this interpretation is impossible.[11]

Added to that is the fact that this covenant is established not only with man, but also with every living soul: with the birds, the cattle, and every beast of the earth.[12]

Certainly there can be no objection to the fact that God establishes this covenant with Noah and his seed, for God always causes His covenant of grace to run historically in such a way that it is established in the line of generations. In Scripture this never means that all, head for head, are reckoned as the true seed of the covenant. The carnal seed is always more numerous than the spiritual seed of the promise. The real objection that Dr. Kuyper has here in seeing the covenant of grace in the true sense is the fact that it was made not only with Noah but also with his sons. This prevents him from seeing that the covenant with Noah is the only covenant. Thus it would be the true covenant only if it were made with Noah and not his sons. The argument comes down to this: Ham and Japheth did not actually belong to the covenant of grace.

There cannot be any objection, either, to the idea that the seed

---

11. Ibid., vol. 1, 17.

12. Kuyper's point here is that because Ham and Japheth were not in the covenant of grace, the covenant with Noah had to be a covenant of *common* grace. Further, Kuyper argues for a covenant of common grace because the covenant was made with the whole creation.

of Ham and Japheth also enter into the inheritance of God's people, that a spiritual seed of the covenant is also found among their descendants. It is not even true that Ham is cursed, but the curse strikes only one of his sons, Canaan. There is, therefore, absolutely no exegetical basis for accepting the idea that at that moment, God's covenant of grace could not have been established with Noah, his three sons, and their seed.

Because of Ham's sin, and in harmony with the nature of the evil committed against his father, punishment is laid upon Ham in one of his children. It is only later that the line of God's covenant is limited to the descendants of Shem. This is already prophetically announced in this chapter, but the historical reality still lies in the future. Therefore, it can very well be explained that at this moment the covenant of grace is established with Noah and his three sons with their seed. It can also be explained that very soon after this, the covenant is for a time limited to the seed of Shem in Abram, but that in the distant future it will again be realized in the generations of all men. Thus the Word of the covenant to Noah and his sons, with their sons included, was certainly literally carried out. One can speak of the spiritual seed of the covenant with Ham and Japheth included.

As far as the fact that this covenant was made with every living thing is concerned, even that need not cause us to wonder. Why should it not belong to the covenant of grace that God saves every living soul and in time glorifies His whole creation? If the dumb animals sigh and long for the freedom of the glory of the children of God (Rom. 8:19–22), what is so strange about it that God includes all flesh in the covenant of grace made with Noah? And we must add that God calls this covenant that He establishes with Noah and every living soul not a temporal, but an eternal covenant.

"And the bow shall be in the cloud; and I will look upon it, that I may remember the everlasting covenant between God and every living creature of all flesh that is upon the earth" [paraphrase of Gen. 9:13–15]. Thus, this covenant also included a promise that there would be no flood upon the earth. But the covenant itself was not limited to this. When we repeatedly read, "And I, behold, I establish my covenant with you, and with your seed after you" (Gen. 6:18; Gen. 9:9, 11, 15), an expression that cannot be defined as "a certain kind of covenant," those words refer to the one covenant of grace (see Gen. 17). And when we read that this covenant is an eternal covenant, this has no other interpretation than that God here reveals the covenant of grace, a covenant that includes all the creatures of the earth, that He in time gives life to every living soul, and that soon He glorifies them.

The bow in the clouds is a sign of this eternal, all-inclusive covenant (Gen. 9:16). That is also how the rainbow appears in every other passage of Scripture where it is mentioned. That is the case in Ezekiel 1 and Revelation 4 and 10. Thus we can understand how Scripture can refer to the flood as a sign of holy baptism (1 Pet. 3:21), which our fathers understood so well that they took up this idea in the prayer before baptism.[13] Therefore, there is absolutely no exegetical objection to it, but all of Scripture speaks in favor of seeing the one covenant of grace in the covenant established with Noah. It is also revealed in other forms, but always remains the same and will attain its full realization only in eternity.

The Prologue of John's Gospel

We can safely go to a discussion of the passages in the New Testament that Dr. Kuyper considers as the most important Scripture passages in proof of common grace. We refer to the prologue of the Gospel of John, Romans 1, and Acts 14:16, 17. It can readily be

---

13. The reference is to the prayer in the Form for the Administration of Baptism used in Reformed churches. It reads: "Thou, who hast according to thy severe judgment punished the unbelieving and unrepentant world with the flood, and hast according to thy great mercy saved and protected believing Noah and his family ... by which baptism was signified." From *The Psalter*, 87 (liturgical section).

surmised why these passages, especially the first two, should be regarded as so extremely important for this doctrine of common
grace. Kuyper repeatedly states that common grace is actually the
restraint of sin, and the resisting or slowing down of the operation
of death. Some think common grace is so clearly expressed in
these Scripture passages that no doubt can remain about the doctrine.

The words at issue in the first chapter of John are found especially in verses 4 and 5: "In him was life; and the life was the light
of men. And the light shineth in darkness; and the darkness comprehended it not."

Dr. Kuyper makes this remark:

> In paradise there was no darkness. As soon as you speak of dark-
> ness, you imply a world sunken away into sin.
>
> Now in that darkness there naturally *was* the eternal Word, even
> as that eternal Word is in the outer darkness of hell. But the Evange-
> list does not speak of that.
>
> He speaks of a deliberate act of the eternal Word. He does not say
> that the Word *was* also in the darkness. This was simply a fact. But he
> testifies that the Word *shone in* the darkness, shone in such a way that
> total darkness could no longer continue. There remained a *dusk* amid
> the darkness. And that dusk amid the darkness, having cast rays of
> light through the mist into the darkness, is common grace.
>
> In a deeper sense, the darkness, which stood over against this
> streaming light, did not drink or suck it in, even though it attempted,
> in its own interests, to banish the light in its own willful blindness.[14]

If that were all Kuyper said, we would gladly endorse it, with
this exception: we would rather speak of a general revelation than
of common grace.[15] The light shines, and the mind of the natural

---

14. Kuyper, *DGG*, vol. 1, 395.
15. Hoeksema was later to repudiate the concept *general revelation* as well.
See the chapter "General Grace and Revelation" in Hanko, *For Thy Truth's Sake*,
141 ff.

man is so darkened and so blind that he does not apprehend the light, but rejects it. But there is still no mention of grace. The blind man will always be offended by that light. The passage is explained by Dr. Kuyper himself in such a way that it actually argues against his own proposition.

Later, this is different. Dr. Kuyper writes in connection with his explanation of Romans 1: "Thanks to common grace, spiritual light has not disappeared completely from the soul's eye of the sinner," and therefore it is not merely a shining, but also an apprehending and a grasping of the light.[16]

Now it is, perhaps, not necessary for our purpose to enter into all the details of the interpretation of the prologue of the Gospel of John. There are difficulties here, concerning which all interpreters of Scripture are by no means in agreement. But it is hardly necessary to enter into all this for a solution to the problem pending among us. Nevertheless, a few more important elements must be clarified for a proper understanding of the issue.

In the first place, it is necessary that we try to grasp in some measure what John has in mind when he speaks of *light*. Dr. Kuyper says:

> The apostle John expresses himself in this manner, that life first becomes *light* in man. And what can this mean but that life in the individual enlightens and clarifies itself and becomes *self-consciousness*, consciousness of the creation round about him, and a consciousness of *his* God. This takes place through the eternal Word that operates within him and by which he exists.[17]

Dr. Kuyper finds the meaning of John's favorite figure in the consciousness of the individual.

Now it is true that this is included in John's figure. Consciousness—self-consciousness, and consciousness of God and of the

---

16. Kuyper, *DGG*, vol. 1, 409.
17. Ibid., vol. 1, 393, 394.

world—belong also to the light. It is also through the Word that
the individual has his existence and is a conscious, a self-con-
scious, being. Through the Word he has natural light. Through
the Word he possesses the light of reason, can reason logically, can
be aware of and investigate things outside of himself and have a
consciousness of God. Also, in the objective sense, the Word reveals and causes the eternal power and Godhead of the Creator to
shine in the creation. It is possible, although also here opinions
vary, that this is the meaning of the ninth verse.

But you also realize at once that this cannot exhaust the concept. You realize this immediately when you take note of the
contrast which John often makes with another concept, namely,
darkness. Dr. Kuyper himself says:

> Also the outer darkness, even as the pitch black night, hides the
> majesty of the Lord LORD. Now everything has become darkness.[18]

In hell there is, therefore, no light. If one holds to the interpretation that the figure of light refers to self-consciousness and the
consciousness of God and all things, one realizes immediately that
there cannot even be darkness in hell. Self-consciousness and
consciousness of God are even in outer darkness. The suffering of
hell suggests this. But if that is the case, that is, if the absence of
light does not mean removal of consciousness, then the light has,
in contrast to the darkness, another, a richer and more positive
meaning.

And that is true. Light is not only a formal concept, and is not
to be considered in a merely formal sense as referring to conscious
existence and knowledge. It certainly has a positive, ethical-spir-
itual significance in Scripture. This is evident from John's first
epistle. Read, for example, in 1 John 1:5–7:

---

18. Ibid., vol. 1, 395. The last two words of the first sentence in the Dutch
are Heeren HEEREN."

This then is the message which we have heard of him, and declare unto you, that God is light, and in him is no darkness at all. If we say that we have fellowship with him, and walk in darkness, we lie, and do not the truth: But if we walk in the light, as he is in the light, we have fellowship one with another, and the blood of Jesus Christ his Son cleanseth us from all sin.

One realizes that light here cannot signify consciousness or self-consciousness as such. Then the text would say, "In God is absolute consciousness. If we have fellowship with Him, then the consciousness in us comes to clearer light, but if we have no self-consciousness, that is a proof that we have no fellowship with God." That makes no sense.

Light has a much broader significance, a much richer content. It is the absolute contrast to darkness. When Scripture says that God is light and that in Him is no darkness whatever, that does not merely refer to God's absolute self-consciousness, but to the full, pure, holy, divine life in all its significance. It also means that God is truth and there is absolutely no lie in Him; that He is righteousness and there is absolutely no unrighteousness in Him; that God is love and there is absolutely no hatred in Him (also God's hatred is love, even as love apart from God is hatred); that He is holiness, purity, faithfulness, veracity, and goodness and that in Him is absolutely no unholiness or impurity, no unfaithfulness or wickedness, no lie, no hatred or envy, no unrighteousness or impurity. That is all from the devil, who therefore is called the prince of darkness, the king who rules in the realm of darkness. But to the light belong love, truth, holiness, and purity. All this is in God. According to His essence, He is Light. It is not as if it can be said of Him that He *loves* and *possesses* righteousness, holiness, and the like, but He *is*, according to His essence, love, holiness, truth, and all that is good. And because He is this according to His essence, He lives as triune God an eternal, perfect light-life, a life of divinely perfect love, truth, holiness, and spotless purity.

Now the Word is the perfect reflection of that light-life. Through Him that light also shines externally. And through Him, that light becomes the light of the creature who is created according to His image, and is therefore inclined in a creaturely measure to live the life of God and have fellowship with Him. If we also live in love, truth, righteousness, and holiness, that is only because we have fellowship with Him. Then we walk in the light and also have fellowship with one another.

Darkness is the absolute contrast to this life of God. It is not an existence apart from God. That would not be possible; apart from God is non-existence. But it is an existence against Him. Even after the fall, the Logos continued to sustain man. Also in sin, man remains a creature who is formally inclined toward God and could possess true life only in fellowship with Him. Yet because of sin, he is absolute darkness. He is darkness in his understanding, so that he loves the lie. He is darkness in his heart, will, and inclinations, so that his thoughts are enmity against God. He lives in unrighteousness, impurity, hatred, and envy. In one word, he walks in darkness and will continue to do that eternally, unless by the grace of God he is born again.

If we apply this to what John states in His prologue, everything is entirely clear. The Light does shine in the darkness. The Light, which in the true sense of the word is the life of man, continues to shine also after the fall. In fact, God not only reveals His eternal power and Godhead since the creation of the world in such a manner that everyone can see it, but He also reveals it in such a way that the same creation reveals much more of God when our eyes are again enlightened by the grace of God. This is evident from the many psalms that glorify God in creation. But that is not the issue when we are speaking of common grace. It is not the question whether the light that is the life of mankind *continues to shine*, whether the darkness in man was somewhat changed by that light, so that he also begins to walk somewhat in that Light and also has some sort of fellowship with that Light. Then death was indeed somewhat restrained by common grace. If this theory is true, then darkness is not absolute.

But notice that this is exactly what John denies. The point at issue, in the notion that common grace is taught in John 1, is that the darkness is somewhat enlightened and death is somewhat restrained in its operation. But John emphatically denies this in the prologue of his gospel. What he does say is this:

1. The Light did shine, and there can, therefore, be no excuse for walking in darkness.
2. This, however, did not change or improve the darkness in the least. It remained darkness. The darkness did not comprehend it. In the original a word is used that actually means "grasping, taking hold, making one's own." The darkness, that is, man as he is in sin, did not do this. The darkness remained darkness amid the rich revelation of light. Therefore, the darkness was without excuse.

In this way the passage testifies against the common grace view, which teaches that by the shining of the light, darkness is indeed changed. Thus it is still a fact that man in paradise actually died, is indeed become absolute darkness, and so, as our confessions express it, *all the light that is in us is darkness*. Natural light is spiritual darkness.

Romans 1

The situation is even more precarious in Kuyper's interpretation of Romans 1.

Kuyper's explanation,[19] comes down to this:

---

19. Summarized from Ibid., vol. 1, 404ff.

1. In the old dispensation a certain operation of common grace was revealed from heaven that checked sin and restrained the operation of destruction.

2. However, God gradually caused this restraining operation to dwindle. This is evident from the term "gave them over" that appears repeatedly in this chapter (Rom. 1). This word means that God withdrew Himself. And by this withdrawal, by this dwindling of common grace, man fell into all kinds of debauchery, which the apostle sums up in this chapter.

3. That God caused His common grace to dwindle had its reason in idolatry. Mankind represented God as a man, a beast, and a creeping animal. As punishment, God now held back His common grace, and sinful man cast himself into the debauchery and impurity mentioned here by Paul.

We wish to remark, first of all, that regardless of the exegetical problems, this is actually no explanation at all. The reasoning of Kuyper is that by God's gracious restraint of sin, man still knew God and still possessed the light of God's revelation in creation. Now a question arises: If the restraint of sin also implied that man knew God and thereby was kept from idolatry, how did he arrive at the first step in which he represented God as a beast or creeping animal? Before man could come to that, a dwindling of common grace must have already occurred. There is no other possibility, unless you make the restraint of sin a resistible grace; and if it is that, then no dwindling is necessary, for then man can overcome God's resistible grace.

The situation is therefore this, according to Kuyper's viewpoint. God first had to cause His common grace to dwindle so that man fell into idolatry. Then God caused His common grace to dwindle still more, so that man fell into the debauchery and filthiness mentioned in this chapter. But if that is the case, the question arises, Why did God cause His common grace to dwindle at all? Dr. Kuyper still owes us the answer to that. This certainly is not an explanation.

But exegetically this explanation is completely impossible.

We will briefly follow the apostle in his argument.

The apostle is separated unto the gospel of God (v. 1). The content of that gospel that he must proclaim in the world is that there is a righteousness of God, a righteousness prepared by God, a righteousness also given by God alone, and given only through faith. The gospel is therefore a power of God unto salvation.

Now the apostle says that he is not ashamed of the gospel of God. On the one hand, he is not ashamed of it because it is a power of God unto salvation. It gives a righteousness that is only from God and can only be accepted by God. On the other hand, he is not ashamed of the gospel because the world is in need of that righteousness. It has no righteousness of its own. Therefore, it also has no blessing. It has only wrath and the curse: "For the wrath of God is revealed from heaven against all ungodliness and unrighteousness of men, who hold the truth in unrighteousness" [Rom. 1:18]. Take note: the wrath of God is *revealed* from heaven. Paul sees in the world and its situation and history a revelation of the operation of God's wrath. God's wrath is over *all* ungodliness and unrighteousness of mankind.

The question is: In what does the apostle see that revelation of the wrath of God?

When the apostle looks around in the world, he sees amazing things. From a religious point of view, man has become a fool. In fact, here he sees someone bowing before an ox; there someone humbly bows before a snake; yonder man worships a frog; and elsewhere he lies in the dust in front of a man. Thus man is become foolish. He is confused, totally darkened. In this way the wisdom of the world becomes a horrible spectacle. "Professing themselves to be wise, they became fools" (Rom. 1:22).

But there is still more. The apostle sees how, not only from a spiritual point of view man has become foolish and bows before man and beast, before four-footed and creeping animals, but also from a moral point of view he has fallen into the horrible depths of debauchery. Men with men work that which is unseemly;

women with women perpetrate impurity; men burn with lust toward each other and sink lower than the animal. There is no sin in the ethical realm which, according to the apostle, does not reveal itself in the deed (Rom. 1:26–32). That is how the apostle regards the world of his time: not the world of the Kaffir or Hottentot, but of the Greek and the Roman.[20]

Now the apostle sets himself before the question, How did that come about? If you say no more, you can never explain this condition out of sin as such. That a man bows down before a frog or a snake is more than sin. It is also foolishness. That has not always been the case. Cain was just as spiritually dead as the Greek and the Roman. But he surely would not bow before a cow. He still knew God; he even spoke with Him. Thus that life of debauchery is more than sin; it is deep misery, a horrible degeneration below the beast. Therefore, the question is this: How did sin develop to the point that man became so foolish, so miserable?

To that the apostle answers, "The wrath of God is revealed from heaven" [Rom. 1:18]. There has been an organic development of sin. On the one hand, the situation was such that God's eternal power and Godhead were revealed in creation. Man stood amid the plain speech of God. Nor was it true that he did not know that speech. He clearly saw God in His work. He had natural light. He knew that God is eternal in power and godliness. He was aware that God must be served. Sin is not insanity; darkness is not ignorance. "Because that which may be known of God is manifest in them; for God hath shewed it unto them. For the invisible things of him from the creation of the world are clearly seen, being understood by the things that are made, even his eternal power and Godhead; so that they are without excuse: Because that, when they knew God..." (Rom. 1:19–21).

---

20. The authors refer to the races of Kaffir and Hottentot of South Africa, formally uneducated peoples in 1923 when the authors wrote this book. In contrast, Paul was making his point regarding the cultured Greek and Roman civilizations of his own day.

But even though that was the case, even though there was a manifestation of God, even though the light shone and man also saw this light, the darkness of sin was that he, sinful man, despised that light. Darkness is no ignorance, no lack of the consciousness of God, but rather enmity against God. That is what man revealed when he refused to bow before God and would not glorify or thank Him as God. Neither did Cain want this, although he was not as foolish as the Roman. That was man's sin, for which he has no excuse. Is it not true, therefore, that God stood on the opposite side, revealing His wrath upon all ungodliness and unrighteousness? And the influence of that wrath of God upon that God-despising godlessness of man was such that man became foolish. God spoke in history: "If you, oh man, standing amid my revelation, will not honor and thank Me as God, I cast you down in foolishness until you bow down before a frog and a snake." Thus, there is no restraining grace, but a wrath of God that in all the history steadily pushes deeper and deeper. This is taught by the apostle in Romans 1. That operation of wrath worked continually. God does not allow Himself, never allows Himself, to be mocked, not for a single moment in all history. He always remains the same. And the man who assaults Him is pushed away by Him (unless saving grace intervenes) until he finally ends up in outer darkness.

Therefore, God also gave them over to dissoluteness and filthiness whereby they continually became more miserable. Nor is the argument of the apostle that God stood idly by, withholding His restraining hand. The idea is rather that He revealed Himself in wrath in such a way that the bold sinner finally sank away into that which was lower than the animal. The "giving up" [Rom. 1:24] is not passive, but active; not negative, but positive. And then, obviously, not in this way: that God is the cause of sin. He does not cause man to sin, but in His divine wrath He guides the development of sin in such a direction that man makes himself dissolute.

This shows plainly that Romans 1 does not teach a restraint of sin, but an organic development of wickedness under the constant influence of the wrath of God, humiliating man and bringing him to foolishness and debauchery.

Acts 14:16, 17

After all that we have said, we can be brief in the explanation of Acts 14:16, 17. There we read: "Who in times past suffered all nations to walk in their own ways. Nevertheless he left not himself without witness, in that he did good, and gave us rain from heaven, and fruitful seasons, filling our hearts with food and gladness."

First of all, we wish to remark that we fully understand the reasoning of some in regard to this text. They say that God did good. In doing good in the old dispensation, He gave rain and fruitful times, food and gladness also to the heathen. Now the heathen had no right to that. Therefore, because they receive something which they did not deserve, God gave the heathen *grace*—common grace.

Naturally, we agree wholeheartedly that God gives the gifts of this natural life to all. All men have in common the whole of natural life as it develops out of creation. We do not deny that these gifts of natural life are good. Who would deny that God does good? Who would deny that God always does what is good? Therefore, everything that comes from God is also good. The heathen receive from God good rain and good fruitful times, good food and good gladness. There is no difference whatever in that regard.

The question is whether God also gave *grace* to the heathen. That is exactly what we deny and Scripture never teaches. If at the moment when the murderer lifts his arm to strike the victim, God did not give him good strength, that cruel arm would at that very moment drop lamely. God therefore also does good in that instance, for He gives good strength. But who will say that God gives him grace? When God gives to the Greek artistic skills, and He gives him the good marble, and the Greek then makes an idol, who would dare to assert that God gave grace along with the skill and the marble? When God gives to the Roman the sword and natural jurisprudence, and that Roman stands before Jesus and says, "You are innocent, but I crucify you," who calls that grace? And when God gives to the world a glad heart, and that world turns away from God with that glad heart to wild pleasure and revelries, who will say that grace is hidden in that gladness of the world? Therefore, let it be said again: grace is not in things, but in the good favor of God, who works blessing in and through the means. The things are always common in this world, but grace is never common.

Besides that, we must not forget that this idea does not even touch the actual point of common grace. That actual point, according to the doctrine of common grace, is always that sin is restrained and that the natural man is thereby qualified to live a somewhat good life in creation before the face of God. What does Acts 14 tell us? We have seen that common grace is denied in the prologue of the gospel of John. The light did shine, but the darkness was not improved by it and did not grasp the light. It was no different in Romans 1. Far from teaching that a certain operation of God's common grace can be detected in the history of the heathen world whereby sin is restrained in its course, Paul rather teaches us that the wrath of God is revealed from heaven, whereby the heathen world became foolish and debauched. That is the very opposite.

Is it different in Acts 14:16, 17? Absolutely not. Just listen: "Who in times past suffered all nations to walk in their own ways." Is that not surely the very opposite of restraining the wicked in their way? The ways of the heathen were sinful ways, and God allowed them to walk in these ways. He did not restrain them, did not hold them back in their walk, but allowed them to continue. And this was true even though they were not without a witness of God. For God did not leave Himself without witness in that heathen world. No, He revealed Himself in rain and fruitful times, in food and gladness, as a God who did good. But that brought no change whatever in the ways of the heathen. If a change should be brought about, God would have to give them grace. But that is exactly what He did not do.

Thus we have, in our opinion, treated the most important passages of Scripture to which some appeal is made for proof of a common grace that restrains sin and causes man to practice, in a measure, that which is good. We always come to the same conclusion. Scripture does not teach a restraint of sin by grace but an organic development of sin. The whole of natural life is a place to serve that purpose. Spiritual death works from within, so that the total depravity of the natural man continues to develop in all wickedness. The whole of natural life stands at his disposal, and he subjects it to the service of sin. And from heaven the wrath of God is revealed against the sin and godlessness of mankind, and directs and punishes it in such a manner that man becomes ever more foolish and more debauched, unless divine grace intervenes. "He that believeth on the Son hath everlasting life; and he that believeth not the Son shall not see life; but the wrath of God *abideth* on him."

The Authors

Henry Danhof (1879–1952)

Rev. Henry Danhof and Rev. Herman Hoeksema were born in the Netherlands, but immigrated to America in their teens. They both attended Calvin College and Seminary, were graduated from the seminary, and were ordained ministers in the Christian Reformed Church.

The problem of common grace came to the foreground during their ministries, and they opposed the doctrine on the grounds that it was both unscriptural and non-confessional. Their agreement on the doctrine of sovereign and particular grace led them to collaborate on several writings, the most important of which was *Van Zonde in Genade*, translated into English in this volume under the title *Sin and Grace*.

For their stand, both were deposed from their ministerial offices in the Christian Reformed Church.

After cooperating in the formation of the Protestant Reformed Churches and in the early work of the Protestant Reformed Seminary, Rev. Danhof left the Protestant Reformed Churches. The rest of his career was that of pastor of a small, independent church in Kalamazoo, Michigan.

Herman Hoeksema (1886–1965)

For Further Reading

⌘

Books on the History of the
Protestant Reformed Churches

Hanko, Herman. *For Thy Truth's Sake: A Doctrinal History of the Protestant Reformed Churches*. Grandville, Mich.: Reformed Free Publishing Association, c. 2000.

Hoeksema, Gertrude, editor. *God's Covenant Faithfulness: The 50ᵗʰ Anniversary of the Protestant Reformed Churches in America*. Grand Rapids, Mich.: Reformed Free Publishing Association, c. 1975.

Hoeksema, Gertrude. *Therefore Have I Spoken: A Biography of Herman Hoeksema*. Grand Rapids, Mich.: Reformed Free Publishing Association, c. 1969.

Hoeksema, Gertrude. *A Watered Garden: A Brief History of the Protestant Reformed Churches in America*. Grand Rapids, Mich.: Reformed Free Publishing Association, c. 1992.

Hoeksema, Herman. *The Protestant Reformed Churches in America: Their Origin, Early History and Doctrine*. Grand Rapids, Mich.: First Protestant Reformed Church of Grand Rapids, Mich., [1936].

Books in English by Herman Hoeksema
(published by the RFPA)

Behold, He Cometh!: An Exposition of the Book of Revelation. Edited and partially revised by Homer C. Hoeksema. Second edition. 2000.

Believers and Their Seed: Children in the Covenant. Revised edition. 1997.

In the Sanctuary: Expository Sermons on the Lord's Prayer. Edited by Homer C. Hoeksema. 1981.

The Mystery of Bethlehem: Devotional Reading for the Christmas Season. Edited by Homer C. Hoeksema. 1986.

Ready to Give An Answer: A Catechism of Reformed Distinctives (section

of questions and answers regarding the errors of the well-meant offer of the gospel and common grace). 1997. The Hoeksema section
on common grace is taken from his book *The Protestant Reformed
Churches in America.*

Reformed Dogmatics. Edited by Homer C. Hoeksema. 1966.

Righteous by Faith Alone: A Devotional Commentary on Romans. Edited by
David J. Engelsma. 2002.

Sin and Grace. Translated by Cornelius Hanko and edited by Herman
Hanko. 2003.

The Triple Knowledge: An Exposition of the Heidelberg Catechism. Edited
by Homer C. Hoeksema. 3 vols. 1970, 1971, and 1972.

When I Survey . . . : A Lenten Anthology. Edited by Homer C. Hoeksema.
1977.

"Whosoever Will." Second edition. 2002.

The Wonder of Grace. 1982.